ELECTRONIC COLONIALISM

Volume 126, Sage Library of Social Research

RECENT VOLUMES IN
SAGE LIBRARY OF SOCIAL RESEARCH

95 Roberts **Afro-Arab Fraternity**
96 Rutman **Planning Useful Evaluations**
97 Shimanoff **Communication Rules**
98 Laguerre **Voodoo Heritage**
99 Macarov **Work and Welfare**
100 Bolton **The Pregnant Adolescent**
101 Rothman **Using Research in Organizations**
102 Sellin **The Penalty of Death**
103 Studer/Chubin **The Cancer Mission**
104 Beardsley **Redefining Rigor**
105 Small **Was War Necessary?**
106 Sanders **Rape & Woman's Identity**
107 Watkins **The Practice of Urban Economics**
108 Clubb/Flanigan/Zingale **Partisan Realignment**
109 Gittell **Limits to Citizen Participation**
110 Finsterbusch **Understanding Social Impacts**
111 Scanzoni/Szinovacz **Family Decision-Making**
112 Lidz/Walker **Heroin, Deviance and Morality**
113 Shupe/Bromley **The New Vigilantes**
114 Monahan **Predicting Violent Behavior**
115 Britan **Bureaucracy and Innovation**
116 Massarik/Kaback **Genetic Disease Control**
117 Levi **The Coming End of War**
118 Beardsley **Conflicting Ideologies in Political Economy**
119 LaRossa/LaRossa **Transition to Parenthood**
120 Alexandroff **The Logic of Diplomacy**
121 Tittle **Careers and Family**
122 Reardon **Persuasion**
123 Hindelang/Hirschi/Weis **Measuring Delinquency**
124 Skogan/Maxfield **Coping With Crime**
125 Weiner **Cultural Marxism and Political Sociology**
126 McPhail **Electronic Colonialism**

ELECTRONIC COLONIALISM

The Future of International Broadcasting and Communication

THOMAS L. McPHAIL

Foreword by Everett M. Rogers

Volume 126
SAGE LIBRARY OF
SOCIAL RESEARCH

 SAGE PUBLICATIONS   Beverly Hills   London

For information address:

SAGE Publications, Inc.
275 South Beverly Drive
Beverly Hills, California 90212

SAGE Publications Ltd
28 Banner Street
London EC1Y 8QE, England

Printed in the United States of America

Library of Congress Cataloging in Publication Data

McPhail, Thomas L.
　Electronic colonialism.

　(Sage library of social research ; v. 126)
　Bibliography: p.
　Includes index.
　1. Communication, International.　I. Title.
II. Series.
P96.I5M36　　　　　302.2'3　　　　　81-5622
ISBN 0-8039-1602-7　　　　　　　　AACR2
ISBN 0-8039-1603-5 (pbk.)

FIRST PRINTING

CONTENTS

Foreword by Everett M. Rogers   7

Preface   9

1. The New World Information Order   13

2. Freedom of the Press   39

3. A Misguided Start: The Media and Development
   Research Traditions   61

4. The Role of UNESCO   89

5. The Message: The 20th and 21st General
   Assembly of UNESCO   109

6. The Medium: International Telecommunications Union and
   the World Administration Radio Conference   149

7. The Wire Service, DBS, and Related International Issues   171

8. The MacBride International Commission   207

9. Conclusions and Summary   241

Appendix A   251

Appendix B   253

Index   257

About the Author   260

FOREWORD

Here is a book about the New World Information Order (NWIO), a topic that most North American professors and students of mass communication may only begin to understand. Western media generally have given scant attention to this international debate, and our public is poorly informed about the rise of power by less-developed countries in United Nations agencies like UNESCO. Needed is an objective, detailed account of this process by which the politics of international communication shifted away from the United States and Western Europe.

The basic issue here is freedom of the press versus government control of the media. Everyone agrees that following the former principle in the past has not led to a very perfect system of international communication. Our news from developing countries in Latin America, Africa, and Asia concentrates on disasters and coups, hardly a balanced account. Developing nations' broadcasting systems carry a diet of "Kojak" and "I Love Lucy," content that distorts the image of the West. The magnificent potential of the mass media for fostering socioeconomic development is largely wasted. What the Third World tried to do about these problems of international communication through the NWIO debate, and how the United States and other Western governments reacted, is the story of this book.

Tom McPhail gives us an insider's account of the NWIO debate of the 1970s and early 1980s, balanced by his perspective as a communication scientist. He demonstrates an unusual ability to sift through the mass of materials about this topic, much of it written in what he calls "UNESCOese," and to distill a highly readable account. Much of Professor McPhail's background material and personal respondents are colored by their extreme positions on the debate. But in my opinion, the present book is both balanced and readable. In fact, this is the best account of the NWIO debate that I have seen.

Everett M. Rogers
Stanford University

PREFACE

Students and professionals are facing a rapidly changing environment in international broadcasting and telecommunications. The label of the New World Information Order (NWIO) has become synonymous with much of the concern and rhetoric between Western industrialized nations and Third World countries covering disparate pasts and conflicting philosophies about the proper role of media systems in domestic and international affairs.

This book accounts for the impetus toward an NWIO. With the rise of nationalism in emerging Third World nation-states during the late 1950s and 1960s, a parallel concern for control of their economies and culture was established. This concern presented itself in many ways, but crystallized on two major considerations. One was the flow and accuracy of media messages entering or leaving such countries (with the major wire services—Associated Press, United Press International, Agence-France Presse, and Reuter's—being central to this concern); and the other concern was with the fear of future broadcasting technologies, particularly direct broadcast satellites (DBS).

Many personalities, events, meetings, and countries are involved in the international media story. But when all is said and done about the international information environment of the 1980s, it will most likely be that UNESCO (United Nations Educational, Scientific and Cultural Organization) will have been the most prominent institution. A strong supporting role will have been played by the MacBride International Commission for Study of Communication Problems.

The following is an overview of the major events which surprisingly have gone largely unnoticed by many Western countries and students of communication, sociology, political science, and journalism. Yet, the ability to collect and disseminate information about foreign countries, especially those in the Third World, may well rest on the outcome of this international debate.

The stakes are high for Western nations with democratically elected governments. When one realizes that currently 1 out of every 20 jobs in North America is connected with exports to the developing world, then understanding these nations becomes critical. In addition, Western foreign policy initiatives are based largely upon their acceptance by the general public. Yet, in turn, the public's image of societies beyond their immediate surroundings is based upon what the mass media present. If less developed countries (LDC's) begin to exclude, censor, or limit the media agencies of the West, then it will be increasingly difficult, if not impossible, to build public opinion to support substantial foreign policy initiatives by the West.

With a world population growth rate of one million people every five days, adequate and accurate coverage of LDC's is more imperative now than ever. Some say that the NWIO will result in less rather than more coverage of LDC's in the 1980s—the exact opposite of what is needed.

For example, the Camp David accord could not have occurred without the media. Nor would the American public have accepted the considerable financial and political burden involved if it were not for the realization, through extensive press coverage, of the need for strong and direct foreign policy initiatives affecting nations thousands of miles away from U.S. shores.

Will a "Camp David" type summit be a policy option for Western leaders to solve foreign problems in Asia, Africa, or

Latin America in the future? Clearly it may be possible if
their constituencies are aware of the underlying problems,
disparities, or even bloodshed in countries far removed from
their day-to-day concerns. Today the impact of foreign
affairs is as close as the corner gas station.

Finally, a Canadian perspective is unique and most applicable to the NWIO. With the introduction of radio at the
beginning of the 20th century to current concerns over
transnational data flows affecting its sovereignty in the Information Age, Canada has tried to protect and support its
domestic cultural industries. The protection is from U.S.
cultural domination for the most part. Yet, at the same time,
as Prime Minister Pierre Trudeau asserts, Canada is like a
mouse sleeping beside an elephant. The United States' prox-
imity brings competition, a high standard of living, and a
continental culture that is now being exported far beyond
North America. That is why Canadian students of communication and culture understand the Third World's concerns;
they have been there. The history of Canadian broadcasting
has been a story of countering U.S. radio, television, film,
and magazine influence; the writings of Canadians like Harold
Innis and Marshall McLuhan are based on the crucial relationship of culture and communication.

"Information is the oil of the 1980's" was an expression
that I heard frequently while at UNESCO Headquarters in
Paris during 1978. Attending the 20th General Assembly of
UNESCO during October and November of 1978 in Paris
enabled me to acquire insights and materials concerning the
various positions being taken about foreign media coverage
and the NWIO. I was able to interview many reporters,
delegates to the UNESCO General Assembly, and senior staff
members of the large UNESCO bureaucracy.

Particularly useful, related books are Rosemary Righter's
Whose News?, Anthony Smith's *The Geopolitics Of Information*, and Mort Rosenblum's *Coups and Earthquakes*.

Thanks go to the many people both here and abroad who assisted with the gathering and criticisms of the material.

Finally, special thanks go to Wilfred Kesterton for his excellent comments on earlier drafts and to Jeffrey Mahoney who provided research materials.

Financial assistance from Carleton University permitted the author to both travel in Europe and collect materials that would have otherwise been impossible to obtain. The Canadian Commission for UNESCO and Ms. Betty Zimmerman of The MacBride Commission were most cooperative. Of course, all materials, interpretations, and limitations are the sole responsibility of the author.

Chapter 1

THE NEW WORLD INFORMATION ORDER

Lord Cooper, publisher, to William Boot, foreign correspondent:

> With regard to policy, I expect you already have your own views. I never hamper my correspondents in any way. What the British Public wants first, last, and all the time is News. Remember that the Patriots are in the right and are going to win quickly. *The Beast* stands by them four-square. But they must win quickly. The British public has no interest in a war which drags on indecisively. A few sharp victories, some conspicuous acts of personal bravery on the Patriot side and a colourful entry into the capital. That is *The Beast* policy for the war.
>
> *Scoop* by Evelyn Waugh

Introduction

International communication is undergoing a major reexamination and analysis. The outcome of this wide-ranging investigation may substantially alter the nature and flow of all types of international information in the future.

This book outlines the major institutions, individuals, conferences, and issues that are altering the international information, telecommunication, and broadcasting order. This includes all types of mass media activities—wire services, daily newspapers, satellites, journalists, film, radio, television, and advertising. Traditional assumptions about media flows are being challenged and altered. What follows is a descriptive and analytical portrayal of how certain events, some very recent, are affecting the information environment of the future.

UNESCO, the International Telecommunications Union (ITU), the New International Economic Order (NIEO), the concept of development journalism, the origins of a "free press" in Western societies, the International Program for the Development of Communication, and emerging new communication technologies are but some of the interrelated issues that are evolving in such a way as to cause concern to some and hope to others. Much depends on the perspective one takes. In the final analysis, the New World Information Order (NWIO) may produce significant problems in the collection and dissemination of international news since the underlying philosophical stances of the major parties are totally incompatible.

The NWIO is an evolutionary process seeking a more just and equitable balance in the flow and content of information, a right to national self-determination of domestic communication policies, and, finally, at the international level, a two-way information flow reflecting more accurately the aspirations and activities of the less developed countries (LDC's).[1]

The NWIO seeks a restructured system of media and telecommunication priorities in order for them to obtain greater influence over their information, economic, and political systems. To the LDC's the current world communication system is an outgrowth of prior colonial patterns reflecting

commercial imperatives of former times. Now the LDC's
want to remove the last vestige of colonial control by promoting the NWIO. But

> Western governments and news organizations vigorously oppose
> the plan, fearing it will bring increased interference with freedom
> of the press. But in October [1980], officials of the United
> Nations Educational, Scientific and Cultural Organization, where
> the third world enjoys large voting majorities, were authorized to
> draw up concrete proposals. Outvoted Western delegates, while
> remaining critical, agreed that further study should proceed on
> the form a new order would take [New York Times, 1981: E3].

In seeking to attain movement toward an NWIO, critics from
LDC's have postulated potential mechanisms that clash with
strongly held journalistic traditions in the West. The call for
government responsibility and control of the media—limiting
reporters' access to foreign events, journalistic codes, licensing of reporters, and taxation of the radio spectrum—are
moves which the West adhors. (More details on Western press
traditions are presented in Chapter 2.) Even the call for a
balanced flow, which was approved by UNESCO in 1978, is
disliked by many who claim that it interferes with the free
market mechanisms and that only an open and free flow of
information is consistent with the goals of a truly free press.
   Many LDC critics attack the Western press as if it were a
monolithic, rational system. They fail to realize that what
eventually winds up in Western newspapers or on radio or
television is determined by a complex, and not entirely
consistent, process of decision making. Rosenblum puts it
this way:

> Correspondents play an important part in selection by determin-
> ing what to cover in the first place. But most of the process is in
> the hands of editors at different stages. These are the gatekeepers.
> Each medium and each type of correspondent operates in a
> different fashion, but the principle is the same. A correspondent's
> dispatch first goes to one gatekeeper and then what emerges—if

anything—goes on to others. All along the way, the original
dispatch may be shortened, lengthened, rewritten or thrown away
entirely. This series of editors determines what is to be eventually
shared with the public; and they decide what the American
people may never know [1979: 7-8].

This is an important point. What people in Western soceities
currently learn about LDC's is meager and the result of
several gatekeepers. With the NWIO, the Western press fears
that this situation will become even worse. Licensing of
foreign correspondents, as discussed by UNESCO in February
1981, or by any agency is seen as the first of many steps
which will collectively result in both fewer reporters being
acceptable to LDC's and only favorable, pro government
news stories being permitted out of many LDC's. The NWIO,
which is just evolving as a significant aspect of world communication, has the potential for substantially altering the front
pages or national newscasts for American and European citizens alike. The problem is, and this is what the book details,
that the coverage of LDC's in the future is going to change
but no one knows whether it is going to improve in accuracy,
quantity, and quality or whether it will be restricted, biased,
or heavily censored. That is why awareness of the NWIO is
central to understanding world communication.

What makes this successive diminution of information
ironic is that both technically and theoretically there is more
international information available today than ever before.
Satellites, portable teletype terminals, videotext, video-discs,
minicomputers, high frequency radio, and direct long-
distance dialing have collectively replaced slow and cumber-
some dispatches of the past.

But practically the story is quite different. The average
mass circulation newspaper in the West now carries less and
less international news. There are several contributing factors.
The major ones are simply high costs, roughly $100,000 to
place and equip a single foreign correspondent abroad for a
year. This has led to a net reduction of reporters that wire
services, networks, or individual papers are willing to place

abroad; second, restrictions, ranging from outright bans to censorship of certain pieces, to withholding critical interviews past filing time, to threats of physical abuse unless "proper" slants are evident, jailing, or even death all serve to reduce or limit the amount of available copy. Third, the high turnover of foreign correspondents and the "pack journalism" phenomenon (Crouse, 1972; Epstein, 1973) make editors and publishers reluctant to extend time and money to significantly increase foreign coverage. Finally, the lack of public concern—as reflected in the trend toward "disco journalism" where people move their hips rather than their lips as they read—reduces the incentive by editors or demand by readers for any coverage, let alone in-depth and continuous coverage, of a broad range of foreign issues.

The exceptional and unusual still dominate what is reported. Indepth front page pieces on population, education, health care, and other development successes are a long way off. Rosenblum, in talking about "The System," makes this point:

> Foreign correspondents do often seem to be mad as loons, waiting on some source for hours in the rain so they can write a dispatch which might well end up blotting spilled coffee on an editorial desk back home. Editors seem madder still, suffering hypertension over whether their own man reached some obscure capital in time to duplicate stories available to them by other means. And their combined effort, when it reaches breakfast tables and living rooms across the United States, often appears to be supercilious and sloppy.

> This system is geared as much to amuse and divert as it is to inform, and it responds inadequately when suddenly called upon to explain something so complex and menacing as a dollar collapse—or a war in Asia. Yet it is the American citizen's only alternative to ignorance about the world.

> Because of the system—and in spite of it—most Americans are out of touch with events which directly affect their lives. When crisis impends, they are not warned. When it strikes, they are not prepared. They know little about decisions taken on their behalf

which lessen their earnings, restrict their free freedoms and
threaten their security [1979: 1-2].

Why is this the case? What are the implications? In an era
of so much information, why is there so little useful information? That is what this book addresses.

Traditionally, mass media research looked at either select
issues, such as agenda setting, ownership, or violence, or at a
select medium, for example, television. Only from time to
time do individuals deal with the macro and larger aspects of
the overall mass communication system. Harold Innis, Marshall McLuhan, and Jacques Ellul are representative of the
latter school. Yet recently the concept of a "new world
information order" has emerged in several forums, which
may ultimately alter the "ground rules" for international
information and mass communication systems. The major
wire services, Associated Press, United Press International,
Reuter's, and Agence-France Presse, are central actors, some
say, victims of the emerging NWIO movement. The international debate over a shift from the "free flow of information philosophy" to the "free and balanced flow" with the
possibility of government control via licensing of journalists
merits much additional attention.

The following outlines the major events in the origins of
the demand for an NWIO. The concept of "electronic
colonialism" reflects much of the current concern and is a
good concept with which to begin.

Electronic Colonialism

Over the course of history there have been but a few major
trends in empire building. The first era was characterized by
military conquests; these occurred during the Greco-Roman
period. The second era involved militant Christianity; the
Crusades of the Middle Ages are typical of this expansion
movement. The third era commenced with significant inventions in the 17th century and came to a rather abrupt end

toward the middle of the 20th century. It was essentially mercantile colonialism fueled by the Industrial Revolution and a desire to both import raw materials and find export markets for finished products. Asia, Africa, the Caribbean, and the Americas became objects of conquest by the European powers. France, Great Britain, Spain, Portugal, and Nordic nations systematically set about to extend their influence. These expanding empires of Europe sought raw materials and other goods unavailable at home and, in return, sent colonial administrators, immigrants, finished products—and a language, educational system, religion, philosophy and lifestyle that frequently did not suit the invaded country. During the latter part of this third era, industrialized nations sought to extend their influence through transnational corporations which supplemented and extended more traditional means of control. But the common denominator was a desire for trade links (involving raw materials, cheap labor, expanding markets, and so on) that carried with them many commercial imperatives and governmental practices that suited the larger and more powerful industrialized nations rather than their foreign colonies or customers.

World Wars I and II not only brought an end to major military expansion movements but also placed the industrialized nations of the West in command of vital trade routes and practices. During the 1950s the business and economic climate allowed transnational corporations to increase and solidify domestic and foreign markets based upon production of goods, from cereals to computers. Basically the industrialized revolution took its logical course. But two major changes occurred during the late 1950s and early 1960s which have set the stage for the fourth and current era of empire expansion.

The two major changes are the rise of nationalism, centered mainly in the Third World, and the shift to a service-based economy in the West which relies substantially on telecommunication systems, where traditionally geographical borders and barriers to international communications are being rendered obsolete. The postindustrial society, with information-related services being the cornerstone, has significant implications for industrial and nonindustrial nations alike. Military and mercantile colonialism of the past may be replaced by "electronic colonialism" in the future. A nation-state may now be able to go from the Stone Age to the Information Age without having passed through the intervening steps of industrialization.

Electronic colonialism is the dependency relationship established by the importation of communication hardware, foreign-produced software, along with engineers, technicians, and related information protocols, that vicariously establish a set of foreign norms, values, and expectations which, in varying degrees, may alter the domestic cultures and socialization processes. Comic books to satellites, computers to lasers, along with more traditional fare such as radio programs, theater, movies, and wire services to television shows demonstrate the wide range of information activities which make up the broad configuration of what is possible to send and thus to receive—and there lies the rub (Read, 1976; Tunstall, 1977).

Essentially how much of the foreign and imported material rubs off on the receiver is the critical issue. The displacement, rejection, altering, or forgetting of domestic and native materials is a major concern for the Third World. Electronic colonialism of the 20th century is just as dreaded as mercantile colonialism of the 18th and 19th centuries.

The recent rise of nationalism in many Third World countries has resulted in a parallel concern for political, economic, as well as cultural control over their own destinies. Leaving aside the political aspects, it is with the cultural issues that students of journalism and telecommunication find theoretical and research interest. For example, two of the largest issues of international concern that link the Third World and the West, and frequently on opposing sides, are the performance of the major wire services and direct broadcast satellites (DBS). The flow, accuracy, emphasis, and content of the major Western wire services in reporting Third World items have come under considerable criticism and scrutiny, particularly at UNESCO.[2]

The other fear deals with a future broadcasting technology—DBS. It represents to date the ultimate mind- and culture-invading mechanism that is being developed by Canada, Japan, and the United States and the Soviet Union alike. In the field of international communications, DBS is to the future what Gutenberg was to the past. DBS may go far beyond the technical and economic aspects of message transmission to create another set of issues which are cultural, political, and sociological in diversity. Before detailing the several critical conferences of the 1960s which have propelled the issue of creating a new set of ground rules for journalism in LDC's, a few comments about "development journalism" are appropriate.

Development Journalism

The demands of a mature press differ substantially from those of an infant press. To impose the legal, economic, or regulatory models of one onto the other fails to appreciate the underlying differences in needs that are a result of a combination of historical and cultural forces. "Development Journalism" is the concept that attempts to deal with the needs, strengths, and aspirations of journalistic endeavors in emerging nation-states of the Third World. It is a media theory that encourages an engineered or committed press, committed to government set priorities and objectives.

The rationale for development journalism is:

All national resources—including the resource of information—must be directed toward development. If information is allowed to cause dissent or loss of international prestige, it detracts from the greater goal. By this reasoning, the control of news is not only a legitimate right but also a national necessity [Rosenblum, 1979: 206].

Although the seeds of a theory of development journalism were sown in the 1960s, it was the 1970s which saw the debate about the role of the mass media being conducted in several forums; it will be in the 1980s that we will see the results of both the debate and the role of Western press standards and news-gathering activities in light of the consequences of both development journalism and its counterpart, the NWIO.

Who are the actors? What are the issues? Why is "objective journalism" viewed as a myth by many critics? What underlies the fear of advanced communication technologies? Why is Western advertising seen as a threat to the Third World? These are but few of the questions which cumulatively will provide the framework for the emerging international information environment of the 1980s.

Concern about the impact of communications, whether in the form of folklore transmitted orally down to color television transmitted live via satellite, has heightened the need for a detailed background to the various events and positions that will alter the markets for Western media offerings as well as what the West may be able to cover, collect, and transmit from Third World and Socialist countries in the future.

From a broad perspective, the West values freedom of the press, free speech, and the free flow of information. LDC's reject most of these and other related values, some with considerable rhetorical vehemence. The LDC's claim that they cannot afford the luxury of a multitude of competing media systems, that many are lucky to have a single medium, usually radio. The high illiteracy rate makes a printed press a distant dream if not an illusion for many emerging nation-states. In fact, illiteracy on a world scale is still increasing. Most LDC's lack the necessary telecommunications infra-structure required for modern media systems.

The LDC's position on the role of government control of the media is diametrically opposed to traditional Western views. For over two centuries the West, taking much of its conception of the press from British traditions and laws, has fought in the streets and in the courts for a press free from government control.[3] The LDC's, on the other hand, look for, encourage, and, in many countries, have no choice but to accept and repeat the official governmental position.

The argument goes this way. Newly emerging nations tend to come from the less advanced areas of the world, many being from Africa or small islands with low per capita income, high illiteracy, and almost nonexistent media systems. The infrastructure to support an advanced telecommunications system is a dream for many. In order to rapidly improve the LDC's economic and social position, a concerted effort by *both* government and media is required. The "luxury" of competing or critical views on government policies and programs by media is viewed as detrimental to the tremendous "catching-up" task facing the LDC's.

Rosenblum discusses the weaknesses of Third World coverage and concludes:

> There are deep philosophical differences over the role of the press and government in society. Whoever is right or wrong, few Third World leaders are prepared to accept the way Western correspondents feel they are obliged to report world news [1979: 204].

In order to correct the imbalances and mistaken impressions created by the Western press, LDC's are promoting their media theory, development journalism (Righter, 1978; Smith, 1980a). To give one an idea of the growing power of the LDC's, when the UN specialized agency, UNESCO, was founded in 1946, there were 20 member states; at the close of the 20th General Assembly of UNESCO in 1978, there were 146 states—the vast majority being LDC's. Development journalism, therefore, is a modern philosophy and practice adhered to by many nation-states.

Development Journalism and the Canadian
Situation: A Case Study

THE FREE PRESS AND CAPITALISM

Although development journalism is a concept applied to the aspirations of communication activities in the Third World, that is not its only application. From a theoretical point of view, the concept of a "free press," or the "free flow of information" philosophy, reflects a situation where the "free press" is basically a development press in favor of free enterprise and a capitalistic social system. The ideological role of the mass media in Western nations is to protect, perpetuate, and enlarge the role and influence of the capitalistic system in all phases of decision making. Indeed, editorials and feature columnists continually call for less government control and less regulation in order that market forces be allowed to control the economy in the spirit of the 19th century Spencerian philosophy.

But in the 20th century the mass media system serves to portray a value system that will create a climate favorable to the economic system of Western nations. The Western news is not value-free, since it is ideologically supportive of the economic system which makes the press a profitable enterprise. Without going through the extensive literature on such phenomena as "gate-keeping," "agenda-setting," and "cross-ownership" of the mass media in the West, it suffices to say that the Western press is a development press and has, in fact, successfully developed itself into an ideological arm of the capitalistic and free enterprise system. In essence it provides free and paid for (via advertising) support of a social and political system consistent with basically maintaining the status quo (Klapper, 1960).

In *The Vertical Mosaic,* (1965) a landmark in Canadian sociology, Porter suggests that one social rule of the Canadian mass media is to restate and generalize a value system that will provide for cohesion and unity in society, confer a sense of rightness on the social order, and ascribe legitimacy to certain social practices. This ideological function

> must provide the justification for the economic system, the political system, and so forth, and this it does by attempting to show that the existing arrangements conform with the traditional value system [Porter, 1965: 460].

Porter goes on to point out that "Canada's mass media are operated as big business. Many of them, particularly in the large cities, are closely linked with corporate enterprise." After reviewing the ownership and control of private media (to the mid-1960s) he concludes:

> The ownership group in their selection of personnel to run their newspapers and periodicals have to concern themselves not only with technical competence, but also with ideological acceptability which means sharing the attitudes and values of the owner. Thus the image of Canada, inasmuch as the mass media contribute to that image, is created by the British charter group as represented by the upper class owning group or the successful middle class journalists [Porter, 1965: 486].

Thus, it is possible to surmise from Porter's analysis that the manifest function of the private media in Canada is akin to other corporate goals, primarily profit; but, in addition, the press has a latent goal to convey an ideology that will continue to create a climate for a profitable press. Similar manifest and latent objectives are true of the press in other industrial nations.

MEDIA CONCENTRATION

Clement, in *The Canadian Corporate Elite* (1975), extends Porter's thesis and argues that control of this ideological role is vested in a media elite that is virtually indistinguishable from other corporate elite. Clement not only updates the continuing trend toward media concentration among chain-

ownership groups but he also refers to the standardization
caused by the usage and reliance upon a single wire service:

> A further way news is concentrated in Canada, beyond the
> limited number of dailies and media groups, is through the
> Canadian Press (CP) wireservices. . . . According to the Senate
> Report, 'More than 70 papers rely on CP for all the news they
> publish beyond what is written locally by their own staffs'
> (I:230). . . . The basic source of news for most of the newspapers
> in Canada turns out to be identical for each of them [Clement,
> 1975: 301].

The Canadian Special Senate Committee on Mass Media
(1971) also expressed concern about press concentration:

> But the trend towards fewer and fewer owners of our sources of
> news and information is already well entrenched. There are only
> five cities in the country where genuine competition between
> newspapers exists; and in all five cities, some or all of these
> competing dailies are owned by chains [Davey, 1970: 5].

With the closing of the *Montreal Star, Ottawa Journal,* and
Winnipeg Tribune, another Royal Commission on the Press
was established in 1980 to investigate possible government
action. In addition, old distinctions are beginning to be
blurred. A noted British student of the media, states:

> Until recently it was thought possible to distinguish broadly
> between on the one hand systems controlled by government and
> on the other hand systems linked to business through private
> enterprise and advertising. Yet there was always a third type of
> system, represented formidably by the BBC, where it was neither
> government control nor business underpinning it. This system,
> which was widely copied, was seldom copied in its entirety, and it
> now has many variants. In many countries also there are now dual
> or multiple systems, in some cases, but not in all, subject to
> common "supervision"; and in all countries there are degrees and
> nuances of control whether by governments or by market forces.

The United States system, which is important not only in itself but because of the influence it has through exports of programmes and through diffusion of broadcasting styles, is itself a complex system—containing as it does multiplicity of agencies and a changing public service element. It is hoped that United States experience will be covered in a later volume.

Alongside such complex structures, the products of time and place and in many cases deeply resistant to fundamental change, there are, of course, many new broadcasting structures in the world, including many which have come into existence in new countries.

Many of these structures reveal themselves as extremely complex, too, when they are subjected to careful scrutiny. Nor are they necessarily very malleable. The more governments set out to chart and carry through conscious "communication policies"—often related directly to their planning policies—the more they are compelled to consider the relationship of "traditional" modes of communication to new technologies. The more, too, they are forced to establish priorities [Briggs, 1977: vii].

Briggs underscores the link between forces, whether government or business, that affect the tone of Western information systems. A closer look at the Canadian system is illuminating.

COUNTERACTING IMPORTED MEDIA

Historically, Canada has faced the media flow from the United States since the beginning of the 20th century. Although Canada inherited much of its press traditions from both Great Britain and France in the 19th century, and now is influenced extensively by U.S. media, it still has a mixed model of government and business media systems (Rutherford, 1978). Yet is is interesting to note that from the early part of the 20th century, media systems in Canada developed in such a way as to be an early example and case study of "development journalism."

Beginning with the problems of radio in the 1920s with both microwave frequency interference and programming taste interference from the United States, the first Canadian Royal Commission on Broadcasting in 1929 set the precedent. It recognized that the federal government had a distinct role to play in fostering a unique Canadian broadcasting system in the public interest. The Royal Commission's final report pointed directly to a major plank of the development journalism philosophy—self-determination of a nation's culture. From the first Aird Royal Commission:

> In our survey of conditions in Canada, we have heard the present radio situation discussed from many angles with considerable diversity of opinion. There has, however, been unanimity on one fundamental question—Canadian radio listeners want Canadian broadcasting. . . .
>
> At present, the majority of programs heard are from sources outside of Canada. It has been emphasized to us that the continued reception of these has a tendency to mould the minds of the young people in the home to ideals and opinions that are not Canadian. In a country of the vast geographical dimensions of Canada, broadcasting will undoubtedly become a great force in fostering a national spirit and interpreting national citizenship [Canada, 1929: 6].

This was to be the first of several investigations of the Canadian mass media. But the media problems were not solved. Consider the Fowler Royal Commission on Broadcasting:

> But as a nation we cannot accept, in these powerful and persuasive media, the natural and complete flow of another nation's culture without danger to our national identity. Can we resist the tidal wave of American cultural activity? Can we retain a Canadian identity, art and culture—a Canadian nationhood? . . . Is it possible to have a Canadian nation at all? The Canadian answer, irrespective of party or race, has been uniformly the same for nearly a century. We are prepared, by measures of assistance, financial aid and a conscious stimulation, to compensate for our disabilities of geography, sparse population and vast distances,

and we have accepted this as a legitimate role of government in Canada [Canada, 1957: 8-9].

In 1935 the federal government created the Canadian Broadcasting Corporation (CBC) and in 1939 the National Film Board (NFB) under John Grierson. These are examples of the federal government's becoming directly involved in production and distribution in order to create a Canadian awareness and presence both at home and abroad.

In the 1950s the Massey Royal Commission on Culture and the Arts further developed regulatory cultural agencies to insure a Canadian presence. This eventually resulted in the creation of Canadian content rules for radio and television.

In 1968 the government created the federal Ministry of Communications. It also created Telesat Canada, the Canadian domestic satellite organization. Canada, along with the USSR, were the prime movers in the domestic broadcast satellites area. A major incentive for Canada to enter the satellite race was not only to provide broadcasting to remote northern areas but also to tie up prime parking spaces in the much sought after band 22,800 miles above the equator.

In the same year, 1968, the creation of the Canadian Film Development Corporation (CFDC) was a major step into the feature film industry. Its purpose was, once again, to counteract strong domination of American Hollywood films. Canadian movie houses, also dominated by foreign chains, show basically Hollywood films. Although the CFDC had a slow and mixed start, recent changes in the tax status allowing 100% write-offs as capital cost allowances for movie investment has rapidly altered this situation. Canada finds itself as a major feature film industry with many international stars now shooting films in Montreal, Toronto, and Vancouver.

Another example of development journalism and fostering culture by regulation is a recent change in the Revenue Act requiring Canadian ownership in the magazine industry. *Time, TV Guide,* and *Readers Digest* were affected most. It was hoped that by altering the tax status of these foreign magazines that their advertising would shift to a Canadian domestic magazine, namely *Maclean's.* It was hoped that

Maclean's would be able to grow and foster a Canadian orientation in the weekly magazine field. Traditionally, it was believed that *Maclean's* would not be able to compete against the strength and presence of large U.S. weekly magazines. To some extent this has not worked out. *Time* (U.S. edition) is now making more profit in Canada and *Maclean's* is still a losing enterprise more than five years after the original tax legislation became law.

CANADA'S FUTURE

A recent minicommission was created by the federal government to look at the future of communications. Their report is known as *Telecommunications and Canada: The Consultative Committee on the Implications of Telecommunications for Canadian Sovereignty*, headed by J. V. Clyne. It has a great deal to say about the role of new communication services and Canadian identity in the future. Essentially the report maps out what impact communication in the future will have on the Canadian business and cultural climate. A growing foreign penetration in computers and data control industries illustrates that aspects of Canada's future are foreign controlled, and transnational data flows are considered by some to be a threat to future sovereignty. Canada does not want to become an information colony of another nation. The Clyne Report states:

> Canadian sovereignty in the next generation will depend heavily on telecommunications. If we wish to have an independent culture, then we will have to continue to express it through radio and television. If we wish to control our economy then we will require a sophisticated telecommunications sector developed and owned in Canada to meet specific Canadian requirements. To maintain our Canadian identity and independence we must ensure an adequate measure of control over data banks, trans-border data flow, and the content of information services available in Canada. . . .
>
> In approaching telecommunications we should realize that its importance demands we view it in a special way. Telecommunications, as the foundation of the future society, cannot always be left to the vagaries of the market [Canada, 1979: 2].

The report uses unusually strong language for a government report when it deals with controlling future communication activities:

> Unless positive action is initiated now, the sovereignty of Canada will be jeopardized in two main fields. First, Canadians are already being swamped with foreign broadcast programming and a new approach to the problem is urgently required; at the same time, there is a danger that foreign interests may achieve a predominant share of the market for data processing services and far too much of the information stored in databanks will be of foreign origin. Second, Canada is heavily dependent on imports in telecommunication technology. In certain sectors, such as communication satellites and information exchange, Canada is in the forefront of competitive technological developments. The exploitation of developments requires public support that does not entail a vast expenditure of public funds; this is an industrial sector that can create jobs and be competitive on an international scale. The timing is important. It may not be possible to do tomorrow what we fail to do today [Canada, 1979: 5].

In sum, we are able to see that a developed Western nation like Canada had been actively involved in activities consistent with a development journalism philosophy. Other nations, such as Australia, have also been very active in attempting to influence its media culture by insisting on Australia content rules so that the pervasiveness of U.S. television does not overwhelm their native cultural identity. Europe, with the growth of cable technology, now shares similar concerns.

Finally, the major points are, first, the Western press is basically a development press on behalf of the free enterprise system. This is even more the case with the totally unregulated newspaper industry. Yet as newspapers turn into electronic newspapers, given the advances in videotex systems, then existing government regulation of radio and television will also be extended to communication services. Therefore the last bastion of the free press (i.e., an independent newspaper system) will slowly evolve into an electronic system.

Second, Canada is an early and excellent case study of a First World nation having attempted actions being called for by the Third World, as reflected in the MacBride International Commission for the Study of Communication Problems Final Report[4] and by the NWIO. Since Canada is the most cabled nation in the world, with 70% of the urban homes having access to cable, it has been on the forefront of change that may serve as a model for other nations just embarking upon "wired-city" technologies.

Breadth of the Problem

The range of communication, broadcasting, media, and information activities covered by the NWIO is extensive. On the one hand, there is a large group of Third World countries concerned about basics such as the introduction of first radio services, or the introduction of telephones. High illiteracy makes the introduction of print a difficult problem for many.

On the other hand, other nations, some industrialized for over a century, also have communication concerns. Basically they are concerned with their own role and survival in the Information Age. They do not want to become an information colony of another nation. The questions of transnational data flows, computers, data processing, privacy, and computerization effects on the work place and labor are central to policy concerns of several industrialized nations. This is highlighted by the fact that now more than 50% of the U.S. gross national product relates to information-based services. This means that employment is now directly related to the ability to supply all phases of the information process, both hardware and software, necessary to participate in the Information Age. The concept of some nations becoming information colonies of other nations is central to the Information Age.

Clearly, for Western nations, issues of national sovereignty and electronic colonialism relate to questions of a free and balanced flow. Aspects of government intervention and regulation in such areas as the "electronic newspaper" (Com-

paine, 1980; Smith, 1980b), interactive cable, tariffs, distribution of satellite signals, and other regulatory decisions
offer a different set of propositions and outcomes that are, at
first glance, remote from the concerns of the Third World
and their information disparities and problems. Yet the
NWIO covers all these aspects.

Another relevant point is, has a "free flow" ever existed?
Probably not.[5] Initially, custom laws, tariffs, visas, telecommunications regulations, preferential rates, and availability of
transatlantic cable had an impact on early international dispatches. Reuters tried to block competing wire services, particularly American ones, so also other competitive and
commercial pressures have affected news flow from the
beginning. Currently the major national supporters of the
"free flow" philosophy are governments responding to pressures from multinational corporate interests, ranging from
American Express to Xerox, to protect or extend their corporate, and not necessarily national, interests. What is good
for IBM World Trade, for example, in selling computer
systems to the USSR, is not necessarily good for the national,
or indeed international, interests of the United States. Yet
some individuals and firms are holding tenaciously to the old
information order.

Ironically a great deal of the pressure and support for the
"free flow" is coming largely from print groups, both daily
newspapers and major weekly magazines. Their concern is
intense and historically genuine. Yet technology is quickly
moving them toward government involvement of some type
that they vehemently reject or even abhor. Electronic information systems to the home will bring print media under
some type of regulatory control. The electronic newspaper is
no longer a case of if, only when. William Paley, Chairman of
CBS, states the case well:

This new era of information plenty, with its convergence of
delivery mechanisms for news and information, raises anew some

critical First Amendment questions about our freedom which merit comprehensive rethinking. Once the print media comes into the home through the television set, or an attachment, with an impact and basic content similar to that which the broadcasters now deliver, then the question of government regulation becomes paramount for print as well.

Too many of us in print and broadcasting have imagined that we had separate destinies and separate problems, but the destinies and the problems of each are becoming the same [1980: 24].

This is where, upon closer analysis, the NWIO links the LDC's and the West. Whereas the former are actively seeking a role for government, the latter through technological innovations are increasingly finding themselves affected more and more by government decisions or indecision. The granting of cable franchises is but one example of the central role of governmental bodies, whether they be a city council or a national regulatory agency.

The fact is that today the print and electronic media are still running on separate legal and regulatory tracks. On the one hand, the print media are increasingly restrained by the actions of the courts; on the other, broadcast journalism is restrained, not only by the same courts, but even more by such obsolete legislative and regulatory restrictions as the 'equal time' and fairness doctrine provisions, the inhibiting effects which are clearly inconsistent with the spirit of the First Amendment.

Broadcasters and print people have been so busy improving and defending their own turf that it has escaped some of us how much we are being drawn together by the vast revolution in "electronification" that is changing the fact of the media today, and thereby bringing the issue of government control for both of us into even sharper focus [Paley, 1980: 24].

That is why the focus on the NWIO of government responsibility or at least an enlarged role in the overall decision-making process is probably more related to future Western delivery systems and services rather than the myopic concern of just concentrating on the "free press" and the traditional daily newspaper as we know it.

Just as the technology of the print press is evolving into some form of electronic publishing in a videotex format, so also are parallel decisions being made that will have some impact upon information that crosses borders electronically. In the future nearly all information will cross borders electronically whether it be by a terrestrial microwave network or via satellite. For example, at the June 1980 World Conference on Transborder Data Flow held in Rome, many items concerned balance, sensitivity to national concerns, and items similar to the debate about the NWIO. Informatics, an item described in the MacBride Report, is a computer-based information system.

Consider the results and call for additional action of the June 1980 conference on transnational data flow.

a) A definitive progress in the description of the different technical, legal, sociocultural and economic aspects of the transnational data flows.

b) The verification that transnational data flows are an important international dimension of informatics that must be included and integrated in the national strategies and policies for informatics.

c) The acknowledgement that even more important than the role of transnational data flows in informatics is its impact in the informatization of societies.

d) The proof that it is possible that developed and developing countries can discuss among themselves looking for solutions in a constructive way and also that representatives of the governmental and private sectors can work together in a positive context towards solutions.

e) It became evident that around the subject many problems and possible solutions exist and to achieve appropriate results at the international level requires the participation of many intergovernmental organizations.

f)   To take advantage of the opportunities that transnational
     data flows can offer it is necessary that the regulatory condi-
     tions at the national level do not become too complicated
     and to obtain a high degree of harmonization at the inter-
     national level [Ahumada, 1980: 7-8].

The significant point is that the original concerns about the
NWIO dealt extensively with the printed press and international news agencies but in the 1980s there will be a shift
to electronic information of all forms in the West and thus
the debate about the NWIO in many ways is only beginning.

Format for the Balance of the Book

Chapter 2 goes into considerable detail about the historical
origins of both the concept of freedom of the press and the
social forces that assisted the removal of government control
of the press in the West.

Chapter 3 outlines the research traditions of both development theory and mass communication theory and how they
have failed to provide the hoped for models and empirical
verification necessary to aid LDC development. In addition,
there is some discussion of the LDC's rejection not only of
the West's free press philosophy but also of the West's academic traditions in the communications and development
theory domain.

Chapters 4 and 5 deal more directly and in some detail
with the role of UNESCO and the NWIO. The 1980 UNESCO
General Assembly held in Belgrade is detailed here.

Chapter 6 discusses the spectrum debate involving the ITU
and how this problem of the medium is related to UNESCO's
debate about the message.

Chapter 7 provides additional details about the major
international wire services, direct broadcast satellites, a profile of Latin American concerns, and some added points
about the United States information policy.

Chapter 8 examines the origins and background activities of the International Commission for the Study of Communication Problems (also called the MacBride Report). Details are provided about the Final Report of the commission and a new major communication agency, the IPDC, being established by UNESCO.

Chapter 9 discusses the potential impact of the NWIO, the implications of the new UNESCO initiatives, and the implications of these various activities for the future of international broadcasting and communication.

NOTES

1. Nomenclature: There are several ways of defining and categorizing the nations of the world. Frequent dichotomies are North-South, East-West, developed-underdeveloped, Socialist-Capitalist, Industrialized-Third World, and Western and Socialist countries. Although far from being perfect, this book will use the following: Western nations will include the industrialized nations, which according to the World Bank are Australia, Britain, Canada, Finland, France, Italy, Japan, Netherlands, Sweden, Switzerland, United States, and West Germany. Most of these fall in the North. The LDC's are mainly located in Asia, Africa, and Latin America or generally in the South. There is no derogatory meaning attached to the term *less* in LDC's; in fact, some critics maintain that the LDC's are fortunate in having avoided the major industrialization problems, such as pollution or high energy consumption, of the West.

A final point: Nations are continually obtaining independence or moving back and forth on both the political and economic scale; examples are Iran, Mexico, Afghanistan, and Poland. No definition will fit accurately over time; therefore, the terms *West* and *LDC* will be used in this book for the sake of convenience since they reflect fairly well the major parties involved in the debate about the NWIO.

2. Additional details about both the wire services and DBS appear later in the book; some may wish to refer to these sections now.

3. A major section is devoted to this tradition later in order to provide a frame of reference upon which to view the divergent concepts of the role of the press, from both a historical and contemporary perspective.

4. The MacBride Report is the major document in the overall debate between the West and the LDC's. Background on its establishment and what it covered are discussed in detail in Chapter 8.

5. Communication lawyer and academic Charles Dalfen has presented similar arguments.

REFERENCES

AHUMADA, R. S. (1980) "The IBI world conference on transborder data flow policies: An overview of its main results."

BRIGGS, A. (1977) "Foreward," in E. Hallman, Broadcasting in Canada. Toronto: General Publishing.

Canada (1979) Telecommunications and Canada: The Consultative Committee on the Implications of Telecommunications for Canadian Sovereignty. Ottawa: Minister of Supply and Services.

Canada (1957) Fowler Royal Commission on Broadcasting (Vol. 1). Ottawa: Government Printing Office.

Canada (1929) Aird Royal Commission on Broadcasting. Ottawa: Government Printing Office.

CLEMENT, W. (1975) The Canadian Corporate Elite. Toronto: McClelland and Stewart.

COMPAINE, B. (1980) The Newspaper Industry in the 1980's. White Plains, NY: Knowledge Industry Publications.

CROUSE, T. (1972) The Boys on the Bus. New York: Random House.

DAVEY, K. (1970) Mass media (Vol. 1). Ottawa: Information Canada.

"Debate sharpens on a New World Information Order" (1981) New York Times (February 15): E3.

EPSTEIN, J. (1973) News from Nowhere. New York: Random House.

KLAPPER, J. (1960) The Effects of Mass Communication. New York: Free Press.

PALEY, W. (1980) "Paley warns of print regulation by government." Editor and Publisher (June 14).

PORTER, J. (1965) The Vertical Mosaic. Toronto: University of Toronto Press.

READ, W. (1976) America's Mass Media Merchants. Baltimore: Johns Hopkins University Press.

RIGHTER, R. (1978) Whose News? Politics, the Press and the Third World. London: Burnett Books.

ROSENBLUM, M. (1979) Coups and Earthquakes: Reporting the World for America. New York: Harper & Row.

RUTHERFORD, P. (1978) The Making of the Canadian Media. Toronto: McGraw-Hill Ryerson.

SMITH, A. (1980a) The Geopolitics of Information. London: Faber and Faber.

SMITH, A. (1980b) Goodbye Gutenberg. New York: Oxford University Press.

TUNSTALL, J. (1977) The Media are American. London: Constable.

Chapter 2

FREEDOM OF THE PRESS

> The main controversy at the UNESCO conference at Belgrade involved the role of communications—of the press. I think it took a beating. I think the United States took a beating [Bullen, 1980: 1].

One of the more contentious aspects of the call and movement toward an NWIO is the threat of government control. Various UNESCO discussions and drafts of mass media declarations have from time to time referred to control, responsibility, or licensing power over correspondents, for a code of ethics establishing certain standards and sanctions for violations, or state involvement with the press. Socialist countries have little difficulty with such a requirement since TASS is a government-controlled and operated news agency. But the Western press rejects as nonnegotiable the call for government control.[1]

Indeed, the history of the press, as it emerged in Great Britain and was exported to its colonial empire, is one of unshackling government control. Because of the long struggle to free the press from government control in the West and the ironic shift to place it back under some type of government control as called for by UNESCO from time to time, a detailed history of the struggle for a free press is provided.

Western Standards

Central to the controversy over the NWIO is the question of the appropriateness of Western standards of freedom of press and speech for the LDC's. The freedoms of press and speech are among the most cherished values of the Western world; it is an almost universally accepted principle in the West that a free press is imperative to the proper working of democracy. It has become a major part of the system of "checks and balances," and the print press is not referred to as the "Fourth Estate" by accident. The press must be free from government regulation or influence in order to function effectively. Indeed, this is one of the chief principles or assumptions about freedom of the press, that it keep government power in check.

Siebert observes that "Like other theories of the status and function of the mass media of communication in society, the libertarian doctrine is a development of the philosophical principles which provide the basis for the social and political structure within which the media operate" (1956: 39). The philosophical principles underlying this theory of the press are those usually associated with the rise of liberalism in the West between the 16th and 18th centuries. Before looking at these principles, some of the major social, religious, and political experiences and conditions of the era are outlined. It is important to understand this background in order to appreciate the high social value attached to the concept of the freedom of press.

Background

THE ROLE OF RELIGION

Bury (1952: 61) notes that in the 16th century the declining power of the Pope in Europe, the decay of the Holy

Roman Empire, the flagrancy of the Church's suppression of opposition, and the growth of strong monarchies more interested in worldly power than ecclesiastical policy contributed to the success of the Reformation. Most of the leaders of the Reformation, such as Calvin and Martin Luther, by no means endorsed liberty of conscience and religious tolerance in general. But they and their followers, in rebelling against the Roman Catholic Church and fighting for the freedom to practice their own faiths, inadvertently encouraged the cause of religious liberty and the right of private judgment for everybody.

Accompanying the Reformation were great strides in science and geographical exploration as well as the rediscovery of classical art and learning which characterized the Renaissance. Copernicus, Galileo, Newton, and others began to explain the universe in terms of mathematical formulations and natural and physical laws which required the exercise of reason, rather than faith, to understand. Rational and mechanistic concepts of the universe were replacing explanations which depended on the clergy and supernatural explanations (Bury, 1952: 66-71).

THE ROLE OF ECONOMICS

In addition, Siebert (1956: 42) says the rise of a commercial class in Europe expanded and influenced the growth of liberalism. Free contract and an open, competitive market system "became the basis of the economic liberalism which the age of expansion demanded." A newly emerging commercial middle class pressed for less state and church control and influence over areas which affected its ability to freely supply the wants of man and for as much individual freedom as the pursuit of laissez-faire economics required. Free enterprise arrived with a strong dislike for any impediments or regulations set by anyone. The struggle to renounce church and state control emerged in this era. This incipient recognition of certain claims to individual and civil liberties and of the power of reason—as well as the loosening of traditional values

and attitudes—furnished the context for the emergence of a
basic philosophy of liberalism. The principles of this philosophy are stated briefly. According to the libertarians, the
state exists to promote the fulfillment of the individual
which is the ultimate goal of society. When the state fails to
add to the enrichment of its individual members or begins to
assume greater importance than them, "it becomes a handi-
cap which should either be abolished or drastically modified"
(Siebert, 1956: 41).

THE ROLE OF LIBERTARIANISM

Besides being an end in himself, man is also a rational
animal, according to liberal theory, and is capable of understanding and dealing with the world around him on his own.
Men, say the libertarians, are endowed with reason, and the
application of this faculty to the evidence of the senses will
yield the truth upon which men can act and which, as Siebert
notes:

> is definite, provable, and acceptable to rational men. The con-
> ception that there is one basic unassailable and demonstrable
> explanation for natural phenomena as developed by mechanistic
> experimentation and observation became the model upon which
> libertarian philosophers proceeded to generalize in all areas of
> knowledge [1956: 41].

Because not all men exercise their faculties of reason with
equal success, a great deal of argument and controversy often
surrounds the truth. But, the libertarians argue, from the free
interplay and competition of conflicting opinions and ideas,
the aggregate reasoning of men in society will eventually
distill the truth.

The main contributions of liberalism as an underpinning
for the philosophy of freedom of the press and of speech
which developed over time were (1) its stress on the concept
that there are natural and inalienable rights—such as freedom
of thought to which every individual is entitled as essential

conditions to his fulfillment and which the state must protect—and (2) its confidence in human reason.

American historian Carl Becker provides the premises
behind the libertarian doctrine of freedom of expression:

> The democratic doctrine of freedom of speech and of the
> press . . . rests upon certain assumptions. One of these is that men
> desire to know the truth and will be disposed to be guided by it.
> Another is that the sole method of arriving at the truth in the
> long run is by the free competition of opinion in the open
> market. Another is that, since men will invariably differ in their
> opinions, each man must be permitted to urge, freely and strenu-
> ously, his own opinion, provided he accords to others the same
> right. And the final assumption is that from this mutual tolera-
> tion and comparison of diverse opinions the one that seems the
> most rational will emerge and be generally accepted [1945:
> 57-58].

Freedom of the Press in Practice

Let us now look at the early development in Britain and
the United States of the actual practice of freedom of the
press in the two countries where the concept was most
clearly felt as an issue and where most of the major battles to
establish it, both legally and in the minds of men, were
fought.

THE EARLY PERIOD

William Caxton set up the first printing press in England in
1476, but "printing was not a social force for about 50 years
after its establishment in England" (Emery, 1978: 5). Not
until 1529 did King Henry VIII begin a long series of
attempts by British governments from that time to the late
18th century to control the press, by drawing up a list of
prohibited books. By a Proclamation on Christmas Day 1534,
printers were required to obtain royal permission before they
could practice their trade. And with the Proclamation of

1538, Henry VIII instituted the first regular royal licensing system for all books printed in English (Siebert, 1952: 48).

The next major episode in the control of printing in England was the establishment of The Stationers company by Queen Mary in 1557 to organize a rapidly expanding printing trade (Clyde, 1934: 2). In return for favors from the Crown such as the granting of "patents of monopoly" whereby the master printers of the company gained exclusive rights to print certain books or classes of books, the officials and wardens of the company were charged with carrying on "a large part of the administration and enforcement of the regulations governing the press" (Siebert, 1952: 64). The company was empowered by the Crown to search the premises of printers suspected of violating these regulations and to seize their equipment.

During most of the Tudor period there were few violations of press regulations and little mention of freedom of the press. However, by the 1580s, during the latter part of Queen Elizabeth I's reign, there were stirrings of discontent among unprivileged printers, that is, those printers who were excluded from the brisk trade in books covered by patents of monopoly (Siebert, 1952: 89-95). Because almost all the books which were profitable to print were already preempted by royal patents granted by the Crown to the established, privileged printers, the unprivileged printers could hardly make a living.

One unprivileged printer, John Wolfe, began reprinting or "pirating" the properties of the privileged printers and made "the first noteworthy statement of the subject's liberty to publish at will" when he asserted that he would print any lawful book regardless of any of the Queen's commandments (Clyde, 1934: 17-18). Wolfe was imprisoned for his attacks on the Queen's prerogative to grant patents, but later, to keep him from agitating further, he was made a privileged printer. Problems of copyright trace their origins to this case.

Peter Wentworth made an impassioned plea for freedom of speech in Parliament in an address to the House of Commons.

His address was provoked by Queen Elizabeth's disregard for the Parliamentary privilege (which was really a privilege in name only at the time) of every member of Parliament to freely discuss any subject in the House when she warned the Commons not to meddle in matters of state which did not concern them (Siebert, 1952: 101).

These were the first faint rumblings for some form of freedom of speech and the press. But they were met by even stricter regulations on the printing trade in the form of the Star Chamber Decree of 1586. The decree announced that:

> The Archbishop of Canterbury and the Bishop of London were appointed licensers, that nothing was to be printed that had not been perused by both or one of them, and that all printing was to be confined to London and the two Universities [Oxford and Cambridge]. The Stationers Company were to search for printing presses . . . and to seize unlawful books. . . . The Company were forbidden to elect new printers without special recommendation from the licensers and severe penalties were fixed for infringements of the law [Clyde, 1934: 20-21].

But even this severe decree did not deter some Puritans from conducting a campaign through the press in which they attacked the Church of England and opposed the established order. The famous Martin Marprelate tracts were part of this campaign and while they were eventually stopped by the government, they "had made a deep impression upon the public consciousness" (Siebert, 1952: 100) and attested to the potential power of the press.

During the early Stuart reign (1603-1640) controls on the press increased somewhat but enforcement of and compliance with these controls diminished. This, Siebert (1952: 3) states, was largely due to the growing rift under the early Stuarts between the Crown on the one hand and the public and the Parliament on the other. The public suspected James I of Papist leanings and the Parliament was pressing for a larger role in governing the country. Moreover, unprivileged printers were becoming even more disenchanted with the

Stationers Company which had by this time "become an autocratic oligarchy principally engaged in pursuing the pecuniary advantage of its officers" (Siebert, 1952: 141). As a result, the disenfranchised printers grew more defiant of the licensing system.

The two most significant controls that the Stuarts introduced were the broadening of the legal concept of seditious libel and the Star Chamber Decree of 1637.

Under James I, the courts, particularly the Star Chamber, were used increasingly to suppress political discussion. Criminal or seditious libel—especially after it was expanded to include true as well as false statements concerning "Great Men of the Realm," along with the penalties attached to it including severe corporal punishment—proved an effective weapon in curbing the expression of unwelcome political and religious opinion.

Under Charles I, the licensing system was updated with the Star Chamber Decree of 1637. The name of the author, printer, and licenser had to appear on every printed work and printers were required to deposit £300 as a safeguard against the printing of unlicensed works.

Another significant development under the early Stuarts was the appearance in 1621 of the first corantos, forerunners of the modern newspaper. Printed in the Netherlands, they contained foreign news and the great demand for them stemmed from an interest among the English in the Thirty Years War. Because the corantos were critical of his foreign policy, James I tried to stamp them out but had little success. Eventually these small newssheets began to include accounts of domestic news and "out of these accounts developed the 'diurnals,' or daily reports of local events" (Emery, 1978: 8).

SHIFTS OF AUTHORITY

In 1641, the Long Parliament abolished the Star Chamber, which through its decrees of 1586 and 1637 and its punishments of seditious libel played a great role in deterring freedom of expression in England. With the shift of authority

from the Crown to Parliament, the authority and enforcement powers of the Stationers Company, which relied
directly on royal prerogative for its mandate and its patents,
began to crumble. The licensing system was also in a state of
suspension while Parliament struggled to wrest the power to
control it and other areas of the printing trade from the
Crown.

As a result of these changes, critical, subversive, and seditious publications became far more common and unprivileged
printers took advantage of the confusion in the Stationers
Company to engage in piracy and infringements of patents to
an unprecedented degree. The Long Parliament, comprised
principally of religious reformers who had no particular commitment to freedom of discussion or the press, finally
responded to these abuses of the press by reinstating the
licensing system with the 1642 Ordinance for the regulating
of printing (Siebert, 1952: 187).

The revival of the licensing system provoked John Milton
to write his famous *Areopagitica,* an appeal to Parliament to
abandon licensing which later became probably the most
frequently cited argument for a free press. Siebert concisely
isolates the main points of Milton's *Areopagitica's* argument
in the classic *Four Theories of the Press:*

> Basic to his argument were the assumptions that men by exercis-
> ing reason can distinguish between right and wrong, good and
> bad, and that to exercise this talent man should have unlimited
> access to the ideas and thoughts of other men. Milton was
> confident that Truth was definite and demonstrable and that it
> had unique powers of survival when permitted to assert itself in a
> "free and open encounter." Out of Milton have developed the
> contemporary concepts of "the open market place of ideas" and
> the "self-righting process": Let all with something to say be free
> to express themselves. The True and sound will survive; the false
> and unsound will be vanquished [1956: 44-45].

However, as Levy (1960: 95-99) points out in *Legacy of
Suppression,* Milton's vision of freedom of the press was

quite limited. He would not extend this freedom to Roman Catholics and possibly not even to the publishers of popular newssheets. Also he suggested that the government has a legitimate claim to suppress, after publication, opinions it considers to be mischievous or which it thinks lessens the esteem the people have for it—in other words, seditious libel.

Many of Milton's contemporaries, such as Henry Robinson, Richard Overton, and the Levellers John Lilburne and William Walwyn, also argued for greater freedom of the press and against licensing. But, Levy notes (1960: 88-100), none of these writers went so far as to advocate freedom to scandalize the government or to express opinions considered dangerous to the state. Freedom of the press meant freedom from prior restraint to most Englishmen during this period and for some time to come.

Unfortunately Milton's *Aeropagitica* and other essays dealing with the concept and philosophy of freedom of the press were not widely read at first and had little effect on their author's contemporaries.

Between 1647 and 1649 control of the nation began to pass into the hands of the Army and by 1652 England had become a Protectorate headed by the Lord Protector Oliver Cromwell. With England under military rule, the Printing Act of 1649 came into effect. This act was designed partly to check the publication of small daily newsbooks such as mercuries and journals which were offsprings of the earlier corantos but which now also reported domestic public affairs and, to some extent, the proceedings of Parliament even though reports of the latter were not permitted.

These newsbooks were very popular and had been multiplying very rapidly with little control. Many of them were critical of the government and expressed royalist sentiments. Under the Printing Act of 1649 the licensed press of the time was replaced by an official press.

When Cromwell took the regulation of the press into his own hands in 1655, he ordered official and unofficial newsbooks banned. Only two newsbooks were suffered to remain.

They were strictly controlled and became, in effect, official organs of Cromwell's government.

With the restoration of Charles II in 1660, control over the press was divided between the King, who retained the power of royal proclamation, and Parliament, which participated through the Regulation of Printing Acts. The most significant measure taken to regulate the press during this period was the Printing Act of 1662. The act restricted printing to the master printers of the Stationers Company and the printers of Cambridge and Oxford universities. All printers had to produce a surety to guard against unlawful printing. The act further stipulated that nothing heretical, seditious, or offensive to the Christian faith or any government official could be printed, imported, or sold (Siebert, 1952: 221-241). An exclusive patent system was also established under Charles II. Siebert describes it:

> The printing patents were monopolistic grants by the crown as distinguished from copyrights which arose out of prior registration in the books of the Stationers Company. The royal grant might vest the ownership of a single book in the author, printer, or stationer, or it might reserve an entire field of the publishing business for the benefit of a particular person or group of persons. The most important patent in reserved fields, aside from the grants to the Stationers Company, was that of royal printer or printer to the king [1952: 245].

THE END OF LICENSING

In 1694 the Printing Act of 1662 expired and with it vanished licensing in England. The refusal of the House of Commons to renew the act and its licensing provisions stemmed not from any profound moral or philosophical objections to the practice of licensing or commitment to a freer press. Instead, the commercial restraints that the monopoly patent system as confirmed by the act were placing on the printing trade, the difficulty of administering and enforcing the licensing system, and the difficulty of determining what books should be categorized as offensive and thus suppressed were the main reasons cited for allowing the legislation to die (Siebert, 1952: 261-262).

The collapse of the licensing system represented the most significant step forward, up to that point in history, for freedom of the press. Also, it marked the start of a series of landmark concessions British governments made during the 18th century to further free the press.

The great inroads made in the name of a free press in the 18th century may be traced to a number of causes. Perhaps the most important was the changing constitutional arrangement in England which started with the overthrow of James II in 1689 and the ensuing ascendancy of Parliament over the Crown. The evolving awareness of the supremacy of a Parliament representing and accountable to public opinion was part of a democratic trend. If Parliament was supposed to consult and be guided by public opinion, the public would have to have wider scope to express its opinion and to learn about the issues of the day.

Also, a two-party system was emerging at this time in England, and "as it became evident that the group in power in government was subject to change under shifts in public opinion, a new theory of the place of the press in society became necessary" (Siebert, 1952: 6). Moreover, there was a rapid growth of daily newspapers in the 18th century, starting with the appearance of the first one in England, *The Daily Courant*, in 1702. The presence and popularity of these papers reflected an awareness of an expanding need and demand for information, discussion, and criticism among a public that had become more responsible and active in affairs of state.

At the beginning of the 18th century, the only legal controls on the press were the law of seditious libel and regulation by Parliament of its proceedings. The relaxation of most of the 17th century controls resulted in a deluge of seditious literature which vexed Queen Anne.

To stem this flood of critical material, Parliament passed the Stamp Act of 1712, which imposed a tax on printed matter. The act was designed to reduce the circulation of pamphlets and newspapers which carried the bulk of the offensive literature. But because of a loophole in the act, most of these publications managed to escape paying most of the tax. Eventually the loopholes were closed and the taxes increased in later years, but it is unclear whether these measures ever really were the deterrent which the government intended.

Between 1720 and 1723 the so-called "Cato" letters, written by John Trenchard and Thomas Gordon under the pseudonym "Cato," appeared in the *London Journal.* They represent one of the most complete and cogent articulations of the principles of the freedom of the press in the 18th century. Cato argued that libel was a necessary evil arising out of a free press but that the benefits to the advancement of liberty, religion, the arts and sciences, and knowledge in general that a free press would bring outweighed the evils of libel. He contended that government should submit to having its deeds openly examined by the public it served.

> On ground that the public had an interest in the truth about public measures and men, Cato argued that truth should be admitted as a defense against a criminal libel charge, in other words, that a defendent who could prove the accuracy of his allegedly seditious utterance should be acquitted [Levy, 1960: 119].

Cato's argument for truth as a defense against libel appeared a decade later in colonial America in the trial of John Peter Zenger, a case which, though it had little effect on legal reform with respect to freedom of the press, did help to mobilize public opinion on the issue (Alexander, 1963).

RESTRICTIONS IN AMERICA

Freedom of the press was not really an operative concept in pre-Zenger America. A quite rigid licensing system under the authority of the governors and councils of each of the colonies had been in effect in the late 17th and early 18th centuries. The first newspaper in the colonies, *Publick Occurrences Both Foreign and Domestic,* did not appear until 1690. After just one edition, the governor and council disallowed any further publication of the paper because it had been published without authority. For the next few decades, most newspapers were published by government-appointed postmasters and usually carried a line stating that they were Published by Authority, which meant the governor or his secretary had approved the contents of the paper before printing (Mott, 1962: 9-14).

Levy also notes,

> Colonial America was the scene of the most extraordinary diversity of opinion on religion, politics, social structure, and other vital subjects, but every community, particularly outside of the few "cities," tended to be a tight little island clutching its own respective orthodoxy and too eager to banish or extralegally punish unwelcome dissidents [1960: 18-19].

He adds that when nonconforming opinions were tolerated by the community, they were often suppressed under law.

While there were hundreds of trials for seditious libel in England in the 17th and 18th centuries, the common law courts in colonial America did not play a very active role in the suppression of unorthodox or critical opinions. The governors with their councils, acting on a quasi-judicial capacity, and the popularly elected legislative assemblies were far more instrumental in quelling seditious opinion. Levy says the assemblies:

> Zealously pursuing its prerogative of being immune to criticism, an Assembly might summon, interrogate, and fix criminal penal-

ties against anyone who had supposedly libeled its members, proceedings, or the government generally. Any words, written, printed or spoken which were imagined to have a tendency of impeaching an Assembly's behavior, questioning its authority, derogating from its honor, affronting its dignity, or defaming its member's individually or together, were regarded as a seditious scandal against the government, punishable as a breach of privilege [1960: 20-21].

Prior to the Zenger trial, there had never been an essay on freedom of the press published by anyone in America and the concept of seditious libel was never questioned. Cato was popular and widely read, "but the colonists gave little independent thought and even less expression to a theory of unfettered debate" (Levy, 1960: 126).

The Zenger trial in 1735 aroused the slowly awakening concern in the colonies over the issue of freedom of the press. Zenger, the printer of the *New York Weekly Journal*, was indicted for seditious libel. Andrew Hamilton, Zenger's defense lawyer, delivered a moving argument for the freedom of the press to expose abuses of power by the government. Hamilton's argument rested on two key points: Truth should constitute a defense against libel and juries should determine the libellous character of the words in question. At the time, truth did not constitute a defense and judges determined the question of libel. Juries determined whether the defendant actually published the words, not whether the words were libellous.

The jury, swept up in the tide of popular support for the cause Zenger represented, returned a verdict of not guilty. But it was not until 1790 that truth as a defense and the right of the jury to decide both the law and the fact in libel cases were legally recognized in America (Emery, 1978: 46).

THE NEW WORLD'S INFLUENCE ON THE OLD

The Zenger trial also caught the imagination of the English. It set an example for British juries to emulate and helped fuel popular dissatisfaction with the narrow view, especially as it was upheld in the courts, that freedom of the press was nothing more than freedom from licensing and was subject to the laws of seditious libel. Seditious libel "was the most useful single weapon available to the government in its conflict with recalcitrant printers and publishers" in the 18th century (Siebert, 1952: 380). The concept was very broad, including any statement which tended to diminish the affection of the people for their government.

Due largely to the relaxation of controls on the press such as licensing and the new constitutional relationship between the crown, Parliament, and the public, the British people at this time were enjoying a greater latitude for discussing and participating in public affairs than they had known before. Seditious libel prosecutions were unpopular. There was a growing feeling in many quarters that the procedural rules in seditious libel cases were out of step with the times and should be changed to enable juries to decide the whole question of libel.

In 1764 John Wilkes was prosecuted and convicted of seditious libel after he insulted the King following his speech of 1763 in the *North Briton*. The public, which rallied to the support of Wilkes and freedom of the press, was once again alerted to the need for reform of the seditious libel laws. However, little or no change of those laws was made as a result of the case (Siebert, 1952: 383-84).

The Wilkes case also drew attention to the general warrants for search and seizure which were often issued in cases of seditious libel. These warrants authorized the arrest of anyone on the mere suspicion of his implication in a libel and authorized the search of homes of all suspects and the seizure of any of their property. Wilkes's private study had been ransacked under a general warrant. In 1765 these general warrants were declared illegal (Levy, 1960: 12). The spotlight was most directly turned on the rules of procedure in trials for seditious libel during the prosecutions of the publishers of one of the famous "Junius" letters in 1770. In the letter in question, Junius, shielded by his anonymity, called upon the King to "admit his mistakes, reverse his policies, dismiss his advisers, and to withdraw from his interference in Parliament" (Siebert, 1952: 385). John Almon, the first publisher to be prosecuted, was convicted. Henry Woodfall, who had first published the letter, was prosecuted next. After more than nine hours of deliberation, the jury returned a verdict of "guilty of printing and publishing only," implying that it did not consider Woodfall guilty of seditious libel. Two more publishers were tried and the jury in both cases returned a verdict of not guilty.

By refusing to convict the publishers simply of publishing the material in question, which they obviously had done, the juries were in effect taking upon themselves the duty, reserved for the judge, of deciding on the criminal nature of the material. Siebert, describes the aftermath of the Junius decisions:

> The public uproar which accompanied the Junius prosecutions convinced both the government attorneys and the justices of the difficulty, if not impossibility, of obtaining convictions for seditious libel in the present state of public opinion. . . . Tactically the battle was won by the London newspapers and their supporters since juries refused to convict; theoretically the law remained as Lord Mansfield and the government prosecutors contended [1952: 389].

Not until Fox's Libel Act in 1792 was the jury's competence to pass a general verdict on the whole issue in a libel case, not just on the publication and innuendoes, legally recognized.

Reporting the Proceedings of Parliament

Another key contest in the battle for freedom of the press was won the year after the Junius prosecutions, 1771. In that year, the press' right to report the proceedings of Parliament was implicitly conceded by the House of Commons. Both

Houses of Parliament had always prohibited accounts of their proceedings. Few significant attempts to test this prohibition were made before the 1730s. In that decade, two monthly magazines, the *Gentleman's Magazine* and the *London Magazine*, began publishing contemporaneous reports of House of Commons proceedings and debates. These accounts proved so popular that the two magazines, which were locked in a heated competition, were encouraged to step up their Parliamentary reporting. Eventually the publishers of both magazines were ordered to appear before the House of Lords and were reprimanded. After that the *Gentleman's Magazine* discontinued its Parliamentary reporting and the *London Magazine* drastically reduced its coverage.

By 1758, monthly magazines were obsolete but they were replaced by a flood of new triweekly newspapers which competed with the older papers. The rigorous competition for survival which these new papers triggered compelled publishers to turn to new of Parliament to stimulate readership. Both houses responded by placing heavy restrictions on this type of journalistic activity (Siebert, 1952: 349-356). But the newspaper publishers were united in their opposition to Parliament's measures. They were supported by the city government in London which was in the hands of the Parliamentary opposition and by the city's representatives in the House of Commons. The issue finally came to a head in 1771 when a number of newspapers not only related a motion made in Parliament but also presented it "from a point of view with the direct objective of influencing the votes of the members of the ancient assembly" (Siebert, 1952: 357).

Three printers of offending papers were arrested in connection with this incident. But, following a preconceived plan, the three printers had themselves brought before the sympathetic city magistrates who immediately released them. For their part in discharging the printers, the lord mayor and two of his aldermen were called before the House of Commons. The lord mayor and one of the aldermen were found guilty by the house of a breach of the house's privilege and committed to the Tower of London. The other alderman was John Wilkes, who was also a member of the House of Commons. He repeatedly refused orders by the house to appear before it to answer charges. Not only were its orders ignored but the house's embarrassment was compounded when the two city officials sent to the Tower were made heroes by the London populace (Siebert, 1952: 359-360).

Siebert explains the effect of this whole episode:

> The House was never again to act in the same arbitrary way to defeat the right of the people to know what was taking place in the highest legislative body of the land. Not that this right was either openly or by indirection recognized. The Commons in 1771 yielded only because it felt it was more important to maintain its hereditary rights in theory than to put them to the test by force against a popularly supported and unified group of newspaper publishers. Secrecy of debate was still enjoined; the power to enforce such secrecy still existed but ceased to be exercised [1952: 361].

In 1775 even the House of Lords opened its door to reporters.

In America during this period the forces of independence were gathering strength and much of their fight against British rule was conducted through the press. This naturally involved marshalling arguments for a freer press in order to expand their latitude for criticizing the British government and the royal governors. But except for men like Thomas Jefferson, who was perhaps the most brilliant exponent of a free press in America at the time, most Americans who advanced the cause of freedom of expression conceived of it as an instrument for spreading the message of independence and did not embrace it so much on philosophical or moral grounds. Nevertheless, it became, by virtue of its high visibility, an integral part of Americans' image of their society at the time. Freedom of the press was recognized as an inalienable right and protected in a number of state constitutions after the Revolution. And in 1791 the First Amendment, guaranteeing that "Congress shall make no law . . . abridging the freedom of speech, or of the press," was ratified.

During the 19th and 20th centuries, the victories that had been won in the name of freedom of the press were consolidated and the concept was broadened. Judicial construction, constitutional provisions, and legislation such as a Parliamentary Act in 1843 in England, which established truth as a defense in libel cases, lifted most of the remaining legal barriers to freedom of the press and speech. Moreover, wide privileges of fair comment and of reporting public proceedings without fear of libel have been generally recognized in Britain and the United States.

Nineteenth century libertarian thinkers such as James Mill and his son John Stuart Mill argued in favor of a wider scope for the free circulation of seditious statements. Through a gradual accumulation of more liberal judicial decisions concerning freedom of the press, seditious libel is by now a weak legal concept at best.

Current Concerns

By the standards that prevailed between the 16th and 18th centuries, the press in most advanced Western democracies today is quite free. However, issues such as the revealing of sources and the extent to which the press should have access to, and the right to report, information pertaining to national security remain. The U.S. Pentagon Papers and the attempts to stop the publication of nuclear-related materials in the *Progressive Magazine* in the late 1970s reflect the continuing debate over the "free press." More recently the United States

Supreme Court's ruling in Stanford Daily case (which holds that police need only search warrants to search washrooms and private homes and offices, even if occupants are not suspected of crimes) and jailing of New York Times reporter M. A. Farber (for refusal to turn over notes to New Jersey Court), have spurred new wave of bills in Congress to protect press. And news that county prosecutor last month invaded newsroom of KBCI-TV Boise, Idaho, with search warrant and seized news tapes may add impetus to drive for such legislation. Also last month, newsman for WBZ-TV Boston was ordered by state court to jail for refusal to reveal sources for his story on judicial misconduct [Broadcasting, 1980: 15].

The concerns over a "free press" and the First and Fourth (unreasonable search) Amendments keep the government involvement with the press an ever-present issue.

In England in 1980 the issue of Granada Television and an investigative piece on the British steel industry also has the press concerned. Lord Denning of the British Court of Appeal initially ruled that the program researcher had to reveal from whom he received inside and confidential British Steel Corporation documents. The researcher, claiming journalistic immunity, refused. Ultimately British Steel dropped its pursuit.

Any claim or move toward government control or responsibility for the media as part of the aims of the NWIO is untenable; indeed, year by year and conflict by conflict, many of which are being resolved by the highest courts, increasing government control and responsibility make Western journalists and publishers more determined and committed to a "Fourth Estate," where a distance from government philosophy dominates rather than even thinking of any possibility of "benefits" from government control.[2]

NOTES

1. Considerable detail is provided later on UNESCO's role in the overall debate about the NWIO and the draft declarations on the mass media receive attention. In addition, the five major international wire services are described later.

2. A related issue in Britain is the possibility of government subsidy to its class papers, *The Times*, the *Observer*, or the *Guardian*. They represent major historical institutions that are continually beleaguered by both financial and labor

problems. Rather than allow them to fold, the government may step in with financial assistance. Such action should bring the issue of government involvement in the press back to a controversial stage. In addition, with electronic papers via videotex systems, such as Prestel, moving beyond the experimental stage, the role of government in media activities is bound to grow rather than decrease despite the 200 years of struggling to separate the two.

REFERENCES

ALEXANDER, J. (1963) A Brief Narrative of the Case and Trial of John Peter Zenger. Cambridge, MA: Harvard University Press.

BECKER, C. (1945) Freedom and Responsibility in the American Way of Life. New York: Alfred A. Knopf.

Broadcasting (1980) "Shield legislation." August 4, p. 15.

BULLEN, D. (1980) "UNESCO and the media: A report on developments at Belgrade." Tufts University, Medford, MA., November 10, pp. 1-9.

BURY, J. (1952) A History of Freedom of Thought. London: Oxford University Press.

CHENERY, W. (1935) Freedom of the Press. New York: Harcourt Brace Jovanovich.

CLYDE, W. (1934) The Struggle for the Freedom of the Press from Caxton to Cromwell. New York: Burt Franklin.

EMERY, E. and M. EMERY (1978) The Press and America. Englewood Cliffs, NJ: Prentice-Hall.

LEVY, L. (1960) Legacy of Suppression. Cambridge, MA: Harvard University Press.

MOTT, F. (1962) American Journalism. New York: Macmillan.

SIEBERT, F. (1952) Freedom of the Press in England 1476-1771. Urbana: University of Illinois Press.

SIEBERT, F., T. PETERSON, and W. SCHRAMM (1956) Four Theories of the Press. Urbana: University of Illinois Press.

Chapter 3

A MISGUIDED START:
The Media and Development Research Traditions

Several apparently unrelated forces are now coming together in such a way as to further the movement toward an NWIO. Among these forces is the dual rejection and failure of modernization theory and practice promulgated since the close of World War II. Simply put, modernization theory has failed to produce.

Within the overall theoretical framework, a substantial component of the mix of factors which cumulatively should have moved the LDC's to an industrialized status is the mass communication system. Herein lies the connection between modernization theory and communication practices.

In retrospect just as educational television in the West did not bring about the projected revolution in the classroom, so also the projection in the 1950s and 1960s of broadcasting as a panacea to rapidly bring about the transformation of LDC's into industrialized nations, and markets, failed to materialize.

Broadcasting has had limited success in LDC's. Indeed
radio, and now television, may have done more cultural harm
than good in aiding the newly formed nations of recent
decades. The appropriateness and cost of foreign content to
meet the needs and objectives of these newly formed nation
is now a central issue. Also, a clear and realistic set of current
development objectives is still a rare phenomenon for many
LDC's. And within these objectives, exactly what role mass
media is to play, other than the vague rhetoric of media being
used to aid development goals, is even more elusive. Finally
some LDC's are pursuing color television as a necessary
system despite its expense and limited uses. It is within this
rather massive reexamination of modernization and communication policies that the NWIO has looked with disfavor on
the bulk of accumulated social science theory and related
media research.

The following attempts to trace the various streams of
theory, both American and European, and major research
trends that are underpinnings of knowledge for students of
international communication; the chapter begins with development theory and then highlights major contributions to
the literature dealing with theoretical and applied aspects of
international mass media research.

Development Theory and the Role of Communication

Wilbur Schramm and Daniel Lerner, discussing development performance in the 1960s and 1970s, state, "The
impressive gains of GNP in many countries evaporated when
restated in per capita terms, for these economic gains were
largely swallowed by the greater increases of population
(1976: 15). Now, unless they have domestic oil reserve
many LDC's are slipping even further behind the industrialized West. The disappointing record of Third World development efforts in general has occasioned rethinking of development theory and approaches to research among students
international and mass communication theory.

Development communication study in the last three decades, it has been charged, has been characterized largely by the application of Western, especially American, generalizations and research methodology about mass communication and the modernization processes (Schiller, 1969: Varis, 1974; Wells, 1974). In other words, it has been accused of having a distinctly "Made-in-America" flavor.

These U.S. and other Western theoretical models of development and communication and approaches to research methodology are now being questioned by both Western and Third World critics alike. Their relevance and sensitivity to the unique (non-Western) problems and conditions in LDC's has brought about a different conceptual design.

The theoretical model or, as it is often called, "paradigm" of development which has dominated thinking and guided most research and even policy making vis-à-vis modernization and aid programs has been drawn from the experience and patterns of European and American expansion, particularly in the 19th and 20th centuries.

Most Western theorists in economics, politics, and communication conceived of patterns and forces which catapulted Europe and America into modernity as being more than part of a culturally specific, one-time historical phenomenon. They concluded from the example of Western progress that modernization is a deterministic, inexorable, and universal process "in which all societies participate or which is inherent in the development of every society" (Eisenstadt, 1976: 38). They argued that modernization has a distinct pattern with certain reappearing characteristics. These characteristics were usually identified by such analysts as those associated with the economic growth and modernization of Western society, such as industrialization, urbanization, literacy and education, mass media, political unification, differentiation and specialization of societal institutions and structures, plus a breakdown of traditions that retarded the industrial process.[1]

Lerner, in his landmark work on development and communication, *The Passing of Traditional Society*, displays this emphasis in early development thinking on the primacy and universal relevancy of many features of the Western model of development and modernization:

> As we shall show, the Western model of modernization exhibits certain components and sequences whose relevance is global. Everywhere, for example, increasing urbanization has tended to raise literacy; rising literacy has tended to increase media exposure; increasing media exposure has "gone with" wider economic participation (per capita income) and political participation (voting). The model evolved in the West is an historical fact. . . . The same basic model reappears in virtually all modernizing societies on all continents of the world, regardless of variations in race, color, creed [1955: 46].

In elaborating on this sequence, he demonstrates that a shift of population from rural to urban settings is the first stage which must occur before there can be a "takeoff" into modernity. Urbanization leads to the next step, increased literacy and mass media exposure, which in turn trigger "empathy," or the ability to imagine oneself as socially mobile. This is a precondition for the final step which is greater economic and political participation. Lerner (1955) understands this sequence of institutional developments to be a natural and historically determined order which governs the way traditional societies make the transition to an industrial state and modernity.

This is consistent with a common feature of the dominant paradigm—namely, the view that the unfolding of the development process generally conforms through some kind of historical or logical necessity to a series of progressive stages which must be passed through on the way to modernity. The order in which these stages are supposed to occur is usually derived from the example of Euroamerican modernization.

THE ECONOMIC GROWTH MODEL

Perhaps the best known categorization of stages of development is the one Rostow (1971) advances in *The Stages of Economic Growth*. He finds that the development process can be divided into five stages: traditional society, establishment of preconditions to takeoff, takeoff into sustained growth, the drive to maturity, and the age of high mass consumption.

A larger evolutionary perspective, characteristic of the dominant paradigm, resonates through these stage conceptions of development. Each stage represents an advance over the preceding one, similar to the stages of biological evolution.

In most versions of this scheme, traditional and modern societies are placed at opposite ends of the evolutionary scale. Development is viewed as evolving beyond traditional structures which supposedly cannot accommodate rapid social change and economic growth; the attitudes, values, and social relationships which support them are frequently conveyed by media and educational systems. Eisenstadt notes that these evolutionary schemes

chiefly attempted to explain the processes, with their variations, in the possible transition from traditional to modern society. The basic model that emerged ... assumed that the conditions for development of a viable, growth-sustaining, modern society were tantamount to continuous extention of modern components and to destruction of all traditional elements. According to this view, the greater its characteristics of structural specialization, the higher a society ranked on various indices of social mobilization. Concommitantly, the more thorough the disintegration of traditional elements, the more able a society would be to "develop" continuously—to deal with perennially new problems and to increase its capacity to absorb change; and, implicitly, to develop other qualitative characteristics of modern societies such as rationality, efficiency, and a predilection to liberty [1976: 33].

Like biological evolution, then, development was assumed to be irreversible. Schramm, summarizing Eisenstadt's description of evolutionary models of development, says:

> Social modernization was able to generate continuing change, and also to absorb the stress of change and adapt itself to changing demands. In other words, the process seemed irreversible. Once the necessary conditions were established for takeoff, a country took off, became modern, stayed modern [1976: 46].

This same dominant paradigm of development did not fulfill the success stories on which governments and aid agencies counted. Criticisms mounted during the 1970s and into the 1980s.

An early critic, Inayatullah, provides one of the most cogent indictments of the paradigm. He questions the validity of the assumption underlying the paradigm that postulates development as a universal process, the internal logic of which forces all societies to approximate Western patterns of modernization and the surrounding values which facilitated it. Also he questions the evolutionary theme of the dominant paradigm which suggests in a somewhat normative and ethno-centric way that advanced Western societies, perched atop the evolutionary ladder, are the ideal, beckoning destination of development and that traditional society, stuck at the bottom of the scale, must be completely relinquished if modernization is ever to occur. Inayatullah's critique goes as follows:

> First it the dominant paradigm presupposes that because the "traditional" societies have not risen to the higher level of technological development (since the Industrial Revolution) in comparison to the Western society, therefore they are sterile, unproductive, uncreative, and hence worth liquidating. It measures the creativity of the "traditional" world with a few limited standards such as urbanization and industrialization, like the person who measures the competence of everybody in terms of his own special competence. It ignores (because it cannot measure it with

its available instrument) the possibility of existence or (at least the potentiality) of nonmaterial areas of creativity.

This point of view also rests on a unilinear view and interpretation of history. It presumes that all history is inexorably moving toward the same destiny, same goals, and same value system as Western man has. It presupposes that the range of combinations of technology and values other than the Western (Judeo-Christian?) one is very limited and insists that modern technology could not be adopted without sacrificing the "traditional" values.... It shows remarkable ethnocentrism by equating modern society with paradise and fails to take into account the "crisis," especially in the realm of personality, which the modern society is facing [1976: 100-101].

The modernity versus tradition dichotomy which he challenges is just one of a number of linear dichotomous continua such as "industrial/agrarian," "Western/non-Western," "developed/underdeveloped" in terms of which modernization was, and for some still is, conceptualized under the dominant paradigm. While these relationships are used purportedly as neutral conceptual tools of scientific analysis, there is a case that their use by Western analysts carries an implicit ideological affinity or cultural bias for the "modern," "industrialized," "Western" poles of the continui (Frey, 1973: 340-342).

Eisenstadt notes that the presence of certain conditions of incipient modernization and even "further extension of these indices does not necessarily assure that continued processes of modernization and the creation of viable political or social structures" (1976: 36). He continues:

Several countries in Central and Eastern Europe, Latin America, and Asia seem to have reached at certain levels a negative correlation between such sociodemographic indices as literacy, spread of mass media, formal education, or urbanization on the one hand and the institutional ability to sustain growth or to develop libertarian or "rational" institutions on the other [1976: 36].

To understand the role that communication and mass media were thought to play in development under the dominant paradigm, it is important to note that perhaps the most prominent feature of the paradigm was the assumption that development could be equated with economic growth, especially the type of rapid growth the West experiences with a capital-intensive and technology-based industrialization.

Rogers points out that "economists were firmly in the driver's seat of development programs. They defined the problem of underdevelopment largely in economic terms, and in turn this perception of the problem as predominantly economic in nature helped to put and to keep economists in charge" (1976: 215). Of course, this also connects the New International Economic Order with the questioning of Western assumptions about the logic and control of the international economic system.

The preoccupation with the economic determinism of Western models of development and modernization is reflected in a major text of the late 1960s by Rogers:

> Economic development measures are a type of directed social change. New ideas are introduced into a social system in order to attain higher per capita incomes and levels of living through more modern production methods and improved social organization. The many government-sponsored development programs designed to introduce technological innovations in agriculture, health, education, and industry are contemporary examples of directed change [1969: 7].

Along with other international development specialists, Rogers views development as "a type of social change in which new ideas are introduced into a social system in order to produce higher per capita incomes and levels of living through modern production methods and improved social organization" (1969: 8-9).

THE INADEQUACY OF THE ECONOMIC GROWTH MODEL

For the most part, the attempts at directed change never materialized. The efforts of the First World to engineer change in the LDC's have been unsuccessful. In fact, the most recent World Bank's Development Report points out that developing countries are still relatively worse off, vis-à-vis the industrialized, in terms of growth. Along with economic stagnation many developing countries have massive illiteracy problems which are also getting worse. Director General M'Bow of UNESCO predicts that there will be 954 million illiterate adults in the world by the end of this century. Currently there are 814 million. M'Bow, in a 14th International Literacy Day speech, stated, "Illiteracy is closely tied to poverty. Throughout the world the illiterates are the poor, or make up poor societies. But illiteracy is not only an effect of misery, it is also one of the causes" (1979: 14). This illiteracy also renders certain mass media—newspapers, magazines, books—useless to an ever-increasing proportion of the LDC's population.

As criticism mounts against the Western economic growth model of development, some alternatives are being developed. For example, Sharp reports:

> So what should be the principal ingredients in a new model of development? As yet there is no formal consensus, but the shape of such a model—its premises and priorities radically different from what has gone before—is now emerging from many strands of research, analysis and discussion [1976: 16].

Sharp concludes:

> The formulation of strategies to match the alternative development model is still at an early stage. A prime difficulty is that the most important distinguishing features of this model relate to intangibles: the nonmaterial dimension, which is anathema to development classicists because it cannot be quantified and because it simply doesn't show up on their intellectual radar [1979: 19].

Several aspects of cultural policies and needs—of which mass media systems are a component—fall within this tangible area. Cultural aspects are difficult to measure accurately and meaningfully; classical linear economic models fail to accommodate salient aspects of culturally based movements aiming for independence. Students of development eventually questioned the traditional propositions underlying development theories. Rogers notes:

> One might think that this overwhelming focus of communication research in Latin America would be consistent with the preoccupation with social change and development. However, this research generally shows that the mass media are not very important, at least directly, in fostering socio-economic development. Explanations may be in the nature of the mass media institutions and in characteristics of those who control them. In any event, the mass media in Latin America contain little content (1) of relevance about appropriate types of development for the mass audience of rural and urban poor, or (2) about the sociostructural changes that are needed if much real development is to occur [1976: 9-10].

A leading Latin American researcher, Luis Ramior Beltran, also notes the underlying problem with the bulk of the LDC media research:

> Understandably and legitimately, the United States designed and constructed, in philosophy, object, and method, the kind of social sciences that fit its particular structural (cultural, economic, and political) circumstances. These were eminently sciences for adjustment—essentially addressed to studying conformity with all the prevailing needs, aims, values and norms of the established social order, so as to help its ruling system, to attain normalcy and avoid deviant behaviours [1976: 23].

What he and several others are doing is calling into question the entire functional school of media theory, dating from the two classics by Lasswell (1948) and Lazarsfeld and Merton (1948). Functional for whom is now the critical question. In general this school uncritically accepted the media elite's position and the reinforcement of the status quo as being legitimate and rational behavior for media systems.

It became evident that economic forces alone could not account for problems of underdevelopment and did not automatically generate the far-reaching structural and attitudinal changes such as acceptance of the "Protestant Ethic" that full development required. Attempted imported economics practices, technologies, and media fare often created confusion because traditional systems and ways were not prepared to deal with them. In turn, some analysts shifted to noneconomic explanations of development, identifying such variables as mass media exposure, political and social structural changes, social mobility, and individual psychology as preconditions of development. Eisenstadt says:

> Initially there was a strong tendancy to assume the primacy of the economic sphere; stress was placed, therefore, on the economic solvent [or pushing force that would ignite the "takeoff" into modernity] for development. However, the assumption of economic primacy was discarded relatively early in the game, when it was realized that the development and effective functioning of a modern economic system could not be understood in economic terms alone [1976: 34].

But even accounts which identified noneconomic influences on development did not as a rule go that far beyond purely economic analyses in their explanatory power or the scope of the insights they provided into development. They tended to pinpoint certain individual variables such as the diffusion of innovations or specific clusters of variables such as Lerner's urbanization-literacy-media exposure-participation grouping as the chief determinants of modernization. They were rarely characterized by a broader systems approach which would aim at measuring the interrelationships among all the variables (or as many as data are available on) which might conceivably affect development. These variables would range from the impact on development of the larger international social, economic, and political order to more microlevel considerations such as communication patterns and networks of social interaction and interpersonal relationships among indi-

viduals in a particular developing community which could
reveal larger structural trends in the developing society as a
whole. (This point will be taken up again at the end of this
chapter.)

Moreover, while noneconomic factors were increasingly
recognized as being as essential to the bringing about of
developmental change as economic ones, economic growth as
measured in gross national product and per capita income
continued to be seen as the most important goal of such
change and its most telling index. For example, diffusion of
innovation theories, which generated the bulk of development communication research in the 1960s, proceeded on
the principle that the spreading, copying, and disseminating
of inventions, new ideas, and new technology through communication channels were the main ingredients in inducing
developmental change. Yet Rogers, as one of the pioneers of
diffusion of innovation research who later questioned the
validity of much of that research, once described the purpose
of diffusion in economic terms. He said, "New ideas are
introduced into a social system in order to attain higher per
capita incomes and levels of living through more modern
production methods and improved social organization."

In a similar vein, Schramm says in his influential book,
Mass Media and National Development, that "the task of the
mass media of information and the 'new media' of education
is to speed and ease the long, slow social transformation
required for economic development" (1964: 27). Rogers
(1976) noted elsewhere that it was not until the late 1960s
and early 1970s that equality of distribution of socioeconomic benefits, village level participation in self-development, and economic planning were urged as goals of development efforts. It was assumed under the dominant paradigm, that central economic planning of development was "a
legitimate and reasonable means by which a nation should
seek development goals" (1976: 215). It was thought that
economic development had to proceed on a grand scale that
could only be orchestrated on a national level. Small-scale,

labor-intensive operations were deemed inefficient. Rogers continues:

> The focus on economic growth carried with it an "aggregate bias" about development: that it had to be planned and executed by national governments. Local communities, of course, would be changed eventually by such development, but their advance was thought to depend upon the provision of information and resource inputs from higher levels. Autonomous self-development was considered unlikely or impossible. In any event, it seemed too slow [1976: 216].

Development was conceived then as a one-way, top-down affair. There was no need to worry about equality of distribution of information and socioeconomic benefits. Let the central government manage the economy and the dissemination of information and, it was assumed, there would be a "trickle down" effect in which eventually the most needy would somehow reap the rewards of top-down development initiatives.

Frey (1973: 370-407) demonstrates that while communication was largely ignored as a development factor by economic theorists, it figured prominently in most political, psychological, and, needless to say, communication theories of development which emerged in the context of the dominant paradigm.

Finally, Beltram (1976: 110) states that some diffusion theories went so far as to suggest that communication could by itself spur development and economic growth.

To summarize, the development of mass communication was portrayed under the dominant paradigm as part of a universal, inevitable sequence or pattern of changes which traditional societies must undergo in the transition to modernity.

Mass communication was thought to function best when in the service of centralized government development agencies; it was supposed to be geared toward raising the public's aspirations and facilitating the acceptance of new ideas, values, and inventions for the purpose of overall economic growth and higher per capita income. Promoting equity of distribution and changes in dysfunctional social structures was not considered under the dominant paradigm as part of its role. Critical questions of foreign mass communication's influence and topics like effects of media ownership and control were not addressed.

The Western understanding of the role of communication in development was affected not only by the way it was conceptualized under the dominant paradigm but also by the methods and attitudes that characterized the research that was undertaken within the framework of that theoretical tradition and model.

The Research Traditions

When communication researchers turned their attention to development, they had a dual heritage. First, they were influenced strongly by the body of theory about the development process that had been built up in other fields, namely, economics, politics, psychology, and sociology. But an equally strong influence on development communication research was the already well-established traditions, directions, and orientations of behavior research on communications in general.

FUNCTIONALISM

These traditions began to take shape with the commercially oriented mass communication research in the 1930s and 1940s in the United States which reflected the marketing concerns of a consumer society. Lazarsfeld (1941), one of the pioneers of mass communication research, described this type of work as "administrative research." Jasperse, characterizes administrative research this way:

> Such research focuses on the media audience, and research goals include identifying the uses of the media and assessing media

impact in varying circumstances, with an eye to providing information that will facilitate fuller realization of media purposes.
Administrative research thus examines conditions within the
framework of the mass media system, and, with its emphasis on
gathering facts about the way the media work, inclines towards
empirical methodologies [1979: 9].

Historically, American mass communication research iso-
lated specific media purposes, messages, programs, and
effects from overall social processes. It did not attempt to
relate communication and communication needs to the overall social, ideological, political, cultural, and economic system
in which they operated. Explanations about the specific
communication data were seldom discussed in terms of the
larger communication system or from a macro theoretical
model. A linear, one-time analysis was indicative of the early
stages of research and still afflicts the discipline.

American mass communication researchers concentrated
on collecting and classifying facts usually in order to illumi-
nate new forms of social control, persuasion, and attitude
change. They did not see it as their function to interpret
these facts and build grand theories about structural and
systemic determinants of communication about them. The
trend which started in the 1930s and is still alive today was
toward a quantitative, empirical, behavioral science method
as opposed to a highly conceptual, speculative, theoretical,
and philosophically or historically discursive approach in
mass communication research (Jasperse, 1979: 13).

This emphasis on quantitative, empirical methodology and
microlevel, as opposed to broad system and social context,
analysis is hardly surprising considering that most early mass
communication research studies were commissioned by
broadcast, political, advertising, and marketing organizations
to deal with specifically defined problems of message effectiveness. These organizations wanted to know what kind of
political propaganda or persuasion techniques would produce
the desired *effect*, that is, votes, purchases, conformity, and
such on the behavior of individuals. They were interested in

hard data on particular messages and programs and their short-term effects on specific audiences, not well-reasoned speculation on how these findings fit into the grand social, ideological, and economic scheme of things. The study of audiences to discover "effects" came to almost monopolize mass communication research (DeFleur and Ball-Rokeach, 1975).

Because of this effects emphasis and functionalist approach, with "adjustment" orientation, American-influenced researchers have tended to accept the system-in-being as a given and implicitly endorse it by failing to see how their understanding of communication could be enriched by questioning such basic characteristics of the system as differential distribution of power and access to the media, conflicts of interest in media power centers, and the ideological support of society's power structures in the content of mass media messages. Herbert Schiller, an American Marxist communication critic, says, "A remarkable vacuum surrounds the structures and the power groups that hire the gatekeepers" (1974: 15). Also, a lack of access to financial data of privately held newspapers and media groups has inhibited researchers in carrying out meaningful studies.

Mass communication research has been taken to task for being so inattentive to these issues. Moreover, the significance of who owns and controls the media and to what ends they are being used escalates in the case of the Third World. Clippinger, in one of the few empirical studies on Third World media systems, examined who owns and controls communication systems and who benefits by them; he looked at communication technology innovations in Algeria and El Salvador and concludes:

> A major finding in both case studies is that the governments of El Salvador and Algeria were the principal beneficiaries of communication development. In part this is not a surprising finding, as governments generally own and manage all major communications systems and are—by and large—the locus of political and economic power [1977: 70].

STRUCTURALISM

Some critics, such as Schiller, have probed perhaps even more deeply into the "who communicates" question and have found that the real source, the real shaper, of Third World communication systems and the messages they produce is the West. Most LDC's do not have the expertise or material resources to institute domestic communication systems which would genuinely reflect their history, needs, concerns, values, and culture. So they must rely on the transfer (usually through foreign aid programs) of Western communication technology and software such as television series, Hollywood movies, and wire copy which are far cheaper to get than the production of domestic counterparts. In addition, almost all of the international communication industry is owned and controlled by giant Western, mainly American-based, transnational media and telecommunications conglomerates. These are tied closely into a subtle and invisible network of Western political, ideological, and economic elites which use the communication industry, whether on purpose or not, to perpetuate demand and need for the products, tastes, values, attitudes, and cultural modes which keep them on top. So when an LDC imports, either through purchase, loan, or donation, a telecommunications infrastructure (from simple shortwave radio equipment, to printing presses, to ground stations for color television via satellite) or other software, it imports a way of life. Schiller describes this as cultural imperialism or penetration and says it is

> becoming steadily more important, and more *deliberate*, in the exercise of American power. . . .
>
> The marketing system developed to sell industry's outpouring of (largely inauthentic) consumer goods is now applied as well to selling globally ideas, tastes, preferences, and beliefs. In fact, in advanced capitalism's present stage, the production and dissemination of what it likes to term 'information' become major and indispensable activities, by any measure, in the overall system. Made-in-America messages, imagery, lifestyles, and information

techniques are being internationally circulated and, equally important, globally imitated.

Today, multinational corporations are the global organizers of the world economy; and information and communications are vital components in the system of administration and control.

Communication, it needs to be said, includes much more than messages and the recognizable circuits through which the messages flow. It defines social reality and thus influences the organization of work, the character of technology, the curriculum of the educational system, formal and informal, and the use of "free time"—actually, the basic social arrangements of living [1976: 3].

He says elsewhere:

The concept of cultural imperialism today best describes the sum of the processes by which a society is brought into the modern world system and how its dominating structure is attracted, pressured, forced and sometimes bribed into shaping social institutions to correspond to, or even promote, the values and structures of the dominating center of the system [1976: 9].

Others, like Guback (1969), give an account of how cultural imperialism applies in the case of the film industry in *The International Film Industry*; another work (Curran et al., 1977) suggests that alternative models are indeed being generated.

PROFESSIONALIZATION

An integral but seldom discussed instrument of cultural imperialism is the technocratic baggage—including technicians, engineers, producers, directors, behind-the-scenes personnel, writers, broadcasters, commentators, and so on—which is required for the technical maintenance and operation of an imported communication infrastructure. These technocrats are usually loaned from the West or trained there and bring to developing countries value systems and attitudes, associated with professionalism, about how communication systems should be run that may deflect the purpose or goal of broadcasting in the LDC's. Clippinger states:

> A technocratic "elite" is required to manage and maintain these technologies, and the interests of this group may be different from the interests of those whom the technologies are eventually intended to serve. Certainly when the population being served by the technologies is an uneducated one with relatively little understanding of Western technologies and attitudes, it cannot readily articulate, much less effectively represent, its own interests. Hence, it may be that advanced communications technologies such as ETV, satellite, and telephony, by their capital intensive and technologically sophisticated nature, introduce a complex array of factors into the development process which hamper rather than facilitate certain desired outcomes [1977: 72].

Cruise O'Brien also notes that "the professionalization of broadcasting—which is based on exclusiveness and control and reflects transnational patterns of socialization, has been detrimental to initiative and adaptation" (1977: 153).

Given its predilection with audience research, American mass communication study has not concentrated upon research investigating the ties which bind media institutions to other sources and structures of power, whether domestic or international. In essence, development communication experts have taken for granted that more Western-type technology and communication hardware was beneficial to more Western-type economic growth which was equated with development. In fact, the policies they supported did not advance development and the quality of life, but in fact tended to foster a colonial-type dependence on the West, to aggravate an unbalanced distribution of benefits by concentrating new communication power in the hands of ruling elites, and to create tensions and frustration in LDC's by promoting inappropriate and inaccessible Western ideals and further expand the economic gap between the West and the LDC's.

The European tradition offers a "critical" as opposed to "administrative" school and research tradition. Jasperse says about this critical school: "The critical researcher's task is to formulate a general theory explaining the dominant social and economic forces and to show how, within a particular system, human needs—including communication needs—are met, neglected, or abused" (1979: 10). Critical research operates within a more holistic framework in which communication is examined in relation to broader sociological issues; it is placed within historical, philosophical, and socioeconomic frames of reference reflecting a macrosociological approach. The British scholar Raymond Williams (1974) has argued that communication study should be regarded as a "cultural science" or a part of "cultural studies." According to Peter Golding and Graham Murdock (1978), of the Leicester school, cultural studies try to relate the social order to the totality of symbolic forms which express that order such as religion, fashion, language, media products, and so on.

WESTERN FAILINGS

These exhaustive approaches, focusing on structural, contextual, and procedural determinants of communication, have been low priority concerns in the United States. American students of communication have never strived for a conceptual inventory which would provide a basis for explaining communication in the context of an overall social system. This failure to recognize communication as inextricably tied to social structure appears in development communication research and, particularly in the most prominent variety of it, diffusion of innovation research. Beltran writes:

One basic assumption of the diffusion approach is that communication by itself can generate development, regardless of socioeconomic and political conditions. Another assumption is that increased production and consumption of goods and services constitute the essence of development, and that a fair distribution of income and opportunities will necessarily derive in due time. A third assumption is that the key to increased productivity is technological innovation, regardless of whom it may benefit and whom it may harm (1976: 110].

The interview, sample survey, and content analysis which have been the dominant research tools of diffusion studies have been one of the greatest obstacles to the exploration of social structure as a key factor in the communication process. A preoccupation with methodological precision took precedence over macrotheoretical formulations. Beltran argues:

> What prevented most U.S. social scientists, including communicologists, from engaging in relevant macrosocial studies kept them at the level of small entities were mainly their use of the survey and their concentration on "adjustment" problems. . . . The sample survey is of modest usefulness when the researcher needs to obtain complex information about large entities like total societies or their major subsystems. Interviews best capture *individual* actions and reactions of isolated communication actors, but do not fully capture the *transactions* among them. It is these interactive relationships which may "speak" for society, rather than the electronically accumulated independent and "destructured" behaviors of its components [1976: 121].

This brings us to another feature of most communication study, including diffusion research, which militates against the adoption of a macrosocial approach which considers the role of structural and organizational variables. Western theoretical models of development, following the assumption of individual blame, have tended to locate internal sources of problems in developing countries and "were less likely to recognize the importance of external constraints on a nation's development: international terms of trade, the economic imperialism of international corporations, and vulnerability and dependence of the recipients of technical assistance programs" (Rogers, 1976: 219).

An example of a content analysis study of Third World media is Barghouti's (1974) investigation of Jordan's print and electronic media. Detailing the frequency with which certain topics such as politics and agricultural information appeared in these media and then relating it to the results of an audience survey, the study was effective in demonstrating that the amount of agricultural news was insignificant in relation to other categories, that Jordanian farmers consequently were not getting their agricultural information from the media, and that therefore the media were not contributing as effectively as they might to agricultural development.

However, these types of content analysis studies leave untouched the deeper information structures and communication implications latent in the overt messages. Researchers using content analysis generally fail to examine, as the Leicester school probably would, how the content of mass media messages—through the style in which it is presented and the use of language, metaphor, symbols, and so on— reflects the social order and the structural and ideological properties which characterize it.

A key problem in communication research is dealing with process. While communication usually is defined as a process, it is treated in research in snapshot rather than motion picture fashion. It gives the impression that communication is a mechanistically simple, unilinear, nonprocess affair in which the working of social structural forces over time on acts of communication does not figure.

It was suggested earlier that the lack of an adequate focus on structure in development communication research in particular and American communication studies in general is related to a conservative acceptance by researchers of the premises of the system-in-being as given. This acceptance made it difficult for them to perceive the point of questioning the structure and organization of that system and directed them to concentrate their attention on how mass communication could act upon audiences in such a way as to promote conformity and adjustment to the social order.

One could pose the argument that the lack of a structural focus stemmed also from the heavily empirical, quantitative slant of American communication research and a corresponding reluctance to theorize. The influence on communication of ideological and value systems, patterns of social organization, and subtle, often invisible matrices of power and social interaction are much harder to quantify with empirical precision and less subject to rigorous measurements than the effects of specific messages on specific audiences. Study of these influences necessarily involves some theorizing, hypothesizing, and a speculative thinking not always firmly rooted in hard data. But such modes of understanding run against the grain of the behaviorally exact science tradition of American communication research. Nordenstreng says, "A more or less common misconception about theory among 'hyperscientists' is that anything that goes beyond the empirical or statistical evidence is 'subjective speculation' and not 'exact science' " (1968: 213).

This claim of scientific neutrality is being challenged by a growing number of critics precisely because—by not passing judgment on the system and by placing questions about subtle, often unquantifiable structural, ideological, and systematic dynamics outside the realm of legitimate "scientific" inquiry—researchers who claim such neutrality are in fact passing judgment in favor of the status quo. As a leading British student of the media, Halloran says:

> It seems clear that, on the whole, these "neutral" enquiries have served to maintain the status quo. If it is inevitable that built into our whole research exercise are components which work in this conservative way, then at least let us face up to it and not feign neutrality which is impossible [1974: 13].

New Departures

Development communication theory and research methodology alike have been found wanting in some respects. Critics have not been slack in recommending alternatives to them. On the theoretical side, Rogers (1976: 222-223) has pointed out four main elements in a new conception of development which is beginning to emerge. They are (1) the equality of distribution of information, socioeconomic benefits, and so forth; (2) popular participation in self-development planning and execution, usually accompanied by the decentralization of certain of these activities to the village level; (3) self-reliance and independence in development, with an emphasis upon the potential of local resources; and (4) integration of traditional with modern systems, so that modernization is a syncretization of old and new ideas, with the exact mixture somewhat different in each locale. These four conditions of development strongly contrast with the economic growth, central planning, and overall modernization priorities of the earlier dominant paradigm.

Marxist models of development and the role of communication have also sprung up in the last decade. In these models, the causes of underdevelopment have to be traced back to international imbalances caused by the dominance of Western capitalist systems and the imperialist control they exercise over the Third World. Radical change both within LDC's and in the present international economic system is seen as necessary for real development to occur.

Connected with these Marxist development schemes is an increasing awareness of the role of multinationals in perpetuating a colonial dependence position in the Third World, both culturally and ideologically, through their economic and political control of the international communication industry. This awareness shows up in many new models of the causes of, and solutions to, underdevelopment which consider the influence of global political and economic power structures on development in detail.

The Maoist model of development has also received attention in the 1970s. This is a model, says Yu:

> that discourages urbanization, that encourages sideline and cottage industries in the countryside, that seeks to remove the

difference between manual and mental labor, between industry
and agriculture, and between city and countryside, and that does
not pour hordes of peasants into big cities but teaches them
about industry in the countryside [1971: 232].

Other models (Schumacher, 1973) of development, some
inspired by the Club of Rome's *The Limits of Growth*,
focused on a "small-is-beautiful" alternative to old-style
grand development schemes.

On the research side, new departures have been in the
direction of finding more sophisticated tools for measuring
the influence of social structure, both at a macro- and microlevel, on development communication. Concern with noneconomic factors of life and culture are receiving increased
attention. In sum, both the theoretical and research traditions of Western scholars are undergoing reexamination by
current students of mass communication.

Finally, Marxist research methodologies and European critical school cultural studies, which have been ignored in
development communication studies, are gaining attention in
the Western Hemisphere.[2]

In sum, both development promises and theoretical
approaches plus media studies of the North American administrative school have failed to provide guidance or sufficient
hope to sustain these approaches. The mostly European-
based critical school offers a significant alternative although
operationalizing their premises into large-scale research projects is still wanting. It is within this vague body of usable
knowledge that the NWIO is finding itself. In essence the
NWIO is not itself a research methodology; at best it represents some theoretical alternatives about media flows, cultural sovereignty, and so on that deserve attention by both
students of development and the media as well as media
professionals actively involved in the collection and observa-
tion of LDC news.

NOTES

1. Innis (1951, 1972) describes the breakdown in terms of the oral (time) traditions being replaced by print (space) traditions and concerns. He further maintained that every new communication innovation brought with it certain properties or characteristics which again shifted the societal relationship between time and space concerns.

2. The traditional ethnocentric nature of the American research is reflected also in its media systems (see, for example, Lent, 1977).

REFERENCES

BELTRAN, L. (1976) "Alien premises, objects, and methods in Latin American communication research." Communication Research 3: 107-134.

BARGHOUTI, S. (1974) "The role of communication in Jordan's developments." Journalism Quarterly 51: 418-424.

CLIPPINGER, J. (1977) "Who gains by communications development? Studies of information technologies in developing countries," pp. 65-187 in United States Senate hearings before the Subcommittee in International Operations of the Committee on Foreign Relations, June 8-10.

CRUISE, O'BRIEN, R. (1977) "Professionalism in broadcasting in developing countries." Journal of Communication 27: 150-153.

CURRAN, J., M. GUREVITCH, and J. WOOLLACOTT (1977) Mass Communication and Society. London: Arnold.

DeFLEUR, M. and S. BALL-ROKEACH (1975) Theories of Mass Communication. New York: Longman.

EISENSTADT, S. (1976) "The changing vision of modernization and development," in W. Schramm and D. Lerner (eds.), Communication and Change: The Last Ten Years and the Next. Honolulu: University Press of Hawaii.

FREY, F. (1973) "Communication and development," pp. 337-461 in I. de Sola Pool et al. (eds.), Handbook of Communication. Skokie, IL: Rand McNally.

GOLDING, P. and G. MURDOCK (1978) "Theories of Communication and Theories of Society." Communication Research 5: 339-356.

GUBECK, T. (1969) The International Film Industry. Bloomington: Indiana University Press.

HALLORAM, J. (1974) Mass Media: The Challenge of Research. Leicester, England: Leicester University Press.

INAYATULLAH, I. (1967) "Toward a non-Western model of development," in D. Lerner and W. Schramm (eds.), Communication and Change in Developing Countries. Honolulu: East-West Center Press.

INNIS, H. (1972) Empire and Communications. Toronto: University of Toronto Press.

INNIS, H. (1951) The Bias of Communication. Toronto: University of Toronto Press.

JASPERSE, S. (1979) A comparison of European and American traditions of mass communication research. Presented at the meeting of the Association for Education in Journalism, Houston, August.

LAZARSFELD, P. (1941) "Remarks on administrative and critical communication research." Studies in Philosophy and Social Science 9: 2-16.

LENT, J. (1977) "Foreign news in American media." Journal of Communication 17: 46-66.

LERNER, D. (1955) The Passing of Traditional Society. New York: Free Press.

MEADOWS, D. (1972) Limits to Growth. New York: University Press.

Montreal Gazette (1979) September 19, p. 14.

NORDENSTRENG, K. (1968) "Communication research in the United States: A critical perspective." Gazette 14: 207-216.

ROGERS, E. (1976a) "Communication and development: The passing of the dominant paradigm." Communication Research 3.

ROGERS, E. (1976b) Communication and Development: Critical Perspectives. Beverly Hills, CA: Sage.

ROGERS, E. (1976c) "Where are we in understanding the diffusion of innovation," in W. Schramm and D. Lerner (eds.), Communication and Change: The Last Ten Years and the Next. Honolulu: University Press of Hawaii.

ROGERS, E. (1969) Modernization Among Peasants: The Impact of Communication. New York: Holt, Rinehart and Winston.

ROSTOW, W. (1971) The Stages of Economic Growth. Cambridge, England: Cambridge University Press.

SCHILLER, H. (1976) Communication and Cultural Domination. White Plains, NY: M. E. Sharpe, Inc.

SCHILLER, H. (1974) "Waiting for orders . . . some current trends in mass communication research in the United States." Gazette 20: 11-21.

SCHILLER, H. (1969) Mass Communications and American Empire. New York: A. M. Kelley.

SCHRAMM, W. (1964) Mass Media and National Development. Paris: UNESCO.

SCHRAMM, W. and C. LERNER [eds.] (1976) Communication and Change. The Last Ten Years and the Next. Honolulu: University Press of Hawaii.

SCHUMACHER, E. (1973) Small Is Beautiful. London: Blond.

SHARP, R. (1979) "Towards a new model of development." Populi 6(2): 15-20.

VARIS, T. (1974) "Global traffic in television." Journal of Communication 24: (1): 102-109.

WILLIAMS, R. (1974) "Communication as cultural science." Journal of Communication 24 (3): 17-25.

WELLS, A. [ed.] (1974) Mass Communications: A World View. New York: Orbis.

YU, F. (1976) "Research priorities in development communication," in W. Schramm and D. Lerner (eds.), Communication and Change: The Last Ten Years and the Next. Honolulu: University Press of Hawaii.

Chapter 4

THE ROLE OF UNESCO

Historically, the United Nations Educational, Scientific and Cultural Organization (UNESCO) has avoided controversy. Now, its role and profile in the current international media debate is unmistakable. UNESCO has not only funded crucial meetings and conferences along the way but with research and senior management, headed by Director-General Amadou-Mahtar M'Bow of Senegal, has been directed toward pushing new initiatives in communication. UNESCO has invested too much, backstage as well as publicly, not to be tarnished should the NWIO either veer off course or fail to materialize.

Before describing major meetings held in Bagota, Quito, Costa Rica, Nairobi, Paris, Belgrade and other background details, a few words about UNESCO are useful, since UNESCO has coordinated the international aspects of the issue.

Background

UNESCO is a specialized agency of the United Nations. It began in 1946 with 20 member-states and had grown to 144 at the beginning of the 19th General Assembly in 1978. During the assembly, two additional nations were admitted bringing the total to 146. By 1980 there were 154 member-states.

The General Assembly of all member states meets every two years to decide both programs and budget. The budget of over $200 million comes from these member-states. The program is supervised by a 45-member Executive Board and the day-to-day operations are carried out by the Secretariat. The Secretariat draws personnel from member-states and is based in Paris.[1] Although its mandate covers various activities around the globe, the convening and sponsoring of international ministerial and research conferences is a time-consuming and important task. That is how UNESCO became a major player in the international media debate.

Often quoted is the phrase from UNESCO's constitution which states that "since wars begin in the minds of men, it is in the minds of men that the defenses of peace must be constructed." From that lofty and worthwhile ideal down to its current concern for the New International Economic Order, UNESCO has moved from a passive to an active force in international affairs.

As a brochure on UNESCO states:

> Both on the theoretical and the practical level, UNESCO has a vital role to play. . . . The current economic relations between industrialized and developing countries must, certainly, be transformed, but they cannot on their own change the political and sociocultural factors which shape integrated developments. Thus UNESCO has the task of helping: to enlarge the scientific and technological bases which permit each country to use its natural resources better; . . . to increase and improve communications and information systems; . . . to promote the progress of social sciences so that each society can undertake its own studies and

utilize the instruments of change without losing its own identity
[1977: 3-4].

Although UNESCO originated in Great Britain in November
1945 and was dominated by Western nations, particularly
Britain, France, and the United States, the late 1950s saw a
shift that is still continuing. This shift resulted from the
continual addition of newly emerging nations, mainly from
Asia, Africa, and other Third World areas. During the 1960s a
similar ideological and economic (poor) condition saw the
developing nations form a power bloc or lobby called "The
Group of 77."[2] The number of nations in the group has risen
to over 100 at the beginning of the 1980s. But Hoggart
explains:

> The new nations, who where in general creations of the early
> sixties, tend to take the UN seriously though ambiguously. Since
> the UN was set up by the victorious allied powers, it has the
> stamp of Western ways of thinking. On the other hand, its record
> in anticolonialism is good and it has made a considerable contri-
> bution to the emergence of some new states. Their relationship to
> the UN is therefore rich in ambiguities [1978: 64].

This ambiguity is no better illustrated than in their attitudes
toward information. On the one hand they want, some des-
perately want, to become modern industrialized nations with
color domestic television and all the media trappings that
money and technology permit. Yet most lack even the most
basic of telecommunications infrastructures for telephone or
telegraph let alone sophisticated ground terminals for satellite
television transmission. On the other hand, they want no part
of Western culture. Total rejection of Hollywood films, Madi-
son Avenue commercials, or foreign-produced television programs is mandatory. Only a pure domestic product is acceptable. They may well wind up with the Western technology
with no content to place on the systems. Even for educational, social, or health care uses, the system will be turned
"off." Software is a major issue, or, indeed, problem.

UNESCO has not been without its critics over the years. Part of the criticism has been a spillover from the general negative assessment of the parent United Nations organization. Domination by the West, plus the exclusion of China at the insistence of the United States, has left the UN crippled in key international activities.

Another major event was UNESCO itself, reflecting a new voting alignment by the mid 1970s, excluding Israel from a European regional grouping; this brought a barrage of criticism from the Western press. This same action also led to the United States withholding its share of UNESCO's budget; the amount is almost 30% of the total. The press criticism did not go unnoticed by the Secretariat. It commissioned Roger Heacock and asked the Graduate Institute of International Studies in Geneva "to investigate the claims of the media and the reality to which those claims referred" (Heacock, 1977: 5). What UNESCO's senior officials wanted was:

> independent verification for their belief that the Western press had launched a veritable campaign against the organization, levelling false charges against it in its effort to help restructure world mass communication systems [Heacock, 1977: 5].

In his impressive monograph Heacock maintains that UNESCO lost interest in the study after the United States had paid its arrears:

> I decided nonetheless to publish the study. The subject is a vital one, in an era in which ideological confrontation throughout the Third World is in no way on the wane, Africa being the most prominent current battleground, and when military confrontation between the great powers is increasingly set aside in favour of a war of information and propaganda, the battles being won or lost through the projection of images intended to justify a given model of economic, social and political organization [1977: 6].

He then outlined a series of events that, some say by accident and some by oversight, propelled UNESCO into the middle of an international debate about culture and information.

General Assemblies, Meetings, and Conferences

The worldwide debate over the future of international communication systems was bound to come. But the strength and sophistication of the Third World power bloc were underestimated by multinational corporations involved in communications and by Western governments alike.

At the same time UNESCO was vaguely searching for a *raison d'être*. For the previous decade, research in education had dominated its activities, culminating with the Faure (1972) Commission Report, *Learning to Be*. It was into this vacuumlike atmosphere in the early 1970s that a series of innocent looking resolutions were introduced concerning the development of national media policies.

The following attempts to highlight the major forums where the media debate crystallized. What may be surprising is that UNESCO, despite its ability to obfuscate and to entangle tasks with bureaucratic procedures which are Byzantine in nature, still either directly sponsored, or at least cosponsored, the preliminary critical meetings.

SIXTEENTH GENERAL ASSEMBLY OF UNESCO, OCTOBER-NOVEMBER 1970

As LDC's reached a significant bloc of opinion and influence, they were joined in the media issue by the USSR. In part, the Soviet and other Socialist countries united with the Third World as a means of embarrassing the Western governments. It is important to recall that Tass sees government control as an accepted practice and therefore, when signs of LDC discontent with Western wire services appeared, the Soviets clearly had no journalistic qualms about supporting extended international government control.[3]

Essentially, the 1970 General Assembly outlined the need for articulating national or domestic communication policies. In fact, a series of publications has resulted from this thrust. This examination, by the developing nations in particular, led to a greater awareness and documentation of the one-way flow from the West to the LDC's. Also, national development policies for the LDC's could not be developed in a vacuum when so much of their media systems were controlled in foreign cities, namely, London, Paris, and New York.

SEVENTEENTH GENERAL ASSEMBLY OF UNESCO, OCTOBER-NOVEMBER 1971

Three events of significance occurred during the general assembly. First, the rapid development of communication technology brought the issue of direct broadcast satellites (DBS) before UNESCO. Fear of interrupted transmission from a satellite directly to homes in foreign lands, rather than through ground stations which would permit control or exclusion of alien messages, saw a "prior consent" resolution pass by a 100-to-1 vote, with the United States voting against. Second, a resolution was passed supporting a call for meetings of experts to discuss national communication policies. These meetings were scheduled in Third World countries and not in the West as had been the tradition. Third, the USSR introduced a mass media resolution which was to evolve over several versions during future meetings. At least one title remained unmodified. It was a declaration on "The fundamental principles governing the use of the mass media with a view to strengthening peace and international understanding and combating war propaganda, racialism, and apartheid."

NONALIGNED MOVEMENT

As decolonization placed many newly emerged nations without a larger entity upon which to base or judge foreign policy, a new pressure group emerged to fill the vacuum. A summit meeting in 1973 of Foreign Ministers of Nonaligned Countries met in Algiers. This meeting was particularly significant because several nations sought a foreign policy stance distant from either the United States or the USSR. Among the demands covering the rejection of their colonial past (and aspects of neocolonialism) was a demand for the decolonization of information.

A series of nonaligned conferences followed (Peru in 1975 and Tunisia, Mexico, India, and Sri Lanka in 1976). The rhetoric and action progressed from attacking transnational communication corporations to an action plan for the establishment of a Third World wire service which was a pool of contributing government information services at the outset. More is said about this Third World news agency, Tanjug, elsewhere. Additional clout was achieved as the NIEO and the Organization of Petroleum Exporting Countries shifted international power to a nucleus of nonaligned countries.

Along with the nonaligned summit meeting in 1973 was a related seminar held in Finland. President Kekkoner, speaking at a University of Tampere seminar, also talked of "cultural imperialism." The "free flow" argument was documented as a "one-way flow" and much of the current malaise and rhetoric was established in this era. Indeed, a major document at the Tampere seminar was Nordenstreng and Varis's study revealing the pervasive influence of U.S. and British television sales internationally (UNESCO, 1974).

LATIN AMERICA MEETINGS

While the nonaligned countries were proceeding with their information plans, the UNESCO meetings commenced. They were to investigate the disparities in international information flow, as well as access and participation in determining national communication policies. Although the major meeting was to be held in San Jose, Costa Rica, in July 1976, two background meetings have significant bearing on the movement toward a New World Information Order. These meetings were held in Bogota, Columbia, July 4-13, 1974, and Quito, Ecuador, June 24-30, 1975. Background papers and research documents were presented outlining several media grievances. Foreign wire services, in particular, came in for considerable criticism. The original venue for the meeting, which resulted from a resolution passed at the 17th UNESCO General Assembly, was Asia but the Secretariat had changed it to Latin America, since Latin America has several excellent U.S.-educated researchers and scholars.

It should be emphasized that all parties involved saw these regional conferences as building blocks for an ultimate major conference on media and information. By now just as UNESCO had investigated education (the Faure Commission) for over a decade, so information was to be the area of concern with little awareness of the polarity of opinion (i.e., a free press versus government responsibility) and its possible divisiveness.

The Latin American regional conference proceeded by getting in touch with regional experts for the purpose of assembling background papers. The mandate for the series of conferences was to take a look at the relationship between communication policies and a nation's economic, social, and cultural policies. Here lies the link between government and the media which now dominates the debate. What governments should do to encourage or develop communication policies and practices was advocated during these meetings.

A group of experts met from July 4 to July 13, 1974, in Bogota. This meeting was to discuss Latin America research and media problems. This meeting expanded the underpinnings of development journalism. Some of the research presented outlined the information dependency of Latin America and the control of the media by economic or military elites. Others discussed the cultural imperialism of U.S. television, Hollywood films, and foreign wire services. The original outcome of the meeting was to be limited to UNESCO officials. But a Canadian official obtained the report and turned it over to two major pressure groups, both representing private media interests. In turn, the press began carrying analysis and editorials in the Americas about UNESCO initiatives going against their free press traditions.

Given the heightened profile, the Quito meeting of June 24-30, 1975, attracted considerable attention:

The purpose was to facilitate "fuller news exchange among the countries of the Latin American region" and the "exchange of

information between the region and the rest of the world." ...
The make-up of the observer delegations was similar to that of
the Bogota meeting ... and two U.S. State Department officials,
a fact which revealed the great importance now attached to the
question by the USA [Heacock, 1977: 32].

The Quito report dealt with the disparities in the flow of
information and, given the ongoing shake-up in staff within
UNESCO, the media issue became politically volatile as
events moved toward the main intergovernmental conference
at San Jose, Costa Rica, from July 12 to 21, 1976.

As an indication of the growing press awareness and concern, even the agenda which was distributed 12 days prior to
the San Jose meeting caused a press reaction. Leonard Sussman of the Freedom House, writing in *International News:
Freedom Under Attack,* states:

> These policies ultimately were recognized by journalists as an
> imminent threat when the agenda ... was circulated in March
> 1976. The Inter-American Press Association (IAPA) mounted a
> campaign to alert delegates to the dangers inherent in the
> UNESCO discussion papers. The agenda spoke of the "right to
> communicate" becoming a "central theme of future communica-
> tion policies." The agenda also picked up the proposals for broad
> public "access" and "participation" discussed in the earlier papers
> by UNESCO experts. Perhaps most ominous of all, the agenda
> (UNESCO, 1976b: 5) flatly declared:
>
>> The old notion of the free flow of information must now be
>> extended to include that of the balanced flow of information,
>> which is essential in order that a new, more just international
>> economic order, as defined by resolution 3201 (S-V1) of the
>> United Nations General Assembly, may be brought into being.
>
> The main thrust of the agenda proposals was clear: "a national
> communication policy is necessary in order to help safeguard
> national sovereignty" [UNESCO, 1976b: 5].

The media, particularly the print press, suddenly scrambled
to read the papers and reports of the Bogota and Quito

conferences. UNESCO was becoming a household, and disliked, word among many journalists, and almost all owners of media systems in the Americas.

Sussman demonstrates this:

> The San Jose conference opened in a tense setting. The IAPA's officers, headed by George Beebe and German E. Ornes, established an opposition command post across the street from the UNESCO conference. They held meetings with the press and effectually established an opposition presence. Mr. M'Bow invited the IAPA leadership to discuss the news media issues. There seemed to be some covergence of views but that did not persist once the sessions began. The IAPA adamantly foresaw the undermining of freedom of expression if "communications policies" were approved. "The press of the Americas," said the IAPA (IAPA, 1976: 2), "is before one of the most unusual threats it has ever faced in all its turbulent history" [1979: 121].

The San Jose conference not only dealt with further imbalances of which the wire services were major actors but also a call for regional (Latin America as well as Caribbean) wire services was strongly recommended. Perhaps because of a potential loss of markets, Associated Press and United Press International coverage of events at San Jose were negative and the editorials in the Western press against UNESCO were uniformly harsh.[4]

Other recommendations called for control of satellite distribution, development of national communication policies, national press councils, and journalistic ethics tied to some type of government sanctions for enforcement. The San Jose meeting provided great concern for the wire services and owners of the press in the West. They began working backstage to influence Third World representatives in order to deflect UNESCO's preoccupation with forwarding "national communication policies" as its major policy initiative in the 1970s.

The vital role of information, plus the differing views as to its control, now appeared front-stage at the 19th UNESCO

General Assembly held in Nairobi, Kenya, in 1976. By this time, most Third World countries had abandoned any hope, if they ever had it, for a "free press." They wanted an engineered press, one that would assist in the concerted development of their nation-states. They wanted a cultural stamp of their own making and not one imported from the West or "Made in the USA." M'Bow could not agree more. The major document before the delegates to the Nairobi General Conference with reference to the media was again entitled: "Draft Declaration on Fundamental Principles Governing the Use of the Mass Media in Strengthening Peace and International Understanding and in Combating War Propaganda, Racialism and Apartheid." This declaration, 19 C/91, and Article 12, dealing with government responsibility for all media systems, guaranteed extensive press coverage by the West.

Before outlining the major events that happened in Nairobi, an ironic situation had occurred in the early 1970s that really cemented the strength of the Western perspective, particularly in the United States, of no government control of the press, particularly print. Without dwelling on them, the "Agnew-Watergate" events enshrined the distance the newspapers and the public wanted and deserved from government control. Vice President Spiro Agnew frequently attacked the press and responses to his outbursts provided much concern in the United States about "freedom of the press." This philosophical debate was followed by a major media event, that of two rather junior reporters, Bernstein and Woodward, taking a lead and pursuing it until events, despite White House intervention aimed at stopping the stories, led to the ultimate resignation of Richard Nixon from the Presidency of the United States. The disgust and tarnish of people and events known as "Watergate" was viewed by many as the exact reason why a press free from government control was needed. To talk of government control in the mid-1970s was exactly what the American public and Western journalists did not want to hear. Freedom from government control was now a renewed goal determined by events in the West.

At Nairobi, the role of the media after years of preliminary debates now boiled down to a single draft declaration consisting of 12 articles. Given the heightened profile of the issue in both UNESCO and wire services offices, a move to avoid an out and out confrontation was sought. Leaving aside other issues, it was the single Article 12 calling for state responsibility for media activities that dominated events for days. In the "spirit of Nairobi" a compromise was reached, mainly backstage, to shelve the draft declaration and to reduce pressure among the militants by forming a new group to further examine the issue. This, of course, is Senator Sean MacBride's International Commission for the Study of Communication Problems. Director General M'Bow steered events in such a way as to delay the debate—and vote—to the following General Assembly to be held in Paris in 1978. M'Bow linked the debate for a "new international information order" to the "new international economic order," but he was willing to delay an outright showdown having correctly analyzed the strong Western objection to development journalism.

One other press-related resolution was passed by the General Assembly. Tunisia sponsored a call for financial assistance and other means of support to the nonaligned news pool, Tanjug.

Before describing the 20th UNESCO General Assembly, it is important to introduce, in order to provide a complete picture, the rise of the nonaligned movement and the New International Economic Order.

New International Economic Order

During the early 1970s, the United Nations and its member agencies became major vehicles of change, and to some extent hope, for emerging Third World nations and other "nonaligned" nations.

It is surprising the extent to which the resolve and the magnitude of change adopted by the United Nations was misanalyzed not only in terms of the New International Information Order currently under discussion but also in terms of the underlying New International Economic Order.

Just what is the New International Economic Order that the United Nations and therefore UNESCO are supporting? In effect, it represents a major change for the West which traditionally controlled the United Nations and its organizations. This is clearly not the case any longer. With 146 nations meeting in Paris for five weeks of UNESCO meetings in the fall of 1978, the largest group, 106 member-states, represented Third World or so-called "nonaligned" nations. They were originally labelled the "Group of 77" and this label is still used despite the increased and continually increasing size and influence.

On May 1, 1974, the United Nations adopted a declaration and program of action for the establishment of a New International Economic Order. The fruits of the research and conferences conducted since then are dominating debate and resolutions at all UNESCO meetings. Three major background works have been produced: *Moving Towards Change, The Future of the Third World,* and *The Challenge of the Year 2000.* They outline the background of and need to build a New International Economic Order.

Although the concerns here are centered on issues involving international broadcasting and communications, an international conference on Population and Development sponsored by United Nations in the mid-1970s played a central role in outlining the philosophy of the NIEO. A lack of preparation by the West in terms of confronting the new economic desires and motives of the LDC's was also apparent.

The World Population Conference held in Bucharest, August 1974 examined the controversial issue of the relationship between population and development. The principle organizers, from the West, were almost totally unprepared for the introduction of the concept of NIEO as well as the political strength and resolve of those supporting it.

There are several parallels with this international conference on development and the conferences and UNESCO General Assemblies dealing with the NWIO. Basically, the Bucharest Conference was to adopt a Western resolution calling for additional family planning and population control as a means of controlling development. But the draft plan submitted to the conference was confronted by no fewer than 68 amendments. The West totally miscalculated the impact of the NIEO as a philosophical rationale for developing nations which had decided to reject traditional Western solutions and instead replace them with alternate economic solutions.

The LDC's began to see the industrial nation's domination of markets, raw materials, financial institutions, and the international monetary system as being stacked against its interests. The Bucharest Conference became the earliest landmark of the LDC's putting forward its rationale that dominates United Nations and its affiliates in terms of its perception of how things should move during the balance of this century. That is why an understanding of the NIEO is central to an understanding of the direction and origins of the NWIO.

The other key conference was the first United Nations Conference on Trade and Development (UNCTAD-1) held in 1964.

> At that conference a bloc of African, Asian, Latin American nations (later to be known as the "Group of 77") united in supporting a series of "general propositions" that attempted to redefine the principles governing international economic relations. The Group of 77 had enough votes to establish UNCTAD as a permanent agency of the United Nations, but, lacking the means to implement its goals, UNCTAD remained much more a symbol than a reality [Finkle and Crane, 1975: 92].

Indeed, the future UNCTAD meetings, the most recent of which was held in Manila, have failed to gain significant trade concessions from the West. This lack of concessions has increased the cleavage between the LDC's and the West.

Since economic development and progress was not occurring with any considerable success, the LDC's found an unexpected opportunity and model in late 1973 when the Organization of Petroleum Exporting Countries (OPEC) was able to establish through a cartel a substantial increase in the price of a basic commodity—oil. This, of course, became a model for other Third World nations to emulate in hopes of obtaining the type of economic concessions and financial growth that had escaped them when attempting to work through international organizations and conferences.

Although seldom stated directly, this revised conception of the economic world is dominated by OPEC nations as a result of their cartel and the energy crisis. Indeed, the push for the NIEO now has moved to include sociocultural aspects of life as well as basic economic factors. This is how the press and related media activities have become involved.

Upon analysis it is easy to realize why LDC's, particularly newly created ones, were influenced extensively by the newer, wealthy states. Arab states and OPEC are a model for one-commodity nations to emulate. What the Arab nations have done with the international price of their primary natural resource, oil, other LDC's have hoped to do with their resources, whether they be basic minerals, such as bauxite or copper, or food products, such as coffee or cocoa. But the North-South alliance has not moved in such a way as to complete the shift to an NIEO.[5] In fact, the NIEO is still excessively tied to one commodity, that is, oil. But this has been sufficient to attract power in the short run with UNESCO and at other international meetings and conferences.

Encouraged by the success of OPEC as both a model and a means of frustrating the West, in 1974 a Sixth Special Session of the United Nations General Assembly passed a resolution called "A Declaration on the Establishment of a New International Economic Order." It not only transformed the Bucharest population conference but also became an important instrument in deliberations affecting communications and media trends internationally.

In retrospect few from the West anticipated the NIEO as being central to future United Nations and other international meetings. As Finkle and Crane state:

> Despite the mandate from the Sixth Special Session in April, there was little recognition of its implications on the part of those most directly involved in planning and preparing for Bucharest. Interviews with members of the UN Secretariat as well as delegates from the United States, Canada, Great Britain, and other countries, including some from the Third World, indicate that they had not anticipated that the New International Economic Order would be injected as a major issue into the Conference, or that the Draft Plan would come under such strong attack [1975: 93].

The importance of the Bucharest Conference lay not so much in the amendments to the original draft plan as in the fact that a new political order had emerged to put forward a NIEO. Upon being tested for the first time it was extremely successful and, therefore, the persistence and pace for the NIEO gained speed. The NIEO was quickly interjected into other UN meetings and conferences. Indeed, the rewriting of the documents for the Bucharest Conference in its early days clearly parallels the early days of the WARC Conference in Geneva in 1979.[6] It is also interesting to note that Argentina and Algeria were central at Bucharest in calling for a writing of the draft plan in terminology consistent with the NIEO.

The West was not only surprised but shocked that what they had been aiming at for decades, population reduction through family planning, was now becoming less a priority as compared with the demands for an NIEO. A new sociopolitical order had emerged based upon a different set of

economic principles and goals that was to dominate international debates and goals. Yet, it is ironic to note that "the
scope and the intensity of the Third World demands at
Bucharest were not anticipated by the U.S. delegates despite
the extensive preparation that went into formulating the U.S.
strategy for the Conference" (Finkle and Crane, 1975: 103).
Finkle and Crane state concisely the underlying problem
facing the United States and the West:

> Although the United States is willing to confront Third World
> demands in "appropriate forums," the United States—long with
> most other Western industrialized nations—is simply not prepared
> to accede to the radical transformation of the international eco-
> nomic system as proposed by the developing nations. The
> demand for a New International Economic Order is seen as
> ideologically objectionable as well as a threat to American wealth
> and power. From the American perspective, it is an attempt to
> improve economic conditions in the Third World by distributing
> the existing wealth of the industrialized nations rather than by
> creating new wealth through development [1975: 104].

One could replace the city Bucharest with Nairobi, Paris, or
Belgrade. Miscalculation and underestimation appears to be
the rule rather than exception for Western nations in terms of
the "quantum" change in direction and commitment to new
economic priorities.

The Third World's desire to rewrite the rules for economic
environment received an unanticipated boost in late 1974.
There was another factor seldom mentioned but most
important in creating a power vacuum at UNESCO. This was
the simple act, by the United States, of budgetary withholding of its substantial contribution beginning in December
1974. The budget withholding was over the treatment of
Israel within UNESCO's European regional grouping; the sum
also represented almost one-third of UNESCO's annual
budget.

The United States lost influence and prestige at UNESCO
quickly. First, everyone was affected; internal budgets, pro-

jects, and promotions were slashed or stalled. Even junior employees from European nations felt some antagonism against the United States. Second, the Arab nations, along with Nigeria and Yugoslavia, bailed out UNESCO with short-term loans. This in turn resulted in much greater powers and, indeed, senior posts being assigned to non-Western candidates. As a result, the NIEO was supported from within and at the top and very much continues to be so today. During the U.S. holdout many anti-West, anti-United States in particular, research projects, conferences, and programs commenced. (The United States has now paid all its arrears but this is of modest influence relative to the initial harm sustained.)

The changes in economic orientation brought about in recent years is reflected in all aspects of UNESCO's activities. Everything from the influence of transnational corporations to the role of popular culture is being examined in light of the goals of either the NIEO or the NWIO. The new order is rhetorically harsh on colonial domination, neocolonialism, racial discrimination, apartheid, and violations of human rights. Although the goals are indeed lofty, they blur the attempt to shift international power from the Western nations to a loose coalition of LDC's—Arab, nonaligned, and socialist (namely the USSR) countries. Much of the rhetoric is belligerent and there is little doubt that the NIEO is being set in place. The next move is to alter sociocultural priorities under the protection of the NWIO.

In their analysis, the LDC's realize the influence of the media, not only in conveying capitalist values but also in influencing cultural norms, and they are flexing their new-found political muscles. Greater control of their own destinies, including media content, is a primary goal of those who subscribe to the new order philosophy.

Now we turn to the 20th UNESCO General Assembly held in Paris in 1978. It was totally overwhelmed by concern about the NWIO, media and governments' concern over the mass media declaration, and the MacBride Interim Report.

NOTES

1. For an excellent look at the workings and problems of the Secretariat, see former Assistant Director-General Richard Hoggart's (1978) *An idea and its servants: UNESCO from within.*

2. A list of nonaligned countries is found in Appendix A. Other aspects of the nonaligned movement are discussed in the section dealing with the emergence of the New International Economic Order.

3. One could argue that the debate originated in 1968 with the amended Declaration on Human Rights which included the notion of a "balanced and free flow of information." Interpretation between East and West differed, of course, but it is ironic that the United States initiated the amendment.

4. For an outline of press coverage, see Heacock (1977: 37-54).

5. For additional details refer to the Report on the Independent Commission on International Development Issues chaired by Willy Brandt (1980).

6. The WARC Conference and its relation to the NWIO is discussed later. Some may want to refer to that section now for background detail.

REFERENCES

BRANDT, W. (1980) North-South: A Programme for survival. London: Pan Books.

FAURE, E. (1972) Learning To Be. Paris: UNESCO.

FINKLE, J. and CRANE B. (1975) "The politics of Bucharest: Population development and the New International Economic Order." Population and Development Review 1: 87-114.

HEACOCK, R. (1977) UNESCO and the Media. Geneva: Etudes et Traveux, HEI No. 15.

HOGGART, R. (1978) An Idea and Its Servants: UNESCO from Within. London: Chatto and Windus.

SUSSMAN, L. (1979) "Developmental journalism: The government connection," pp. 110-134 in D. Fascell (ed.), International News: Freedom Under Attack. Beverly Hills, CA: Sage.

UNESCO (1977) What Is UNESCO? Paris: Author.

UNESCO (1974) Television Traffic—a One-Way Street? Report and papers on mass communication 70. Paris: Author.

Chapter 5

THE MESSAGE:
The 20th and 21st General Assembly of UNESCO

The African states had made it plain that they wanted a black African as Head of a major Specialized Agency. The bulk of other nations decided, severally or in groups, that the wish could be acceded to; UNESCO's Director Generalship became vacant at about the right time. As the line became clear, Member States began to say more and more that M'Bow was indisputably the best man who could be found for the job; which was an insupportable claim, since his candidature had not been seriously tested against any others [Hoggart, 1978: 138-139].

The sixth Director General of UNESCO, Amadou Mahtar M'Bow from Senegal, now had his career on the line. Depending upon how he handled the contentious draft declaration on the mass media, his future rested on the resolution. He must have realized that the "spirit of Nairobi" was a false spirit. If anything, it was a spirit of acrimony and distrust. It was worked out backstage at the last moment to avoid a walkout by Western delegations. M'Bow had arranged quickly for the MacBride International Commission to reduce the building pressure. In 1978, the question was, what could M'Bow do to keep UNESCO intact—as well as his career path aimed at the even larger plum—possibly the secretary-generalship of the parent United Nations.

At the end of the 1970s UNESCO's image was tarnished. Within the Secretariat there was a feeling that the Western press, spurred by wire service reports, had decided to emphasize the negative aspects of UNESCO's initiatives and programs. In reality, the Western press had covered both the media issue in Nairobi and the anti-Israel resolution of 1974 in considerable detail. But to some extent the public image of UNESCO was affected by its shift in emphasis from a passive pro-Western agency to an activist, prodevelopment, LDC-oriented agency. Its ideological commitment to fundamental changes (through the NIEO, for example) was little understood and, furthermore, was a threat to the future markets and economic security that the West had taken for granted since UNESCO's inception in the 1940s.

Before dealing with the week-by-week events of the 20th General Assembly in Paris, which are so crucial to an understanding of the NWIO, background on UNESCO's overall force is important.

Basically, UNESCO had no legal force to alter the world's economic or information order. But it does have moral force and votes. It provides an international setting for symbolic actions, via declarations, that are designed to be a guide or ideal. It is an attempt to move beyond the purely economic functions of trade and technology. UNESCO aims to move the debate beyond the cash register to the social, cultural, and human dimensions of international exchanges.

To say whatever UNESCO does in the international media debate is meaningless misses the point. First, UNESCO's Constitution, as explained by its first Director-General, Julian Huxley, is designed to allow nations to act for the benefit of all mankind—not just for local, parochial, or narrow concerns. Second, the media debate in Paris allowed the LDC's to again sharpen their rhetorical skills and determination of purpose for continued encounters at the future meetings, through the MacBride International Commission, at WARC, or through biennial UNESCO General Conferences through the 1980s.

"It was as though they had moved from military colonialism to technological neocolonialism without a thought beyond the purely practical and profitable" (Hoggart, 1978: 193), so a former senior UNESCO official, Richard Hoggart, summarizes the plight of the LDC's. They had rushed to accept Western technology designed for other cultures and other needs and now conceded that technological determinism was not the answer.

The LDC's approached the media and cultural debate with fresh thoughts of what they had covered during the past five years in their quest for an NIEO. Basically, it was "a call for greater distributive justice."

> In a world in which 70 per cent of the population receive 20 per cent of the wealth, in which millions lack bare necessities—adequate food, medical care, employment—in which the rich, mesmerised by the imperative that their already high standard of living should steadily improve, get richer and the poor poorer, it is no wonder that the statesmen of the poorer nations are alarmed and angry [Hoggart, 1978: 193].

The LDC's had flexed their muscles in other areas and now they were prepared to go after the Western mass media.

The 20th General Assembly

The 20th General Assembly lasted from October 24 to November 28, 1978. There was a main plenary session at which the Director-General, M'Bow, opened general policy debate; this was followed by approximately 20 days of responses by each of the 144 member-states and some other officials. Concurrent with the plenary sessions there were five subcommittee sessions of which Culture and Communication was Committee IV. As a result, statements about the media were made in two areas, the plenary session and in Committee IV. It was in the Committee IV meetings that the draft declaration on the media was debated, altered, and passed.

Following the 20-odd plenary sessions there was a major session where the Director-General replied to the general policy debate. Then, in the final week there was the adoption of resolutions and conclusions submitted from the work over the preceding weeks by the various subcommittees. The results set the budgets and priorities for UNESCO until the 21st General Assembly, held in Belgrade, Yugoslavia, in 1980.

The major statement by M'Bow, which opened the plenary session and the general policy debate, both recaps the work of UNESCO since its previous general conference, held in 1976 in Nairobi, Kenya, and also set the framework for future UNESCO work. "The establishment of a new international economic order constitutes... one of the major contexts, and no doubt the largest, within which the activities of the Organization will take place" (UNESCO, 1978: 3). M'Bow continued to point out imbalances between the West and the LDC's since they were not limited to "solely the production and exchange of goods and monetary problems, but also—and inextricably—the creation, dissemination and exchange of information and knowledge" (UNESCO, 1978: 4). Thus the NWIO was further intertwined within the NIEO.

Within the 38-page major address several other topics were reviewed, such as activities in areas of human rights, disarmament, science and technology, and education. In turning to communication, M'Bow states "that the task awaiting the international community in this field over the next few years represents a real challenge, since it is a task which is at one and the same time immense, complex, essential and urgent" (UNESCO, 1978: 14). Then the Director-General proceeded to review the origins of the MacBride Commission and highlighted five areas which required further research and clarification. Because the Director-General is powerful in influencing the way uncommitted members vote and since he provided informal guidance for the second and final year of the Mac-Bride investigation, the five areas outlined are worth mentioning.

They were, first, the philosophical issue of "the dialectical conflict between the notions of freedom and responsibility" (UNESCO, 1978: 15); second, "the apparent paradox existing between the superabundance of goods and services in the information field now becoming increasingly available to industrialized societies" (UNESCO, 1978: 15); third, the disparities in information resources, with highly industrialized nations already having over 50% of their gross national product representing the information industries, and many Third World nations having a very small gross national product, let alone a modern telecommunications infrastructure; fourth, and one that was probably the most important, dealt with "informatics," the interconnecting of computers with telecommunications systems.[1] The fifth question related to content and the power of media for instructional uses to assist solving world problems.

What followed these five questions was an outline of the difficulties and necessity of acting on the draft declaration on the media. M'Bow criticized opponents and states:

> But I believe very sincerely that the draft now before you could meet with a large measure of agreement, provided that it is read objectively and dispassionately, and that form of words are potiently sought which will dispel the ambiguities of hidden motives that some people still read into it. In this way, the large measure of agreement that the General Conference considers necessary could be achieved [UNESCO, 1978: 15].

The Director-General concluded with a mention of a World Conference on Communication for 1981-1982.

He lost ground quickly as nation after nation, in their response to his address, spoke against the submitted draft declaration. Efforts in the plenary sessions, in bars, and in the media cumulatively portrayed a divided UNESCO, based upon East-West lines, with the East (socialist) receiving support from many LDC's.

The controversial draft declaration on the role of the mass media had significant implications for foreign communication activities. It represented a distinct change from the "free flow of information" policy established by the United Nations in the 1940s. M'Bow, at a press conference following his opening address, left no doubt as to where he stood on the issue when he stated "journalists, no matter who they are, are not absolutely neutral."

Before beginning a review of the major speeches, it is important to recall the anti-West premises. The objections to Western media are threefold. The first is a straight anti-capitalist approach complaining about the commercial orientation of press, radio, television, and film industries. The second line of attack deals with basically one-way flow of information that is from the United States, whether it is the wire services or Hollywood productions, to other nations, with very little reciprocal trade. Also it is interesting to note that BBC, Reuters, Spanish, as well as French broadcasting interests are attacked from time to time by LDC's, particularly the African nations, which were formerly colonies of these European powers. The third line of attack is one of cultural domination or fear of electronic colonialism. It is a dislike of the history, norms, mores, and cultural aspects conveyed in the content of the press, radio, television, advertising, and film productions. In order to redress this imbalance, the Asian, African, Latin American, and Caribbean countries have sought to establish their own regional news agencies. In addition, the LDC wire service, Tanjug, is becoming an emerging aspect of the new NWIO. (The historical background of the major wire services is detailed later).

The LDC's realize that given new technologies, particularly powerful satellites, there is some opportunity for them to gain greater control over what is said about their nation-states if they act now. Not only the bad news, the sensational news about coups and earthquakes, but a more balanced flow covering beneficial aspects of their development will be transmitted if they have their say. That was the basic plea by LDC's representatives in Paris.

PRESS COVERAGE

If, as a senior editor of the international edition of *Newsweek* (Behr, 1978: xiii) has observed, "the content of newspapers and magazines, like the shape of women's clothes, follows the vagaries of fashion," then clearly it was fashionable to cover UNESCO's 20th General Assembly. Indeed, the press corps of over 350 represented an almost tenfold increase over the press assigned to the 19th General Assembly in Nairobi.[2]

The major plenary speeches, the press conferences, and the press coverage by major European papers provide significant insight into the international information order debate. The following highlights six weeks of debate that historically may turn out to be the major change in international media practices during this century.

On Monday, October 30th, Judith Hart, M.P., British Minister for Overseas Development, presented the major address representing her government's position. Given the substantial role of Great Britain in UNESCO's brief history, plus the larger role in giving to its former Empire and many Western nations a foundation in both common law and philosophical writings on freedom of the press, the speech attracted considerable attention.[3] In her 11-page speech, fully 10 pages addressed various aspects of journalism and communication. Referring to some problems within the domestic British press and the two Royal Commissions dealing with press issues, she disagreed with the thrust of the media declaration. She was blunt about the "battle of the nipples" raging in the British daily papers for circulation domination. Hart stated:

> The problem we face: That competition for circulation leads to trivialisation, and to an emphasis on sex, crime, entertainment and sensationalism, because the market research men prove that

these sell most papers. Trivialisation plus the pressures of advertising will lead to a real danger that the "pursuit of objective truth" will be completely overlooked [1978: 6].

She then proceeded to talk of government control, as with the BBC, and mentioned the role of journalists in selecting their editors at the major French papers, such as *Le Monde*. Agreeing that the deprivation of the Third World was substantial in areas of communication, she continued:

> What matters is not international agreements on the protection of journalists, but the fact that they so often lack the minimum facilities to collect and disseminate full and fair information. Improved equipment, communications and training will enhance their status and help them in turn to protect the public's right to know and to make choices on a basis of knowledge.
>
> I believe it would be premature for this Conference to try to reach a conclusion at this time on the Draft Declaration [1978: 10].

This movement toward an avoidance of a showdown on the media declaration gathered steam during the next few weeks. So also did Hart's role in the backstage negotiations. She left Paris but returned suddenly as the media declaration issue became more controversial. She was an impressive woman and dealt forthrightly with the press. The quality British papers, which had given a great deal of copy to UNESCO overall, followed her actions and statements closely. (Her activities during the showdown vote later in the conference are covered later in this chapter.)

For several reasons, many already covered, the General Policy Statement by United States Ambassador John E. Reinhardt on November 3 was another major media event. Reinhardt, a black diplomat who also headed the U.S. International Communication Agency (ICA), formerly the U.S. Information Agency, was referred to as an "Uncle Tom" by more than one black African diplomat. Yet Reinhardt was in a tough spot. He had represented the United States in Nairobi and was therefore not unfamiliar with the issues. But although theoretically the United States could pull out of UNESCO as it had the International Labor Organization (ILO) in Geneva, or just temporarily withhold budget funds as it had done before, neither was considered with any seriousness. Given that Reinhardt reported directly to President Carter, and this irked the State Department which otherwise makes foreign policy, the "pack journalism" wisdom concluded that Carter had told Reinhardt to seek a different draft using persuasion and promises rather than threats.

Ironically, Ambassador Reinhardt began with a referral to the "spirit of Nairobi" and a call for a continuation of that spirit. But, in truth, that was a false face-saving spirit that whitewashed the strong divisions among member states. The MacBride group was a last-minute deal to avoid a showdown and, as we shall see, last-minute arrangements still plagued the U.S. delegation in Paris despite the intervening two years when more adequate bilateral and multilateral agreements should have been worked out.

Reinhardt stated that "in culture, we want to participate in strengthening the sense of cultural identity of all peoples and to recognize, at the same time, the contributions of all cultures to the like of all humankind" (1978: 5). But, in a press conference immediately following his address to the plenary session, he modified this stand. The ambassador made a good defense of how state control had led to and not away from war, hostility, and racism.

Two new initiatives were announced in his speech. The first was "to suitably identify regional centres of professional education and training in broadcasting and journalism in the developing world . . . we will undertake to send a senior faculty member or dean of communications to each centre for a year's service" (Reinhardt, 1978: 19). Some British journalists commented that surely this act would strike fear into the hearts of the Third World delegations and that they would suffer anything short of accepting aging deans.

"The second new U.S. project is a major effort to apply the benefits of advanced communications technology—specifically communications satellites—to economic and social needs in the rural areas of developing nations" (Reinhardt, 1978: 20). Although this project represented a major thrust for the United States, it was somewhat surprising to learn, via a hard-working wire service reporter, that in spite of the two years to prepare for such agreements, that the satellite deal had only been worked out the previous evening, November 2, literally at the eleventh hour.

Reinhardt concluded with a strong proposal for a communication consultative group to coordinate the West's cooperation and make sure that aid was going where it was needed most. Unfortunately, this concept slipped through the cracks as the debate on the media resolution focused on "state control and responsibility." The coordinating group idea is worth resurrecting and making operational. Since that time the United States has taken action to help set up a working group that will investigate practical communication initiatives.

On Monday, November 6 the Secretary of State for Canada, John Roberts, M.P., delivered one of the strongest speeches on the media issue during the entire assembly. Roberts stated:

> I am making no secret of my disquiet, and that of the Government of which I am a member, concerning the Draft Declaration on the Mass Media. . . .
>
> On every continent there are some people who think that governments should regulate journalists, should tell them, in the public interest, what to write, or should pass judgement on their accuracy. Canadians do not believe that either politicians or public servants should have anything to say in the management, direction or correction of the media. Quite the contrary. In their view, only a free press can guarantee that the decisions of the state power are in harmony with the wishes of the people. Governments have no means of knowing what the needs of society are for its own well-being, unless they are told by an informed public [1978: 9].

Then he went on to list the reasons for a postponement of the adoption of the contentious text. The address was well-received since Canada has stature beyond expected level—in fact, the President of the plenary sessions was M. N. LeBlanc from the Canadian delegation. Also the Canadian Ambassador to UNESCO, Yvon Beaulne, was a diplomat. (He has since been reassigned to the Vatican.) The wire services from the West gave extensive coverage to Roberts's remarks.

Let us turn now to another significant speech, this one was by George Beebe of the World Press Freedom Committee. In addition to member-states UNESCO allows a certain number of nongovernmental organizations (NGO's) to address delegates during the General Assembly. This is how Beebe got the floor.[4]

Beebe was the first speaker on the afternoon of Wednesday, November 8 and pointed out:

> The World Press Freedom Committee is composed of 32 journalistic organizations on five continents. . . . It is committed to a universal effort to help preserve freedom of expression, to improve the international flow of information and to cooperate with the media of the developing nations in training for journalism and in the improvement of their production facilities [Beebe, 1978: 3].

The committee has 1,000 media volunteers with projects in Africa, Asia, Latin America, and the Caribbean. Beebe was frank about the draft declaration: "We shall certainly continue our programme, whatever happens but this Declaration, if unamended, will dim the enthusiasm of contributors and participants" (1978: 3). His group had a substantial interest in preserving the free flow philosophy to protect their circulation figures and investments.

Since the Third World position has been described in both the development journalism overview as well as in the highlights of the various background conferences, only a few representative highlights will be included here.

A leader of the Caribbean position is former Jamaican Prime Minister Michael Manley. He called the outlook of industrialized nations as being "self-induced myopia." He, like many other LDC leaders, was concerned about the growing disparities between the West and the LDC's, particularly the economic imbalance. He had taken over Radio-Jamaica, which was once privately owned, to spread the word about evils of imperialism. The two privately owned newspapers, the morning *Daily Gleaner* and the afternoon *Star,* opposed Manley strongly. A classic case of media reality being systematically different depending upon to which medium the natives attended.[5]

On Saturday, November 4 Mr. Shihepo spoke on behalf of a liberation group, South West Africa People's Organization (SWAPO). In talking about the mental "decolonialization" of Africa he noted:

> We are pleased to note that UNESCO is debating the role played by the mass media in reporting on developing countries. We as liberation movements have become the victims of continuous and persistent misrepresentation by the Western media. Aggression by the minority regimes is favourably reported, while information on the struggle of the masses is distorted [1978: 4].

Shihepo continued as he pointed out how the West, in particular Great Britain, had armed the white minorities in Africa.

That same morning the Minister of State for Education from Nepal, Mr. Rana, discussed the gap between the West and the underdeveloped world; he stated that:

> Indeed this gap is already so great that even if we had access to a great deal of their technology, much of it would be inappropriate to our scale of need, level of capability, and power of absorption. In so far as learning from the advanced countries is concerned, it is more a question of carefully gauged eclectic access. What is more important is the evolution of a technology adapted to the socioeconomic environment of underdevelopment [1978: 22].

This point of view brings up the question of the Western governments and transnational companies either dumping excess stock or donating obsolete equipment to the Third World as a means of reducing inventory rather than meeting the needs of the underdeveloped world. Clearly it is difficult to assign motives. Yet studies and time will tell.

Finally, Dr. Phillip Muscat from Malta sums up one of the major grievances as well:

> The service that emanates from the big international press and news agencies some time tends to be slanted against the developing countries of the Third World and their leaders. Great prominence is given to certain news items of minor importance, while national achievements in vital sectors are barely mentioned or wrongly reported. Moreover, in certain instances the international press is used as a destabilizing factor against governments whose only crime is generally that of standing up for their rights, their sovereignty and independence [1978: 30].

In sum, this represents the polarity of philosophies on the media.

After the 12 days assigned to the speeches in the plenary session, M'Bow officially replied to the overall general policy debate—in all, 155 statements from delegates and official NGO observers.

It should be recalled that the reply was to the totality of UNESCO's concerns, much of which is contained in the medium-term plan. But the press crowded the back of the main assembly hall for one purpose—to hear the Director-General's remarks about the media situation. M'Bow began with a shot at the press coverage, which he did every time he spoke to the issue. He referred favorably to Mrs. Hart's and Mr. Reinhardt's suggestions but avoided the point of the division between the West and the LDC's stances. M'Bow glossed over the differences by saying, "on the contrary, through the directness of the statements made by the delegates of the Member States, the discussion is based on reciprocal knowledge of the different points of view held by the members of the international community" (1978: 13). Continuing, he referred to the most contentious article in the declaration, the one dealing with government control:

> Some delegates did not conceal their fear that the establishment of a "new international information order" might result in State control over the mass media. If those media can serve a totalitarian ideology, they can, we know only too well, compound the latter's evil effects, as I emphasized in connection with Nazism ... if such a risk is to be held in check, it is essential to lay down a code of ethics to which those who are in charge of the media and communications throughout the world can subscribe [1978: 14].

The call for a code of ethics by the journalistic profession is a separate issue from state control. Enforcement of ethical codes of conduct by other professions, such as law or medicine, also generally demonstrates much of the futility of self-policing. Yet a code could lead to some type of approval system that could be used to restrict journalists from certain nations in even greater numbers than today.

M'Bow concluded with a call for a decision on a final text. Given this public push, the COM IV subcommittee on Communication and Culture had its work cut out for it when it met to discuss and vote on the draft declaration before the delegates.

PRESS CONFERENCES

> To those Britons who since World War II have felt most keenly to the country's loss of an empire and the failure to match the economic achievements of other modern industrialized nations, the contrast between the British strength in high-quality television and the esthetic and moral vulnerability of the programs sent to the United Kingdom from across the Atlantic has been one small area of comfort in a generally uncomfortable world [Dunkley, 1979: 33].

Chris Dunkley, television critic for the *Financial Times* of London, continues by stating that "British schedulers built up an audience with popular American programs early in the evening in the hope of passing it on to more serious programs later." Using the cheaply imported, if not dumped, programs like "Wonder Woman," "Charlie's Angels," "Dallas," "Vegas," and "Starsky and Hutch," British viewers are consuming massive amounts of U.S. shows. In part, it is for this reason that both the press conferences of the United States and Great Britain will be highlighted here. As class shows, such as "Civilisation," "The Ascent of Man," and "Upstairs, Downstairs," travel from the Old World to the New, even industrialized nations see their cultures being affected by foreign imports. So the media flow debate is not solely limited to LDC's concerns. Canada and Australia for years have had import and content controls on select media for cultural reasons. Yet the thrust of the media declaration forced Western delegates to act in unison.

Following his major address to the Plenary Session on November 3, 1978, U.S. Ambassador John Reinhardt held a press conference attended by about 40 reporters. The first question went something like this: "Sir, if the United States puts considerable pressure in broadcasting matters on Canada, such as in the border television advertising dispute, and given Canada's cultural and political problems, how are Third World countries to react to U.S. pressure on their cultures when they lack domestic television networks which Canadians at least have?" The Ambassador swallowed hard and repeated the "free-flow-of-information" argument and said that Canadian materials can flow into the United States and why not United States into Canada. He did not mention the inevitable advantages that accrue to his nation of over 200 million exporting to Canada with slightly more than 20 million (one-third of those being French speaking) and how the free flow masked a one-way flow benefiting both Hollywood and New York production centers.

A Mexican media representative followed with a question dealing with the indirect consequences of accepting U.S. technology and technicians—that a U.S. work ethic would displace native norms and mores established over time. Reinhardt seemed unconcerned and said that the United States should indeed give more aid in the long run to assist LDC's for training in media techniques. In reply to a question from a U.S. wire service representative, he stated that the U.S. domestic media industry had made corrections to better reflect the U.S. mosaic, and Reinhardt gave the increased role of blacks and women as examples.

Ambassador Reinhardt closed his press conference with a veiled threat. In his address he had mentioned two new initiatives: more technical aid and a satellite project. He pointed out that these two projects were outside the regular U.S. funding for UNESCO and that the additional funds would have to be approved by the U.S. Congress. He concluded that "I am not sure Congress will give the necessary funds if the original declaration is passed." Shades of blackmail, some British reporters whispered.

Judith Hart, M.P.: Press Conference. Having departed Paris following her address to the Plenary Session, the British M.P., Judith Hart, returned and called an impromptu press briefing as events picked up steam. With typically British candor, she commenced by stating that there was "slight confusion" over four differing drafts dealing with the media declaration that were being circulated among various delegations. She stated that her government supported the European Economic Community draft calling for an acceptable compromise and that two issues were "highly relevant." The first was that consensus could probably be achieved if a draft omitted state control or power; and a second issue was that two of the four drafts had state control articles within them and were very much alive. Upon questioning, she stated that copies of the various texts were available but were unofficial copies; she went on to point out that "this morning's meeting does not exist." A series of questions then ensued about what could and could not be quoted. Confusion reigned among the press corps again. Hart concluded by stating she was "not unhopeful, but skeptical" about a solution and "it would be a great pity" and hurt UNESCO's image if a state control press declaration was passed.

John Roberts, M.P.: Press Conference. On Monday, November 6, following his address to the plenary session, the Canadian Secretary of State, John Roberts, held an impromptu press conference. It was sparsely attended but the wire service people were there and favorable comments were heard concerning the free bar service. Following his strong speech, Roberts went on to talk of the need to separate press and governments. He criticized the Canadian Press (CP) wire service for closing its Paris bureau and attacked the U.S. film and television industries for dumping U.S. shows in Canada. The Reuter's reporter pursued the cultural invasion issue and Roberts replied at length. Upon finishing, the reporter said that the reply was identical to Tunisia's Ambassador Mosmoudi's stand—that is, governments must control what is shown by the media in order to protect the domestic culture.

Another interesting point occurred in a brief remark by Canadian Ambassador Yvon Beaulne. He complained in his animated fashion about the lack of CBC coverage—the entire bureau it seemed had rushed off to Iran to cover the Shah's demise. But the international wire service representatives admired Roberts for his strong antigovernment control stand—and the press coverage the following day reflected it.

MacBride's Interim Report: Press Conference. The Interim Report of the MacBride International Commission played a strange role during the General Assembly. It was important and unimportant at the same time. It was important because it was the most elaborate and recent statement on the entire new world information order debate, and yet unimportant because the Director-General himself stated that it "had nothing to do with the media declaration" before the assembly.

But on the evening of November 14, in Salle (Room) 2, Senator Sean MacBride, before a packed room of delegates and the press, reported on the commission's progress. He took about 10 minutes to outline his points. He said that the commission was seeking a consensus on the major issues and that the "interim report speaks for itself." He directed special praise to the members of the commission from Yugoslavia and Tunisia. He asked for further comments dealing with oversights and both criticism and elaboration for problems raised in the report.

Raising his voice, he attacked the worn out rhetoric of the Cold War era, calling for a maximum degree of cooperation and understanding. He asserted that the free flow of radio and satellite signals could not be prevented. He concluded with a strong endorsement of rights for investigative journalism and described their role as being necessary for informing objective public opinion and, more important, exposing malpractice, inefficiency, and inertia. Protection of journalists akin to that afforded to international lawyers and diplomats has been a goal of MacBride's for several years.

Following MacBride's statement, the procedure was to allow member states to reply individually to the issues raised or avoided in the interim report. Eighteen speakers were recognized that evening. The balance were heard during the following days. But the media attention dwindled rapidly. Reflecting the worst aspects of UNESCO's procedures, the debate was not of a high philosophical nature dealing with principles of journalism, telecommunications, and informatics, but dealt, endlessly, with trivial aspects of punctuation, spelling, sentence structure, and other picayune matters. Senator MacBride had his moment as a media event and spent the balance of the assembly wandering the halls almost unnoticed.

The Critical COM IV Meetings. On Saturday, November 18, the Communication and Culture Committee (COM IV) finally met to discuss the major item on their agenda—the mass media declaration. In a crowded room somewhere in the bowels of the headquarters, even before the 10:00 starting time, there was not an empty chair; the aisles were crammed with reporters, camera crews, and UNESCO staff, many of whom came in on their day off just to witness the outcome of the debate for themselves. But it was to be a false start.

Here is what happened. The gavel did not come down until 11:20 to commence the session. During that time, and indeed continuing from a late Friday night "secret" meeting, a small group had been trying to work out last-minute details of a compromise.

When the Peruvian chairman of the COM IV session took his seat, a hush came over the chattering audience. He apologized for the delay and understated the situation when he said "there was a problem which had to be solved." He continued to explain that it was a procedural problem that affected the substance of the media debate. Calling for a renewal in the "spirit of Nairobi," he ventured to discuss some new options. The big change was a move to postpone the debate on Item 22 (as the media declaration was known on the COM IV agenda) until Wednesday, November 22. All hell broke loose. Shouts of no, no, filled the hall. Banging his gavel furiously, the chairman finally restored order and continued his explanation.

He stated that there were two reasons for the delay. First, there was a technical reason because a new draft declaration had been received overnight (it was the Soviets that held out the longest, until the morning, but by this time M'Bow himself was involved and so was his career, others speculated). According to UNESCO's rules, an item could not be presented for formal debate until it was translated into the five official languages and this could not be done on Saturday. The second reason given was that a delay would allow heads of delegations to consult with their home governments since many could not vote without direction from their Prime Minister or President. Directions could be sought during the four-day delay.

The alternative was to begin debate on Item 22 at once as originally scheduled. Comments on the issue of starting at once or delaying the debate until Wednesday came fast and furious.

"What has happened since last night? We have been discussing this issue for eight years and there is no reason for any further delay!" was the first response from a socialist delegate. Other socialist delegations responded in a similar vein, calling for debate at once. The Tunisian representative called for closure and a vote on the issue. After further speakers, pro and con, were allowed to speak, a vote was finally taken. At UNESCO a vote is taken by each nation holding up its large name plaque to signify yea or nay. It is by holding up these same boards that speakers are recognized for debate.

At the front of the room is a raised stage for the Chairman and other officials. At the end of the stage two people independently take the vote count and then return to the Chairman in the middle and give him their count. When this happened one could tell that the grimace on the Chairman's usually smiling face meant two differing totals.

The Chairman called the meeting back to order and announced that because of differing totals and the closeness of the votes, he was calling for a roll call vote. Again all hell broke loose. The delegate from Vietnam shouted that democracy was at stake and that the vote results had to be announced and bind the group. Others spoke and it became clear during the confusion that some 10 or 20 delegates had voted one way when they meant to vote the other. A yes vote meant to begin debate now and a no meant delay until Wednesday (which the West wanted). By this point the Chairman had even managed to break his gavel trying to control the erratic events that morning.

A roll call vote was taken. This involved a lengthy process, but about 45 minutes later the official results were announced. The only mirth was the general laughter when China abstained from voting. China could not vote with their socialist brothers while doing its modernization shopping in capitalist nations.

The vote was Yes: 40; No: 55; Abstentions: 16. The West had engineered a delay until Wednesday to work out the details of a compromise declaration on the mass media. This was to be the critical vote. The West had flexed their muscles and won, at least temporarily. The socialist countries and many of their LDC's had laid their cards on the table that Saturday morning and lost. It was a test run of their collective voting power and they came up short. When the chips were down, particularly during the opening role call vote, enough nations switched or abstained to give the Western nations a clear-cut victory. It was a preview of any future vote. Now there was a temporary four day pause in the turmoil.

On Wednesday morning, November 22, the COM IV session was about to begin on time at 10:00 and there was a packed room once again. M'Bow himself took the chair, a step seldom taken; this was indicative of the seriousness of the situation. M'Bow now talked of a new mass media declaration which he was endorsing. The revised declaration had dropped the very contentious article dealing with government control of media systems. But it did include a call for a "free and balanced flow" to replace a solely "free flow philosophy."[6] The Director-General referred to November 9 and his call for consensus being required and how "all possible means and ways" had been resorted to, working both day and night, to overcome obstacles. M'Bow directed that "emotion has not wiped out reason" and that a compromise text "was inevitable." Standing all the while, perhaps 10 minutes, the Director-General concluded with the none-too-subtle directive: The revised resolution will pass. A loud applause followed.

Quickly the various delegations rallied behind the revised text. The first delegate to be recognized by the chair proposed unanimous acceptance without further deliberation. The Polish delegate said it was "a historical moment for UNESCO" and supported the first speaker. This also indicated that the socialist nations had been persuaded to support M'Bow. On behalf of the Nordic countries Finland supported the call for quick adoption. A vote was taken by show of hands: 90 in favor, 3 against. Because of the crowd and confusion, no one was able to figure out for certain which nations had cast the negative votes. A highly unusual standing ovation concluded the brief morning session. M'Bow stood to acknowledge and enjoy the victory. It was over at 11:00.

Ambassador John Reinhardt: Press Conference. On November 22, the day that the compromise media declaration was passed, U.S. Ambassador Reinhardt held a well-attended press conference at 6 p.m. It was also the only press conference held. He began with a lighthearted remark that, as a former English teacher, he bore no responsibility for the poor grammar in the revised declaration. He concluded that the United States played a significant role in the compromise but he did not think that every phrase would satisfy everyone. He stated that the Director-General presented the text and it represented considerable "achievement." Following his opening remarks, his responses to reporters' questions produced some surprises.

The *Washington Post* correspondent inquired about the relationship of the declaration and the ITU-WARC meetings in 1979 (discussed in detail later). Reinhardt stated that he saw no direct connection and, in responding to a series of questions, he stated that the media debate was closed. He maintained that science, education, and culture were new vistas for UNESCO to face. He conceded the point of imbalance in international media flow, but concluded that the new text would affect the status quo but other drafts of the text would have been much more difficult to accept.

MORE PRESS COVERAGE

"The press likes to cover the press" and the media declaration was no exception. This section looks at some of the coverage, mainly in the *International Herald Tribune,* in order to demonstrate the significance attached to the 20th Federal Assembly of UNESCO and the media issue. Although many different media sources were consulted, only a selection will be highlighted here. It should be noted that the selection will not be "balanced" since it will be Western press sources that will be used. The non-Western point of view is included vicariously here but it has been dealt with in detail elsewhere.

The UPI story on M'Bow's opening address and press conference on October 26 dealt with the media declaration. The headline leaves little doubt about M'Bow's position: "UNESCO Head Backs Media-Control Draft." Insightful of M'Bow's personal outlook is the following:

> "Journalists, no matter who they are, are not absolutely neutral," Mr. M'Bow told reporters. He said racism lurks everywhere and must be fought on every front, including the media front. He said feelingly that his own daughter, on a recent train trip in France, was asked by customs and border police officials to show her passport although nobody else in her compartment was asked to do so [*International Herald Tribune*, 1978a: 1].

An Associated Press item in the same edition reported on the United States having paid its overdue UNESCO dues; in turning over more than $17 million it was the first time since 1974 that the United States was paid up.

Ian Murray reported in the London *Times* that M'Bow "did not see any reason to modify the text" (1978a: 7) of the draft declaration. He concluded his item with the donation by the Scandinavian countries of $4 million to aid African communication development.

On Monday, October 30, the British *Daily Telegraph* carried an item that was discussed in the Salle de Presse as reflecting a sensitive Western media concern, particularly with the "balance" concept:

> Tanzania has banned all foreign journalists from entering the country to cover the summit meeting of African heads-of-state which was due to start in Dar-es-Salam yesterday [1978a: 36].

Christopher Munnion covered the events surrounding his exclusion by immigration officials and how his colleague, Eric Marsden of the *Sunday Times,* was also ordered to leave. The following day the *Daily Telegraph* featured an editorial on "UN-NEWS." Fearing the consequences of "a new information order" the editorial stated:

> A motely crew of Third World and Eastern bloc countries—led by that shining example of freedom, the Soviet Union, and frequently (if tacitly) supported by UNESCO director-general, M. Mahta M'Bow of Senegal—have been trying to bring the dissemination of all news under the direct control of the State [1978b: 6].

That same week David Hirst of the *Guardian* was excluded from a Baghdad conference by Iraqi security police. A lengthy editorial piece by Tom Wicker entitled "No, No, UNESCO" labelled it a "dangerous declaration" and mentioned that "the Soviet Union, bastion of truth and human rights that it is, is a strong supervisor of the press declaration." He concludes with a valid point:

> Of course, if the press of the world is to make the claim that truthful reporting, not peace and brotherhood, is its mission, that implies a certain obligation to truthful reporting. And while no reporters can be entirely neutral, as M'Bow observed, he or she can at least approach Third World countries with an open mind, rather than wearing Cold War blinders and burdened with Western assumptions [Wicker, 1978: 6].

That week's British *Economist* (1978: 15-16) went so far as to question UNESCO's own usefulness since UNESCO questioned press freedom and understood so little about the concept.

The UPI coverage of U.S. Ambassador Reinhardt's speech was optimistic: "Hoping to sidetrack a proposal for state control of the world's news media, the United States today offered journalism training and communications satellites to help Third World nations set up competitive news agencies of their own" (*International Herald Tribune,* 1978c: 3). The same item ended with an error, frequent in the overall UPI coverage of the General Assembly: "But the Soviet Union and the United States may find themselves on the same side on the redivision of the world's broadcasting frequencies, the next issue the conference must tackle." It was another conference, ITU-WARC, in the fall of 1979 that had control over frequency allocations and the radio spectrum.

Newsweek devoted a full page to the media issue. Discussing LDC's perception of Western reporting, the article stated:

> As they see it, the Western press views the murder of whites by blacks as headline news and the murder—or oppression—of blacks by whites as no news at all [1978: 61].

Pressure for removal of the offensive media items was extensive:

> As in the past, the U.S. is counting on the threat of Western retaliation—as many as 26 countries could walk out of UNESCO—to head off a confrontation [*Newsweek,* 1978a: 61].

This walkout threat was a creation of the media, not of the Western delegations. And it appeared in much of the copy under the guise of "factual, objective reporting."

Sharing Monday's coverage were an unlikely duet, Mr. Roberts of Canada and Mr. Sendula of Uganda. The latter got the lead—"Hostile Western press Condemned by Ugandan"— and his grievance was quoted:

> Few countries have had to contend with the adverse publicity of a hostile press as my own has. Sophisticated communications media have given some developed countries the advantage to tell deliberate untruths, distort and exaggerate events so as to evoke universal hatred against their less-endowed adversaries [*International Herald Tribune,* 1978d: 2].

Roberts gained notice for his call for delaying the showdown until the 1980 General Assembly. In the same edition there was a four-column analysis on the editorial page entitled: "News, Politics and UNESCO's Wrong Turn," leaving little doubt about its slant.

The following day, the UPI story (IHT, 1978e: 2) discussed a revised text originating from a meeting of 25 Western countries. The press was excluded from the meeting but a delegate confirmed that the state control article had been eliminated. On Thursday, *Le Monde* ran a long article by Francoise Giroud on "Decolonizing Information." That same day, the *International Herald Tribune* reprinted an editorial from the *New York Times:*

> In the name of press freedom, which few of them actually practice, a majority of the world's governments are trying once again to prescribe a code of conduct for all newspapers, press agencies and broadcasters. . . . What on earth have Pravda and The New York Times to bargain about in the definition of news? . . . If it turns out to be impossible to reject this attempt to tamper with our basic principles, there is always the alternative of rejecting UNESCO itself. The good it does is not worth the price it demands [1978f: 1].

Paul Chutkow, the hardworking AP correspondent, after tracking down some of the individuals involved backstage in drafting a compromise media declaration, reported (*International Herald Tribune*, 1978g: 1) that the U.S. initiatives "were labelled a mess and confusing by some West European and Third World diplomats here today." Even Reinhardt confirmed that things were confused but a Western European diplomat put it most emphatically when he stated (*International Herald Tribune*, 1978g: 2): "The negotiating for the Americans or what their real objective is remains a mystery. If their negotiating tactic is to confuse, it's working." Given the lengthy build-up to the debate plus the U.S. investment in the outcome (wire services, video markets, telecommunications equipment sales, and such), such a confusing strategy was remarkable.

The long wait for the formal committee meeting on the draft allowed the various delegations considerable time to attempt to reach a compromise prior to the scheduled meeting. West Germany, heading the European Community (EEC), took over the leadership of the counterdraft movement. In addition, some way had to be found to allow M'Bow to save face in the entire matter because he was so central to and vocal about the need for a new international information order to complement the new international economic order. European diplomats were clearly taking the initiative away from the ill-prepared U.S. delegation. Indicative of the split in strategy is this *International Herald Tribune* article:

> U.S. agreement to support the European text appeared to end, or at least paper over, friction between the U.S. delegation and some European diplomats who were critical of what they said was U.S. naivete in accepting changes in wording while preserving the outline of the original draft declaration [1978h: 2].

The Reuter's copy outlined the parties to the Western draft: the United States, West Germany, Belgium, Canada, France, Greece, Ireland, Luxembourg, the Netherlands, and Switzerland. Great Britain, never feeling totally comfortable with EEC initiatives, had put forward its own draft resolution calling for a delay until the 1980 General Conference in Belgrade.

In order to move LDC's away from the concept "development journalism," some trade-offs were offered as an incentive to accept one of the Western compromise texts. Joseph Fitchett described it this way:

> In effect, a tradeoff is in the making: the Third World would get aid and a renewed commitment to anti-racism while the industrial countries would get unchallenged press rights [*International Herald Tribune*, 1978i: 5].

In the same edition there was an interesting story on the Third World news agency, Tanjug, run by editor Boza Fran-

cuski. Identical stories by the Western wire services and the
Tanjug pool read like they were reporting totally unrelated
events. The concept of an alternative wire service clearly
produced alternate copy:

> Three years after its launching amid expressions of grave dissatis-
> faction with Western news coverage of the Third World, the
> non-aligned pool is caught between conflicting interests and
> limited resources. The most important constraints on its opera-
> tions are the censorship of news for political reasons, poor com-
> munications, the lack of trained journalists and the sheer diversity
> of the countries which participate in the pool. Some regard each
> other as bitter enemies [*International Herald Tribune*, 1978i: 6].

Other critics add that the pool is mainly for government press
releases from the participating 50 countries. The coverage of
the major events of Wednesday, November 22 was important.

Indicative of the relief felt among Western publishers and
editors is the editorial stance of the London *Times*. A three-
column editorial, "UNESCO Avoids the Worst," was almost
scolding in tone; shades of the Empire:

> UNESCO's adoption of the compromise text of the declaration of
> the mass media removes a significant threat to the freedom of the
> international press . . . there is cause for relief and congratulations
> that the relatively few nations possessing a free press were able to
> win acceptance of the principle from many that cannot abide the
> practice. . . . It was the Soviet Union that first began. . . . [*Times*,
> 1978c: 6].

The coverage also referred to an important point. The final
text was loaded with vague rhetoric and some of the key
phrases could be read or interpreted in several ways. The
Times also carried an account by Ian Murray of the recent
events as well as the 11-article text of the media declaration.
The AP wire service copy went as follows:

> UNESCO's 20th general assembly conference approved by unani-
> mous consensus Wednesday a compromise draft declaration on
> the mass media, endorsing the freedom of the press.

The unanimous consensus indicated by thunderous applause before the UNESCO Commission on Culture and Communication, represented a personal victory for UNESCO Director-General Amadou Mahtar M'Bow and a significant diplomatic reversal in favour of the West and moderate developing nations.

This section at least indicates the tone and issues of the copy flowing from the Paris meetings. As had been indicated elsewhere, it was M'Bow who presented, endorsed, and pushed the initial controversial draft, yet in the end the Western press uniformly blamed the Soviets for the attack on the "free press philosophy" and M'Bow received diplomatic praise for engineering the "historic compromise." Both time and the writing of memoirs will reveal how and why the compromise came about. One suspects that M'Bow found his back, and career, against the wall and quickly abandoned what he cherished in October to pacify the Western nations (and their funding) in November. Of course, M'Bow had the 1979 MacBride International Commission and the 1980 21st General Assembly to resurrect and rerun his NWIO tenets once again, not to mention the 22nd UNESCO General Assembly in 1982 or the 23rd in 1984.

21st UNESCO General Assembly: 1980

It is hard to imagine how the delegates to UNESCO general assemblies can continue to put a face of consensus and unanimity on international communication discussions which invariably totter on the brink of open warfare and collapse. It took a reluctantly accepted 11th hour compromise which merely postponed the major issues to pull the 20th General Assembly's session on mass communication out of the fire. The answer in 1980 in Belgrade was a resolution, adopted by consensus when nobody called for a vote on it, which in effect may as well have been two different resolutions in some respects. It was based on the findings of the MacBride Report and set out for the first time, in a preliminary and preparatory fashion, some of the aims and principles of a new

information order, possibly as a framework for fuller elabora-
tions in the future. It is clear that the resolution—which
capped the assembly's discussions on mass communication,
more particularly on the MacBride Report and a new program to deal with development communication—was adopted
by both the West and the LDC's and socialist bloc forces only
because it was couched in language sufficiently ambiguous to
accommodate widely divergent interpretations as to the spirit
and meaning of many of the phrases and principles. In
addition it included concessions to both sides in the form of
recognition of some of the West's cardinal principles and
some of the LDC's concerns, resulting in a rather uneven and
sometimes inconsistent resolution.

Despite the unanimous approval it received largely as a
result of its equivocal language and the reciprocal concessions
that made it appealing to both sides, particularly the few
scraps thrown in to appease the West, the resolution was
"one of the most bitterly fought over in UNESCO's history"
(*New York Times,* 1980b: 14). It appeared, at least on the
basis of serious reservations expressed about some of its
terms particularly by the West, to reveal more about the
extent to which the West and developing world positions on
the NWIO are irreconcilable than about the possibility of
some significant overlapping or balance of interests ever being
achieved. Even though concessions were made by both sides,
the developing world, acting with the Soviet bloc, seemed to
get the better of the West judging by the cautious, reluctant
approval of the resolution by the West and by the comments
of the Western media.

The edge of the developing world-Soviet majority, according to many participants and observers, turned on the inclu-
sion of some principles and the exclusion of others which, if
interpreted in certain way, could prove, in the words of
William Haley (U.S. Information Agency, 1980c: 3-6), the
American negotiator, "exceedingly troublesome," at least
from a Western perspective. Haley, in a statement following
adoption of the resolution, listed the major sore spots. He

remarked that a phrase in the resolution calling for "the widest and most democratic access of all peoples to the functioning of the mass media" (U.S. Information Agency, 1980c: 3) could be a source of concern if interpreted to "imply direct involvement in the editorial process or management of the media" (U.S. Information Agency, 1980c: 3) rather than as the expression of a desire to see "greater participation of the people in all forms and channels of communication" (U.S. Information Agency, 1980c: 2-3), the meaning which Haley said the United States would like to attach to it. Haley also said that the encouragement, embodied in the resolution, to "make communications an integral part of all development strategy is another cause for our concern, since it is subject to varying interpretations, including that governments should use the media for all governmental purposes" (U.S. Information Agency, 1980c: 4). Furthermore, Haley implied that the association of freedom of journalists with the responsibility of journalists could spell restrictions on news gathering and disseminating activities of reporters. The suggestion is that once journalistic freedom is qualified by a formal recognition of responsibilities, there is a danger that such responsibility will eventually be more closely and concretely defined and possibly in such a way as to inhibit the freedom of journalists.

Finally, Haley objected to the resolution's provision for the director-general being asked

> to undertake, without any guidance, studies for the establishment of a new international information order. Also we believe that convening an international meeting of experts (which the resolution calls for) would be wasteful; in the first place, it would be costly; and in the second, there are no "experts" on this particular subject [U.S. Information Agency, 1980c: 5-6].

Other observers identified what was left out of the resolution as the essence of the West's failure and frustration at the conference. For instance, Britain's chief delegate, Lord

Gordon-Lennox, complained that the resolution suffered as much from faults of omission as faults of commission. He said:

> How can we pretend to lay down guiding considerations which omit such fundamental principles as the right to freedom of thought, opinion and expression; the free circulation of information and ideas; the freedom of movement; freedom from censorship and arbitrary government controls and access to all sources of information, unofficial as well as official?" [U.S. Information Agency, 1980c: 4].

He also regretted that the guiding principles of the resolution "concentrated too much on the rights or responsibilities of countries . . . and not enough on the rights of individuals" (U.S. Information Agency, 1980c: 5). Overall, Britain took a strong stand against many aspects of the NWIO but reluctantly supported the final resolution.

There are a number of theories addressing the question of why the West supposedly lost ground at the conference. As Rosemary Righter points out, the developing world exercised its superior voting strength to push through a number of decisions which the West opposed such as the approval of a larger overall UNESCO budget, a veto of

> Western proposals to divert funds from UNESCO's research programme to practical assistance projects—the research seeks to advance several concepts which directly threaten the free press such as exploring the "social responsibility" of the media and pressing for international codes governing reporters; and the approval of a Soviet proposal to hold an international conference of experts on international communication issues mentioned above. But many key elements of the resolution which were objectionable to Western delegations were conceded more or less voluntarily, albeit grudgingly, by their delegates, a factor which occasioned many allegations from the Western media that the Western representatives compromised some of the cherished traditions and principles of a libertarian press and freedom of information. But tactical errors and miscalculations appear to

have been more responsible than any possible lack of resolve or commitment on the part of Western delegates for what were perceived by many as setbacks to freedom of the press and information [1980: 10].

Righter further observed that "Most Western countries had come to Belgrade in the naive belief that they had put to rest the irreconcilable conflict over the role of the press" (1980: 10). While most of the extremist ideological rhetoric that has been a feature of the last couple of UNESCO general assemblies was downplayed, at least in the early portion of the proceedings, the developing world was no less rigorous or insistent in their efforts to generate a stronger impetus for an NWIO and make further inroads toward its establishment and yielded little ground to the West.

As a result, then, of what probably was a misreading of the general mood regarding an NWIO going into Belgrade, the West seems to have found itself backed into a position where it was forced to settle for trade-offs and sacrifices, such as surrendering on the issue of association of development strategies with media uses, in order to accomplish what it really wanted—formal acceptance of the MacBride Report's affirmation of freedom of information and of the press. The West, particularly the U.S. delegation, justified its performance at the conference by balancing the importance of the formal acknowledgment of the principles of freedom of information and of the press against yielding on what it views as disturbing measures, the acceptance of the need to lay out principles for a new information order, for instance.

In fact, the West did not complain much over the principle of an NWIO and the need to work out some of its aims and guiding principles. Of course, the West may argue that what it consents to when it gives its blessing to an NWIO is not the LDC's version, but basically the same order that now exists but with greater and freer flows of a wider diversity of information and with less onesidedness. In the absence of any complete, standard, and official definition of what is called NWIO, this is how the West prefers to think of the NWIO.

Indeed, the West can apply this line of defense across the board. Paul Lewis remarks that the Western countries plan "to interpret ambiguous sections (of the resolution), which can be read as condoning state control of the press, in a liberal sense" (*New York Times*, 1980b: 14). By construing UNESCO language in ways that are consistent with its position and interests, the West could conceivably make the most glaring instances of measures favoring more control over the media appear to be victories. Though the West tried to soften the negative consequences of parts of the resolution by promising to evaluate them in a liberal vein, it was also honest and realistic about the resolution.

All was not bleak for the West, however. They did gain formal adoption of the MacBride Report and the principles of freedom of information and of the press and could count as fairly clear-cut victories (1) the rejection of a Soviet draft resolution which came down hard on Western transnational news agencies, (2) the rejection of Soviet and developing world proposals for "the policing of news and the control of international communications" (Righter, 1980: 10), (3) protection of journalists, and favoritism toward noncommercial types of information and communication.

The launching at the General Assembly of the International Program for Development of Communications (IPDC) stirred up a great deal of controversy and suspicion, particularly in the West and, according to some critics, represents another setback for the West. The IPDC, according to Sarah Powers, a deputy assistant with the U.S. Office of International Organization Affairs, is an attempt to establish a "consultative mechanism in the field of communications and development," a sort of "clearing house for technical information" (U.S. Information Agency, 1980a: 6). It would, according to correspondent James Fuller, "seek to channel manpower, materials, technology and training for the development of communications in Third World countries" (U.S. Information Agency, 1980b: 2).

Robin Chandler Duke, head of the U.S. delegation, asserts "The focus of the IPDC must be on concrete and practical measures relating to infrastructure, equipment and training" (U.S. Information Agency, 1980b: 3). A 35-member intergovernmental council will administer the program and set out priorities and policy. Members would be elected to the council on a rotating basis with regard for regional representation. They will give the LDC's considerable leverage within the IPDC.

The IPDC has been heralded as perhaps the most significant development of the conference. Of course, until it is in place and the precise shape and directions the scheme will assume are known, pronouncements about the promises or threats it holds in store are conjecture. But it is a major mechanism for implementing the NWIO.

Elie Abel, the U.S. representative on the MacBride Commission, believes UNESCO is not the proper structure within which to establish the program. He correctly maintains that such a program would be coordinated jointly by all international organizations which deal with problems in international communication and development. The strongest fear in the West concerning the IPDC is that the director-general will approve the IPDC director and secretariat and that it will be closely integrated with UNESCO's bureaucracy which, according to an article in *The Economist*, "has traditionally been hostile to market economies, multinational corporations and advertising in the media" (1980a: 39). There are voices in the West that worry about the IPDC becoming an institutional weapon within the UNESCO secretariat which will be used to antagonize Western ideas of a free press. Western governments are expected to closely monitor the program for "any moves to use it for ideological ends that might encourage government interference in international news reporting" (*New York Times*, 1980a: 3).

Another focus of controversy concerning the program is funding. Many LDC's moved that an international fund be started within the UNESCO framework. The United States refused to make advanced pledges to such a fund and suggested that the money needed to initiate the program should be diverted from UNESCO's regular mass communication budget. M'Bow did commit $1.5 million of UNESCO's 1981-1983 budget to start-up administrative costs.

The UNESCO 1981-1983 general budget for mass communication was another issue between the West and the LDC's. The West urged that UNESCO postpone controversial programs or divert funds to concrete projects aimed at improving communication technology, infrastructures, and training. However, the LDC's once again prevailed, succeeding in pushing through several resolutions including the approval of studies on advertising in news media and assistance in finding methods for protecting, perhaps licensing, reporting, which the West opposes strongly.

Many observers in the West, particularly in the Western media, took a dramatic view of what happened in Belgrade. One article in *The Economist* announced, "Press freedom suffered a major defeat at the UNESCO conference which ended in Belgrade last weekend" (1980b: 18). Yet in the final analysis, it appears the conference was indeed a humbling experience for the West. However, the extent of the impact of the conference's actions on the practical operations of freedom of the press and of information is easily exaggerated. Lewis, for instance, notes that some Western diplomats have argued that "the West does not recognize UNESCO's jurisdiction in this field and the organization has no means of enforcing its decisions" (*New York Times,* 1980b: 14). Moreover, the UNESCO secretariat has already been directed to continue studies of the NWIO and how far agreement on it is possible. So the principles, aims, and definitions expressed in the resolution, and by the creation of the IPDC, mean that the NWIO in the 1980s, particularly at future UNESCO General Assemblies, will be the major change in international broadcasting and communication since UNESCO (and the United Nations) was created.

NOTES

1. While experts in some nations are talking about the electronic newspapers via satellites and videodisc systems, many other nations have low literacy or only a single, ill-equipped radio station on the air a few hours per day. In fact, informatics represents greater government control, via regulation, in the West, and the debate over "free speech" may become obsolete with advancing technologies. Indications are that the information environment of the West in the future may see considerable government involvement and a renewed interest in government regulation in the public interest. European tradition in this area is systematically distinct from the U.S. tradition (McPhail, 1980).

2. Frequently the beleaguered Salle de Presse staff would comment that the press loves to cover the press. Their half-dozen manual typewriters had never seen so much action; in fact, sometimes there was a queue to get at them; fortunately, the entire press corps was never there all at once; some came only for a day, or a week; others, like the wire service people, were there from start to finish. Most morning sessions began at 10:00 and evening sessions concluded around 11:00; it was a long session for the few who monitored the entire assembly.

It also became clear, in discussion with delegates from several nations, that there was a resentment of the concentration of the press on the media declaration. Some subcommittees received little media attention, if any, despite their major proposals. Even the Associated Press correspondent lamented one day over coffee during about the third week that he had started the assembly filing about six stories daily, was now down to four, and of those the editors were only using one or two at most, and they were the copy that referred to the media issue in either a plenary speech or in the Communication and Culture subcommittee. Most other subcommittee meetings went totally ignored during the final weeks.

3. For similar reasons, the exclusion of Great Britain from the MacBride Commission is of considerable significance. Some argue the deck was stacked against the West from the beginning. Also Great Britain took one of the strongest stands against the NWIO at Belgrade in 1980.

4. Before discussing the stand of the World Press Freedom Committee, a few background details are relevant. Beebe had early morning briefing sessions with his constant companions—Hector Armengal, of the Inter-American Association of Broadcasters' representing private Latin American interests, and two or three others. They always moved about the corridors as a group. The Tass correspondent was frequently bemused by their clustering antics.

At the Paris Hilton on a Saturday evening I noticed a fellow that I recalled seeing at U.S. Ambassador Reinhardt's press conference. Just as I was about to go over and introduce myself, a group came through the door, Beebe plus his followers, and they surrounded the other gentleman who proceeded to pull out his reporter's notebook and took notes. It would have made a great picture for the cover of Tim Crouse's book, *Boys on the Bus*—pack journalism incarnate. As I left I went over and introduced myself; the reporter looked as if he wanted to eat his notebook to get rid of it. He was from *Time*.

5. Manley, like some other socialist leaders, is interesting for another commonality. He holds a British Ph.D. I lost count at the General Assembly of the

number of times that a Third World ambassador or senior government minister upon addressing the plenary session would attack the West and demand a new economic and information order, using the finest British accent and a multitude of polysyllabic phrases. The elite of the LDC's is leading the call for a new order on several fronts.

6. The MacBride Report is covered in detail in Chapter 8; some may prefer to read it at this time since it was a major report discussed at the 21st General Assembly held in Belgrade. The spinoff of MacBride, a new International Program for Development of Communications, is discussed there also.

REFERENCES

BEEBE, G. (1978) UNESCO document 2oc/vr/25 (prov.) November 8.

BEHR, E. (1978) Bearings. New York: Viking Press.

Daily Telegraph (1978a) October 30.

Daily Telegraph (1978b) October 31.

DUNKLEY, C. (1979) "British television." *New York Times,* Section D. February 25.

The Economist (1980a) "Press ganging?" September 20, p. 39.

The Economist (1980b) "Son of MacBride." November 1, p. 18.

The Economist (1978) November 4.

HART, J. (1978) Plenary address. Paris, October 30.

HOGGART, R. (1978) An Idea and Its Servants: UNESCO from Within. London: Chatto and Windus.

International Herald Tribune (1978a) October 27.

International Herald Tribune (1978b) November 2.

International Herald Tribune (1978c) November 4-5.

International Herald Tribune (1978d) November 7.

International Herald Tribune (1978e) November 8.

International Herald Tribune (1978f) November 9.

International Herald Tribune (1978g) November 10.

International Herald Tribune (1978h) November 16.

International Herald Tribune (1978i) November 18-19.

M'BOW, A. (1978) UNESCO document 20 c/info. 10. November 13.

McPHAIL, T. (1980) "Telematics, telejournalism, and public policy concerns," pp. 417-419 in Applications of Telecommunications in the Information Economy. Dedham, MA: Horizon House.

MUSCAT, P. (1978) UNESCO document 20c/vr, 19 (prov.) November 4.

New York Times (1980a) "U.S. backs U.N.'s Third World communications plan." September 27, p. 3.

New York Times (1980b) "U.N. parley adopts principles on news." October 25, p. 14.

Newsweek (1978) November 6.

NIMETZ, M. (1980) Testimony before the Subcommittee on Governmental Information and Individual Rights of the U.S. House Committee on Government Operations. March 27, pp. 1-21.

RANA, T. (1978) UNESCO document 20c/vr 19 (prov.) November 4.

REINHARDT, J. (1978) Plenary address. Paris, November 3.

RIGHTER, R. (1980) "The Third World tightens its hold over the media." *The Times,* October 26, p. 10.

ROBERTS, J. (1978) Plenary address. Paris, November 6.

SHIHEPO, S. (1978) UNESCO document 20c/vr, 19 (prov.) November 4.

Times (1978a) October 27.

Times (1978b) November 23.

UNESCO (1978) 20c/Inf. 9. October 28, 1978. Paris: Author.

U.S. Information Agency (1980a) Sarah Power on UNESCO media issue. September 3, p. 6.

U.S. Information Agency (1980b) UNESCO launches new communications development program. By James Fuller. October 23, p. 2.

U.S. Information Agency (1980c) U.S. statement on UNESCO resolution. October 27, pp. 3-6.

WICKER, T. (1978) "No, No, UNESCO." *International Herald Tribune* (Nov. 2): 6.

Chapter 6

THE MEDIUM:
International Telecommunications Union
and the World Administration Radio Conference

The struggle between the West and the LDC's at the 1978 UNESCO General Assembly over the question of an NWIO ended in a mood of uneasy compromise. The release felt by the Western nations was shortlived.

Observers anticipated that another arena, the World Administrative Radio Conference (WARC), would see another clash between the West and the LDC's. WARC meets once every 20 years, 1959, 1979, 1999, and so on, to assign worldwide frequencies from the usable electromagnetic spectrum available for broadcasting and communication services. (Some technical details are provided at the end of this chapter.) Historically, these meetings attracted little attention as technicians and engineers from various nations around the world sat down and divided the spectrum with great concern for technical matters such as microwave interference between neighboring states, technical standards, and equipment protocol. One can trace the International Telecommunications Union's (ITU) origins to the setting up of international standards for Morse code in the late 19th century. Until only a few years ago, when 152 nations began to plan for WARC meetings in Geneva in late 1979, the industrial nations once again approached matters as merely a technical and engineering meeting with little political, economic, or social concern.

Times have changed. These general WARCs (Howkins, 1979c) occur and are convened and organized by the ITU, a specialized UN agency charged with coordinating international use of telecommunications systems worldwide. The nations represented at WARCs are members of the ITU. Besides certain articles dealing solely with individual radio services such as satellites, which are covered at periodically held specialized WARCs and will increase in importance, general WARCs review and amend the existing ITU International Radio Regulations. For instance, general WARCs are empowered to amend regulatory procedures for settling differences between nations and for notifying, coordinating, and registering radio frequency assignments. Also WARCs are authorized to set new rules concerning technical and performance standards of telecommunication systems. But probably the most significant set of regulations which general WARCs have the scope to revise is the International Table of Frequency Allocation. In other words, WARC 79, as did other general WARCs before it, had the power to alter any of the then-existing uses of any part of the spectrum, from the lowest to the highest frequencies. This is one of the most powerful roles given an international body.

All the general WARCs by virtue of the range of their authority were profoundly significant events. But, for a variety of reasons, WARC 79 was being heralded during the build-up to the conference as potentially the most important ITU meeting ever held. For one thing, the last WARC with a mandate equivalent to that of WARC 79 was held in 1959.

Specialized WARCs such as the 1971 satellite WARC and the 1974 maritime WARC for maritime radio services have been held since 1959. During the years between WARC 59 and WARC 79, technological innovations such as satellites and methods of using more and more of the higher ranges of the spectrum, particularly microwave frequencies, have revolutionized telecommunications. Such new developments in communication now exercise so profound an influence on social, economic, and political organizations and have so radically transformed the way men live and interact with each other and their environment that the present era has come to be known as the information age. According to John Howkins:

> The explosion of telecommunications in the second half of the twentieth century may be compared to the transition that humans made thousands of years ago from hunting to agriculture, or, more recently, from an agricultural society to an industrial society. The transition of industrial societies, via the limbo of the "post-industrial society," into fully-fledged information societies—as we witness now—makes telecommunications the hallmark and defining characteristic of our society. It is the measure of a society's wealth or poverty, and a major factor in a society's capacity for change [1979a: 12].

The chief reasons that more attention and preparation were devoted to WARC 79 by the international community were the increase in the number of countries represented and the fact that the LDC's, which accounted for almost all that increase, have throughout the 1970s constituted a majority in the ITU. In 1959, 96 nations were members of the ITU. By 1979, ITU membership had grown to 154 nations, of which 142 sent delegates to WARC 79. And the level of preparation and negotiating skill that was needed to make a meeting of over 2300 delegates from 142 countries and some 40 independent organizations dealing with issues of unusual complexity in some way manageable was unprecedented in ITU history.

The majority status of the LDC's contributed to that conference's high profile compared to earlier general WARCs because it was expected to be the source of a feature previously unheard of at WARCs—namely, the use of political and ideological criteria in arriving at decisions concerning spectrum management.

Decisions at WARC are taken on a "one-nation, one-vote" basis. The West feared if the LDC's acted in unison they would be able, by virtue of the majority they commanded, to push through measures relating to an NWIO and guarantee access for the developing world to desired spectrum space and geostationary orbits for satellites, measures which the West, particularly the United States, have grave reservations about.

The West had some grounds for their fears. At a Non-Aligned Conference in Havana, Cuba, just two months before WARC 79, member nations drew up a "shopping list" of demands related to an NWIO that they agreed to press for, presumably in a concerted fashion, at the upcoming WARC. Furthermore, at a specialized satellite WARC in 1977, there was talk by the LDC's about reserving certain prime orbital slots for satellites on a nation-by-nation basis, regardless of a country's immediate need, ability, or desire to use such slots, in order to ensure that the limited space for satellites would not be assigned before LDC's had advanced enough to set up their own satellite systems.

While the more prominent issues associated with the NWIO concern cultural imperialism, concentration of ownership, transnational control of mass media, and imbalances in news flow, the LDC's have been quick to point out imbalances in spectrum allocations. For instance, developed countries with only 10% of the world's population have control of 90% of the spectrum. LDC's also note that the "first-come, first-served" approach the ITU has traditionally taken toward managing the spectrum and allocation of satellite parking spaces have favored the West and the USSR, which generally have had the satellite technology and launching rockets to stake early claims on orbital slots and prime spectrum space.

For these reasons, WARC 79 was viewed by LDC's as an important forum in which to press once again the question of a new and more equitable distribution of information and communication resources of all kinds.

Before discussing WARC 79, a brief sketch of the history and structure of the ITU will illustrate the substantial shift in emphasis that has taken place within the specialized agencies of the UN. The introduction of the NIEO and the NWIO has moved the ideological direction and issues that surface, frequently as amendments, to declarations and proposals of an international nature.

History and Structure of the ITU

In 1865, the International Telegraph Union, the ITU's forerunner, was formed under the International Telegraph Convention signed by 20 European states. This makes the ITU the oldest international organization surviving today. At that time the organization dealt exclusively with technical problems. The international standards for the Morse code were among its first endeavors.

The invention and implementation of wireless systems of communication (radio) complicated the process of setting international telecommunications regulations. At the 1906 Berlin Conference, the first international conference to deal with radio and to set standards for equipment and technical uniformity, certain sections of the radio frequency spectrum were allocated to specific radio services, most notably the frequencies used by ships at sea.

The International Radio Telegraph Conference of 1927 held in Washington, D.C., was the site of the next major advance in radio and communication management. At this conference, the Table of Frequency Allocations was created. Howkins points out the rather simple nature of early activities:

> The procedure was simple. Users notified the union about the frequencies which they were already using or wished to use and

the union registered these in its master list. Neither the union nor the user owned the frequency. What happened was that, through the union's processes of registration, the user had a squatter's right to a specific frequency. Furthermore, the union's recognition of a particular usage gave the user some protection in international law [1979a: 14].

This simple squatter's right on a first-come, first-served basis did not take into account the limited nature of the resource. It has been largely responsible for the congestion of uses in some popular frequency banks, a problem which today makes efficient allocation a difficult proposition requiring regional meetings.

Initially the uses of the spectrum were confined to maritime activities such as radio navigation and ship-to-shore communication. During the 1920s, thanks to technological advances and new means of utilizing higher frequencies, the types of services that the radio spectrum enjoyed multiplied rapidly. As new services began to compete for spectrum space, fears grew that unless each new type of service was given a separate and distant band within the spectrum, overcrowding and interference among the services would occur.

The ITU responded to this concern at the 1929 WARC where it was resolved that the various uses being made of the spectrum be coordinated by allocating a certain stretch or band of frequencies to a particular service. By the 1947 Atlantic City Conference, further advances in telecommunications capacity necessitated revision of procedures for registering and securing recognition of spectrum uses. More detailed plans for services were adopted for each of the three newly created regions. They were: Region 1 for Europe and Africa, Region 2 for the Americas, and Region 3 for Asia and the South Pacific.

At the WARC in 1959, the approach of the ITU to telecommunications management came under criticism. For instance, it was noted that huge areas of the spectrum such as the high frequencies bands were unplanned. It was pointed

out that the ITU stepped in to coordinate national assignments of frequencies only after congestion and conflicting
uses had occurred. Generally the ITU gave priority to those
nations which just happened to have the luck or the economic and technological sophistication to occupy a frequency first, not necessarily to the nation which needed the
frequency most. The fortunate nations were primarily from
the West and relied on the "squatter's rights" tradition.

Misgivings about the basic machinery of the ITU and
WARCs have both continued and escalated in the years since
WARC 59. First, the regulations which the ITU had adopted
to make international telecommunications manageable are
becoming either overextended or obsolete with the rapid
introduction of new demands, for example, frequency space
for microwave ovens.

Second, countless "footnotes," which are a device countries use to declare their intention to use a frequency for a
purpose other than that stated in the international table of
allocations, clutter the Regulations (Broadcasting, 1979b:
36). There are allocations in the Regulations to which as
many as 40 countries have entered individual footnotes. For
instance, at WARC 79, the United States tried to enter a
footnote stating that within its borders mobile and fixed
services may be shared on a primary coequal basis with other
uses. It needed a footnote because the international table
provided for only broadcasting as the primary use within
those bands.

When a nation cannot get a footnote approved or otherwise takes exception to any of the Regulations or decisions
adopted by WARCs, they may take a "reservation"—an
extreme measure by which a nation formally gives notice that
it will not be bound by a WARC decision. The United States
took such a reservation when it could not get the abovementioned footnote approved without meeting conditions to
which it could not agree.

Structurally the ITU consists of four permanent bodies:
the General Secretariat, the International Frequency Regis-

tration Board (IFRB), the International Radio Consultative Committee, and the International Telegraph and Telephone Committee (CCIR and CCITT, the latter two's French acronyms).

The IFRB "records all the frequency assignments made by individual countries and checks their conformity with the Radio Regulations and decisions made by administrative radio conferences. On this basis the assignments can be given formal recognition and protection—or be refused such recognition" (Howkins, 1979a: 22). But the procedures for notifying and registering frequency uses have never been adequate. For instance, many frequency assignments on the IFRB's Master Registry have been abandoned and are thus available for new assignment, but the IFRB still has them recorded as occupied. (WARC 79 took measures to correct this situation.) As additional frequencies become registered, the IFRB finds it increasingly difficult to keep up with its work.

The duties of the CCIR and CCITT are to "study technical, operating and tariff questions and to issue recommendations" (Howkins, 1979a: 22). As rapid advances in telecommunications make the problems WARCs address increasingly involved and unwieldy, many items that come up at such conferences are deferred and sent out, usually to the CCIR, for further study. As a result these bodies, especially the CCIR, are becoming overburdened.

To restate the original point, then, while the history of the ITU and the WARCs it has sponsored has been punctuated by difficult problems, and while doubts have been expressed about the efficiency of the structural framework of the ITU, both the problems and the doubts turn on questions which are essentially of a technical or administrative nature. One major reason for this technical orientation was stated in a comment in *The Economist* which noted that "the ITU is full of engineers terrified of controversy and terrified of the press" (1979: 18).

In recent years many critics of ITU and WARC have cautioned that, while this narrow technical focus may have been tolerable when decisions about telecommunications were of concern to only a limited circle of specialists within the industry, now it is simply not adequate. In an age in which telecommunications has become highly politicized because of its profound affects on the complexion of national and international roles, the LDC's are not only concerned about what is said about them but they are also concerned on which medium or frequency it is carried. (See, for example, the section on direct broadcast satellites in the following chapter.)

The ITU has received promptings from many quarters to generate some structural and administrative reforms designed to furnish mechanisms for absorbing and taking into account political inputs. Currently, the ITU has developed neither traditions for dealing with political or ideological concerns nor the necessary administrative circuitry through which such conflicts could be channelled without crippling the ITU in its technical activities.

When many LDC's hinted prior to WARC 79 about turning the conference into an ideological and rhetorical contest, it triggered much speculation that with no history of treating such a development, the talks would collapse before technical issues could be resolved. This would have jeopardized spectrum management decisions and left matters in an uncomfortable state of suspension. Of course, that is the last thing the West wanted, with billions invested in telecommunications systems and thus a keen interest in maintaining a manageable and predictable telecommunications environment.

WARC 79: September 24-December 5, Geneva, Switzerland

Looking at WARC 79 with hindsight, the West had little to worry about. The opening of the conference was delayed three days when the LDC's and the industrialized nations split over the appointment of a chairperson. Many nations from the nonaligned group insisted on a chairperson from an

LDC. The dispute was finally resolved with the choice of Roberto Severini, a widely respected Argentinian delegate. This early episode seemed to confirm the worst fears of the developed countries. But the delegations settled down to highly technical issues for the remainder of the talks.

The industrialized nations at WARC managed to defuse, at least for the time being, the really explosive issues which were expected to divide the First and Third Worlds. Probably the major issue was the matter of LDC proposals that frequency distribution and orbital space slots be planned by allotment on a country-by-country basis. In the build-up to WARC 79 many LDC's made clear their intention to revise IFRB registration and notification procedures "which gave recognition and priority of use to those countries which first register frequency assignments with the ITU" (Robinson, 1979: 155).

FREQUENCY RESERVATIONS

The LDC's wanted to replace this first-come, first-served criteria of spectrum management with a system whereby they could reserve, for future use, frequencies for themselves. This type of prior planning, LDC's have argued, would facilitate fairer and more equal access to the radio spectrum and prime parking spots for their satellites, if and when they are in a position to launch and purchase satellites.

The first-come, first-served approach is often identified as the principal cause of present imbalances in spectrum assignments. Since the older, industrialized nations entered the field of radio telecommunications much earlier than the LDC's, they obtained squatter's rights on prime frequencies. In addition, their technical and scientific communities permitted them to keep at least one step ahead in the race to move in to new, higher frequencies which technological developments brought within their reach. Now the LDC's recognize that radio telecommunications are too important to their progress to rest their chances of meeting future spectrum requirements on the hope that other nations will not have moved first into the frequencies they may want or need. LDC's, in keeping with NWIO, want guarantees now about future costs.

The industrialized nations, particularly the United States, have traditionally shuddered at the prospect of a prior planning of frequency distribution or orbital slots by allotment and reservation or otherwise. They claim it would leave many of the alloted frequencies and orbital slots lying fallow because many LDC's which would benefit from such allotments would not have the facilities, the money, or even the need to use them. Furthermore, scientists and engineers believe reservations could retard technological development in telecommunications, for there would no longer be the incentive to compete for assignments provides, to pursue new methods of squeezing more use out of particular frequency bands (*Broadcasting,* 1979a: 38).

The Western nations also point to previous experience with a prior planning system to make their case. They maintain that the ventures made into a prior planning at a 1974 maritime WARC, at which several maritime frequencies were reserved for landlocked nations while some islands got nothing, was a nightmare from an engineering standpoint (*Business Week,* 1979: 48). At the 1977 satellite WARC, what the United States considers another abortive experiment in planning occurred. Many countries were alloted two, three, four, or five satellite channels independently of their need or ability to utilize them. And some very small nations such as the Republic of Cape Verde and Mali got as many or more channels than the United Kingdom (Howkins, 1979a: 14-15).

But most of the fears and bitter controversy that surrounded the first-come, first-served issue and a prior planning issue gave way to compromise and accommodation once the talks were underway. A mutually satisfactory agreement between the West and the LDC's was worked out on the Radio Regulation articles dealing with procedures for notification and registration of frequency use for its coordination which promoted a first-come, first-served orientation. The compromise managed to evade mention of a prior planning or frequency reservations.

> The essential elements of this compromise were; 1) removal of outdated HF assignments in the Master Frequency Register; 2) reclassification of remaining assignments according to needs and alternative means; 3) finding new frequencies for IIF fixed assignments displaced by allocation changes ("reaccommodation"); 4) increased assistance by the IFRB to countries needing help in finding new frequencies, and in identifying interference; 5) revision of article N12 and related texts, to implement these procedures. The "package" also includes a new resolution to the effect that these provisions are intended essentially for use by the administrations of developing countries should minimize their use of these provisions [IEEE Communications Magazine, 1980: 49].

The question of planning geostationary orbits and other important future space services was delayed and to some extent avoided for the time being. Instead some decisions about significant matters were postponed and scheduled to be taken up again at a two-part space conference to be held in the mid 1980s. This conference will search for ways to "guarantee in practice for all countries equitable access to the geostationary orbit and frequency bands allocated to space services." According to *Inter Media:*

> The conference will "decide which space services and frequency bands should be planned" and then establish guidelines for such planning and related regulatory Procedures.

> The resolution reflects a remarkable compromise by the U.S. delegation. Hitherto, the USA has tended to reject the idea of planning under virtually any circumstances. It is arguable, of course, that the proposed conference could decide that no space services should be planned; but such a result seems unlikely. What is more recommendations not taking effect before 1990 at the earliest; by which time brand-new technologies may enable the richer countries like the USA to move to even higher frequencies that are not affected by the WARC's proposal [1980: 4].

But the West and LDC's factions were not so successful in finding common ground concerning another major barrier, the problem of reallocations in the high frequencies (HF) bands.

HIGH FREQUENCY REALLOCATIONS

The HF bands are very popular among the LDC's for fixed and mobile services. Fixed services, as opposed to broadcasting, cover radio communication between two or more fixed points. Fixed service communication in HF bands may be worked inexpensively with low circuit capacity and equipment that is easy to maintain; thus it provides a cheap means for laying out a society's basic communications infrastructure and connecting remote parts of a country. But because of erratic propagation of HF signals, HF bands are sometimes unreliable. Thus when new techniques made more reliable and efficient microwave frequencies available, the industrialized nations moved their fixed services out of the HF bands. As a result, they have been asking for more use of HF bands for other purposes, particularly shortwave broadcasting such as BBC's External Services, Radio Moscow, Voice of America, and Radio Peking. LDC's have fears, since HF bands are so congested, that concessions to HF broadcasting would have to be made at the expense of essential fixed services.

However, there is no consensus among developing nations about the HF issue. Many LDC's such as Iran, Pakistan, and many African states also want to initiate some shortwave broadcasting in the HF bands in order to balance the influence of the international services of more powerful nations, though they prefer to take frequencies for broadcasting from mobile and amateur rather than fixed services. There have been proposals that the problem of competing services in the HF bands could be alleviated by taking measures to use HF bands more efficiently such as limiting transmitter power and implementing single sideband transmission. But many LDC's cannot, in the foreseeable future, afford to institute such expensive steps as single sideband transmission which requires special receivers. This problem of financing for LDC's entering into more adequate services is a recurring problem.

A number of nations such as the United States and Canada took out reservations declaring that, while they would attempt to operate within the HF broadcasting regulations decided on at WARC 79, they would nevertheless not hesitate to meet their shortwave broadcasting needs in HF bands even if it meant violating those regulations. This is one of five reservations the United States took at WARC 79, more than any other nation. Significantly many nations, including Iran, which wanted greater increases in HF broadcast allocations, took similar reservations. While efforts to win prime HF space for broadcasting did not pan out, those countries interested in upgrading their shortwave services could take some comfort in the prospect of an HF broadcasting conference scheduled for 1984.

Not only did the United States fail to attain shortwave broadcasting frequencies in HF bands that they wanted they also could not secure allocations for maritime mobile services on a primary basis, again due to the priority given at such frequencies to fixed services essential to LDC's. The United States felt strongly enough about the issue to take a reservation noting it will meet its maritime mobile needs in HF bands allocated to the mobile service on a primary basis.

U.S. defense requirements also proved to be a source of WARC conflict. In one case, the United States and a number of other nations obtained a footnote enabling them to operate mobile satellites in bands normally allocated to terrestrial fixed and mobile services. However, LDC's relying on the fixed and mobile services imposed conditions on the special mobile satellite services in the band which would in effect, relegate such satellite services which the United States employs for Navy communication to a secondary use. The United States, together with 12 European countries, took a reservation on the issue.

The United States felt radiolocation (radar) services had also been downgraded to a secondary status in some bands or were forced to share primary status with other uses not compatible with radar. These other uses were incompatible not because they would interfere with radar but because it would be difficult, in the case of radar, to provide these other primary services the protection from interference which under the Radio Regulations is supposed to be guaranteed to all primary services. So the United States took yet another reservation.

Somewhat surprisingly, allocations for earth exploration satellite services did not develop into the controversial issue. NASA's Landsat and Seasat satellites are examples of earth exploration satellites. Such satellites, capable of remote sensing through active and passive sensors, are used to survey the earth's natural resources and provide information about climate, crops, fisheries management, water, and agricultural conditions.

LDC's have expressed fear that they may be used as instruments of espionage and call them "spy satellites." Moreover, frequencies allocated to this type of service has to be done on an exclusive basis because any other telecommunications use at such frequencies would interfere with the highly sensitive passive satellite sensors. But, for whatever reasons, the LDC's gave the United States little argument on the 50 proposals it made regarding remote sensing. These and future remote sensing satellites may provide the West with more up-to-date information about LDC's (crops, roads, exploration, and so on) than the LDC's themselves have.

MOBILE RADIO

Ironically enough, while sharp ideological hostilities did not really surface in a prominent way at WARC 79, a few of the most stubborn issues involved differences between the United States and Canada, two countries which could hardly be more politically, economically, and ideologically akin.

One of the issues had to do with mobile radio services which include maritime, aeronautical, and land services. Mobile radio, especially land mobile service, is a rapidly expanding component of modern telecommunications. Howkins points out that

> Mobile radio epitomises the widespread desire for a communication service that is two-way, personal and flexible, and usually cheap and lightweight. The range of services is very wide—Citizen's Band, bleepers for businessmen, doctors, etc.; two-way radios for taxis, delivery vehicles, the police, service engineers, etc; temporary radio networks in disasters; car telephones; and much else [1979a: 16].

While many LDC's, such as Afghanistan, Turkey, Uganda, and other African countries, oppose the extensive use of mobile radio because its use is so difficult to control, proposals for increased allocations for land mobile services did not emerge as an issue. Most of the proposed allocations for land mobile use of frequencies were in the UHF bands. UHF signals do not travel beyond line-of-sight distances. So, unlike HF signals which, at least at night, reflect off the ionosphere back to earth, back to the ionosphere, and so on and can thereby travel thousands of miles, UHF signals can only cause interference in countries adjacent to them. So the United States, for instance, only has to deal with Canada and Mexico in coordinating use of land mobile services in the UHF band. All in all, WARC 79 was judged at least a mild success by most of the parties involved. The severe ideological pressure to which it was expected to succumb did not materialize in a decisive way.

A TEMPORARY TRUCE

Other industrialized nations managed to satisfy many of their most urgent demands. First, the LDC's staved off efforts by the advanced nations to increase shortwave broadcasting allocations in the HF bands; second, they succeeded in keeping the West alert to the issue of reserving parking spots for satellites with the resolution it pushed through for a significant conference in 1983 to plan geostationary orbits and frequencies for space services; third, five resolutions adopted to streamline notification and registration procedures also answered some LDC's criticisms concerning the ITU's first-come, first-served orientation.

A number of factors discouraged the LDC's from pushing the NWIO concept to its limit in Geneva. First, they realized that there will be other forums sponsored by the ITU in the 1980s for them to state their case and make gains in their movement toward a fairer share of the radio spectrum and orbital parking spaces. Second, many nations, such as the United States and the USSR, applied pressure and collected on debts to ensure that an orderly spectrum remained intact, particularly for satellites. Third, almost all nations have some type of domestic system, regardless of how rudimentary some of them are, and want to see them continue operating without major adjustments. Fourth, very divergent and often conflicting national interests among the LDC's prevented the formation of a powerful, united, and well-orchestrated voting bloc which may have presented resolutions and amendments demanding radical changes in the allocation of the spectrum.

While the talks did not break down, WARC as an institution for setting the ground rules for international radio spectrum management itself showed serious signs of fatigue. The sheer size of the conference and the complexity of the issues resulted in incredible amounts of paperwork; in addition, a tedious tempo with endless arguments in the plenary sessions and often chaotic meetings of the eight major committees, and their spinoff working groups and subgroups, which were set up to review various national proposals and reports, resulted in much frustration. Also, more footnotes and reservations were taken than at any previous WARC and no fewer than nine specialized and regional radio administrative conferences were proposed, many of them to deal with issues that WARC 79 did not have the time or ability to resolve.

There is the uncomfortable suggestion behind all of this that
WARC may be slipping into obsolescence as a forum for
regulating radio telecommunications. Either these regional
conferences will be more significant than the main WARC or
else the idea of meeting every 20 years must be abandoned.

With the pace of technical change accelerating on a daily
basis, the wait to 1999 for the next worldwide WARC is
untenable. Besides, the LDC's and the West alike realize that
despite their philosophical and economic differences, ultimately the international telecommunications system must be
both orderly and workable.

Technology

THE ELECTROMAGNETIC SPECTRUM AND ITS USES

The motion of waves in a body of water provides a helpful,
if somewhat crude point of reference for visualizing electromagnetic energy and its movement. Electromagnetic energy
oscillates (moves in waves) in roughly the same manner as
water in the ocean. Electromagnetic (radio) waves can be
measured by the number of times they pass a given point per
second (frequency) or by the distance from one wavecrest to
the next (wavelength). There is a definite covariation
between frequency and wavelength. One can arrive at the
frequency of an electromagnetic wave by dividing the speed
of the wave, which is always about 300,000 kilometers per
second, by its wavelength. Wavelength is measured metrically
and frequency is measured in terms of Hertz, after the
German radio pioneer Heinrich Hertz. A frequency of one
Hertz refers to electromagnetic radiation that passes a given
point at the rate of one wave (one cycle) per second. One
kilohertz equals a thousand Hertz, one megahertz equals a
million Hertz, and one gigahertz equals a billion Hertz.

The electromagnetic spectrum represents all the possible
frequencies and wavelengths at which radio waves oscillate.
The spectrum is arbitrarily divided into bands ranging from

TABLE 1.1

Wavelength	Frequency	Band
100 kilometres - 10 km	3 kilohertz - 30 kHz	(VHF) very low frequency
10 km - 1 km	30 kHz - 300 kHz	(LF) low frequency
1 km - 100 metres	300 kHz - 3 megahertz	(MF) medium frequency
100 m - 10 m	3 MHz - 30 Mhz	(HF) high frequency
10 m - 1 m	30 MHz - 300 MHz	(VHF) very high frequency
1 m - 10 centimetres	300 MHz - 3 gigahertz	(UHF) ultra high frequency
10 cm - 1 cm	3 GHz - 30 GHz	(SHF) super high frequency
1 cm - 1 millimetre	30 GHz - 300 GHz	(EHF) extra high frequency

the very low frequency band to the extra high one (see Table 1). Any stretch of frequencies within any of these larger bands represented in Table 1 is also referred to as a band.

Information such as voice, music, video, and so on must be modulated into radio waves before it is transmitted. Thus the information which radio waves carry increases as the frequency of the waves increases and hence the wavelength shortens since this means that more waves are passing through a given point per second and the distance between their crests is smaller. John Howkins writes:

The development of telecommunications can be seen as a constant push to use higher frequencies, since the higher the frequency the greater the capacity to transmit information ... the capacities of the main regions of the spectrum can be compared in terms of the bandwidth necessary to operate a single color television channel, i.e., 6 MHz of spectrum. The whole of the VLF (very low frequency) band could transmit only a three-hundredth of one TV channel, LF (low frequency) a twentieth, and MF (medium frequency) a half of one channel. The HF (high frequency) band, however, can accommodate the equivalent of four TV channels, VHF (very high frequency) 45 channels, UHF (ultra high frequency) 450 channels, SHF (super high frequency) 4500 channels, and the EHF (extra high frequency) as many as 34,000 channels [1979c: 145].

Thus, different bands of frequencies are more appropriate for different uses. Some uses are amateur radio; television and radio broadcasting; fixed satellite (point-to-point); broadcast satellite; aeronautical; land, marine, and satellite mobile; radio navigation or radar; space research; earth exploration satellite (which includes remote sensing), and radio astronomy. Table 2 lists typical radio services for which each band of the spectrum is used.

The ITU allocates certain stretches or bands of frequencies for a particular use or uses and may apply such allocations on a worldwide or regional level. Different radio services are often allocated the same stretch of frequencies. In such cases the ITU determines which services have priority by giving each service either "primary" status, "permitted" status, or "secondary" status. Primary status means the service shares equal rights to a band of frequencies with a "permitted" service but has prior choice of frequencies when frequency plans are made. Permitted status means the service has the same rights as a primary service and must not cause interference with them.

GEOSTATIONARY ORBITS

Generally the most effective positioning of a communication satellite is 22,300 miles above the equator in a geostationary or geosynchronous orbit. This means that because it is at such an altitude, the satellite completes one orbit of the

TABLE 2

Frequency Range	Typical Service
30 - 300 kHz (LF)	Navigation
300 - 30,000 kHz (MF)	Broadcast
3 - 30 MHz (HF)	Fixed Aero Mobile Maritime Mobile Amateur
30 - 300 MHz (VHF)	Broadcast Mobile
300 - 3,000 MHz (UHF)	Broadcast Land Mobile Mobile Satellite
3 - 30 GHz (SHF)	Fixed Satellite Navigation Radar
30 - 300 GHz (EHF)	Radio Astronomy Earth Exploration Satellite

earth in the same time as the earth revolves once around its axis, that is, once every 24 hours. Because the satellite is travelling at the same speed as the earth is moving, it always appears to be hovering over the same area on earth and thus it can provide continuous communications service. Other satellites placed at lower altitudes such as 5,000 to 10,000 miles above the earth do not travel at the same speed as the earth and disappear over the horizon. To provide continuous communications with such satellites, as one satellite disappears over the horizon, another one must simultaneously appear to replace it. This requires expensive and elaborate antennae or receivers which can track this new satellite as it enters view. Because synchronous satellites are always over the same spot on earth, simpler receivers or ground stations are able to pick up their signals. Moreover, because of the altitude of synchronous satellites, their beams cover much greater amounts of territory (foot print) than their lower altitude counterparts can.

Unfortunately, there is limited space for satellites in the thin slice 22,300 miles above the equator in which such satellites can operate or park. This is why the question of allotting orbital slots on a country-by-country basis in advance has become such a pressing one for developing countries which trail far behind in satellite technology. If and when they catch up, there may not be sufficient or usable parking spots remaining for additional geostationary satellites.

REFERENCES

Broadcasting (1979a) "WARC '79: Curtain going up on telecommunications future." September 17, p. 38.

Broadcasting (1979b) "WARC '79: The penultimate week." December 3, p. 36.

Business Week (1979) "The hassle over sharing the radio waves." May 7, p. 48.

Economist (1979) "Will you keep my space?" September No. 7100, p. 18.

HOWKINS, J. (1979a) "The management of the spectrum." Inter Media 7(5): 12-16.

HOWKINS, J. (1979b) "How the ITU works." Inter Media 7(5): 22-23.

HOWKINS, J. (1979c) "What is the World Administrative Radio Conference?" Journal of Communication 29: 144-149.

IEEE Communications Magazine (1980) "WARC: The outcome—a U.S. perspective." January, p. 49.

Inter Media (1980) "WARC: More conferences will be held." 8(1): 3-4.

ROBINSON, G. (1979) "The U.S. position." Journal of Communication 29: 150-157.

Chapter 7

THE WIRE SERVICE, DBS, AND
RELATED INTERNATIONAL ISSUES

The rather rapid development of the NWIO and the previously untested strength of its advocates has resulted in
significant potential changes in international broadcasting
and communication. Areas of additional impact will be outlined here; they are: (1) the major wire services, (2) direct
broadcast satellites, (3) Latin America concerns, and (4)
aspects of U.S. information policy.

The Major Wire Services: Perpetrators or Victims?

The Western media, according to LDC critics and even by
their own admission, have not covered the NIEO debate and
other pressing development issues adequately. Many critics
claim that the Western media, when they do direct their
resources to dealing with such issues, betray their Western
biases and their involvement in Western power structures.

The LDC's think that they have no proper platform in the West and that their positions are hopelessly misrepresented.

Increasingly the blame for this situation is placed on the heads of the major international news agencies, which have been accused of exerting a monopolistic stranglehold over the flow of news, of distorting the news, or serving, whether unconsciously or not, the political and economic interests of the West, and finally of blocking the development of rival news services operated by non-Western agencies (Report of the Twentieth Century Fund Task Force on the International Flow of News, 1978: 27).

Some Third World spokesmen have gone so far as to allege that the major Western agencies deliberately distort the news from LDC's either because of subscriber demands for stories dealing with coups and catastrophes and other sensational and stereotyped depictions of the LDC's or because of some suspected overall complicity among the ideological, political, and economic establishments of the West.

Such accusations, especially those concerning international manipulation, cast doubt on the four major Western news agencies' adherence to the "sacred" values of objectivity and accuracy on which those agencies have long prided themselves.

Given the numbers and diversity of these agencies' subscribers, accurate, valuefree, and nonjudgmental reporting is regarded by those in the news agency business as essential if clients with conflicting ideologies and interests are to be kept in the field. Wire services' activities have received much scrutiny in the NWIO debate.

The four major Western agencies are the Associated Press (AP) and United Press International (UPI) based in the United States, Reuter's in the United Kingdom, and Agence France Press (AFP) in France. The "Big Four" Western agencies and Telegrafnoye Agentsivo Sovietskovo Soyuzo (TASS), the official news agency of the Soviet Union, collectively dwarf all other news agencies and news pools.

AP, based in New York, is generally held to be the largest
of the five. Six New York newspaper publishers founded the
agency in 1848 as a nonprofit cooperative which it still
claims to be today. According to Bruce Nathan, AP's promotion manager, AP's board now consists of 18 newspaper
publishers and three broadcasting executives and about 1200
U.S. newspapers make up the voting membership of the
agency. Over 10,000 newspapers and broadcasters subscribe
to AP's services. The agency has a fulltime news and photo
staff of about 1032 domestically and 498 abroad. Its 1980
operating budget is over $130 million.

UPI, formed by E. W. Scripts in 1907, is a privately
owned, New York-based company. It has approximately
6000 subscribers to its news services alone, according to Kevi
Nolan, the agency's public relations director. Among these
subscribers are about 1100 U.S. newspapers, 3300 U.S. radio
stations, and another 1,000 U.S. television and cable operations, 695 foreign newspapers, 188 foreign news agencies,
and 90 foreign radio and television operations make up the
balance. UPI employs a fulltime staff of 1725 journalists
worldwide, 1265 of which work in the United States. Of the
rest, 135 are posted in Latin America, 9 in Mexico, 119 in
Asia, 8 in Africa, 28 in the Middle East, and 148 in Europe.
The agency has an operating budget in the neighborhood of
$900 million. It was put up for sale in 1980.

The United Kingdom's international news agency,
Reuter's, is an exclusively international agency. It has 532
fulltime news staff abroad with almost 1000 stringers around
the world covering 159 countries, more than any other news
service. Reuter's turnover in 1979 was 76,300,000. According to S. Guebenlian, Reuter's publicity manager, the number
of subscribers to the agency's news services is difficult to
determine since they generally deal with national news agencies which resell the service. The number of subscribers to
Reuter's economic information services, from which the
agency attracts by far the bulk of its revenue, is easier to

determine. There are almost 7,000 subscribers to each of Reuter's Economic Service Teleprinter system and the Reuter Monitor System.

While Reuter's economic services account for most of its income, the French AFP has bureaus in 118 countries, 200 AFP foreign correspondents and 1,200 stringers are scattered over roughly 170 to 200 nations. Of these correspondents, 102 are stationed in the LDC's (22 in Latin America and Mexico and 80 in Africa and Asia). AFP's LDC's coverage is not a lucrative proposition but the agency's operations are subsidized by the income received from the many official government and embassy subscriptions. This income represents 60% of AFP's $80 million budget. Because the French government has such a significant input, it has three representatives on AFP's 15-member Board of Directors. The other 12 are newspaper publishers. There are no available figures on how many clients, besides the French government, subscribe to AFP's news services, for the same reasons as Reuter's cites.

TASS has 325 foreign subscribers and according to Uri Romantsov, chief of its New York bureau, fields about 200 correspondents abroad and covers about 120 countries. TASS and the four major Western agencies differ sharply in their perceptions of their roles. According to Anthony Smith:

> It [TASS] exists to serve the interests of the Soviet state and was tutored from its earliest days in the Leninist art of poemic, the art of struggle. Unlike the other agencies, it proclaims that it exists to form public opinion, to orientate the people "correctly" and to do so with information which is topical and truthful, but 'socially meaningful' at the same time. It is directly responsible to the Council of Minister of the USSR, and, in a statement to UNESCO, defined its own role overseas as being "to systematically" explain to foreign readers the peaceloving foreign policy of the CPSU and the Soviet government . . . disseminate information about the achievements of real socialism in economy, science and culture, publicize the Soviet way of life, expose the concoctions and slander of bourgeois ideology [1980: 83].

To the charge that these agencies, particularly the Big Four Western ones, monopolize international news flow, there is no convincing defense. No other news gathering and dissemination operation has the money, the manpower, or the technological means to provide anywhere near the extensiveness of world coverage that the Big Four and to some extent TASS offer. Thus, most LDC's, having very meager domestic or government resources for collecting news, must rely on the major agencies if they are to keep abreast of developments from around the world, including their next door neighbors, on which their interests and welfare might vitally depend. Rosemary Righter states:

> It is not an adequate response to say that no agency, however powerful, can force a client to take its services, or most developed countries, the choice is between isolation and choosing among the Big Four (and/or TASS) [1978: 52].

The grip that the Big Four and TASS have on the international news market has resulted in serious inequalities and onesidedness in global news flow. LDC's are forced to look to the West for both reporting "to" and "about" them at the international level.

Two complaints commonly crop up concerning the news that the Big Four report about the LDC's. For one, there simply is not enough of it. LDC's are swamped by news originating in the West but industrialized countries give relatively little play to stories originating elsewhere. For example, a background paper prepared for the MacBride Commission said:

> While there is a flood of news on the East-West axis between North America and Europe, as well as, albeit on a lower level, between Socialist and Western countries, the much lesser flow that exists between the North and South can hardly be called an exchange due to the imbalance [*World of News Agencies*, 1978: 16].

One reason for this is the high costs to the major Western agencies of setting up news gathering operations in remote areas of the world where LDC's are generally located. Not only is it very expensive—between $80,000 and $140,000 according to Mort Rosenblum (1979: 9)—to send a single journalist to cover an LDC for a year. Yet there is also very little demand, sometimes even among LDC's themselves, for news about the Third World. Moreover, Western journalists are increasingly encountering government intimidation around the world. The reporting of LDC's is in fact so unprofitable that most agencies must subsidize such coverage with their profits from other services they provide.

The other criticism frequently levelled at the agencies in connection with their reporting is that what there is of it tends to be sensationalistic, insensitive to the goals and values of the LDC's, and distorted, usually by the application of Western stereotypes, biases, norms, cultural perspectives, and even ideological designs about the nations and materials being covered.[1]

In general the Western and the major wire services have, it is charged, focused their coverage on disasters, crime, violence, and drastic social upheavals such as revolution. Their preoccupation is with the unusual or negative aspects of life. The Western media appear to be blind to more gradual, directed, yet richly significant developments and social changes in LDC's. Improvements in health care, education, transportation, cultural heritage, and so on might represent a breakthrough in an LDC's struggle for development and modernization. Yet such gains generally go unnoticed by the Western media, unattuned as they are to the development objectives and needs of such societies.

Both the selection and content of the stories that the Big Four and the Western media in general carry about the Third World, the argument runs, reflect Western capitalist orientation, and the values, assumptions, and standards of industrialized liberal democratic societies as well as their criteria of news worthiness are less acceptable to LDC's supporting the NWIO.

Even if an agency reporter in an LDC could avoid distortion by neutralizing even unconscious Western habits of thought, perception, and evaluation, his/her material would still have to pass through a New York, London, or Paris desk where editors tailor the copy to meet market demands, Western expectations and interests, or even their own individual assumptions about the subject of the story. Righter states:

> It is alleged that stories originating in developing countries, if honestly and fairly written, go through editing in New York which twists them according to U.S. private or governmental interests before sending them bouncing back to the country of origin [1978: 62].

American coverage of the events surrounding the 1978 revolt in Iran which led to the ousting of the Shah has been cited as an example of the distortions and preestablishment sentiment of the Western media.[2]

The agencies generally deny both the accusation of bias and distortion yet Righter comments:

> The agencies insist that they report from no country's viewpoint; most of the complaints, they say, come from governments who simply want a better public relations job done for their country. Yet all judgments as to what is news must have some anchor. And the agencies must work both in and for societies which differ—at least officially—in their criteria. It is possible to play neutral, to say that "we try to see countries and peoples as they see themselves." But when it comes to filing the report, which audience, which set of cultural criteria ultimately influence the selection of the story and the way it is written? The agencies face two simultaneous dilemmas: they must be sensitive to local values, yet meet the requirements of a consistent style to which their international claim to objectivity is based [1978: 57-58].

As a result of the bias and distortion that characterizes Western wire service coverage of the Third World, many LDC's feel they are misunderstood not only in the West but

also in other developing countries that subscribe to these
same Western wire services. Even development news about
successful growth and aid projects in neighboring nations
goes uncovered and thus potential models for LDC development are underutilized and not reported by the Western
series.

Third World spokesmen apply the same charge of Western
bias and distortion in agency news about LDC's to news that
the agencies disseminate "to" them. They claim that incom-
ing wire service news is written with little regard or respect
for national traditions and values and is rarely characterized
by local angles or geared to local needs and interests.

But most Westerners consider charges of deliberate distortion and intentional manipulation of news by the wire services as, if not totally unfounded, at least terribly exaggerated. Agency spokesmen continually reject claims by NWIO
proponents about distortion.

In the West, largely due to practical and economic reasons,
the day has become the functional unit of time for most
print media. As a result, discrete, self-contained stories which
transpire within the space of 24 hours or that can be easily
broken up into such time frames are at a premium. Western
news structures are not particularly favorable to placing
events carefully and thoughtfully in the context of an overall
process which gives the events meaning and relates them with
gradual trends and less obvious social conditions. Western
news systems are far better adapted to dealing with exceptional or unusual events such as revolution, and disasters
which generally have a distinct beginning, middle, and end
and can be quickly quantified in terms of lives lost or
economic consequences. The 30-second clip or "inverted
pyramid" dominate the newsgathering process. In addition,
Anthony Smith notes:

> The centre of the problem is really the definition of news itself.
> We have seen a little of how the agencies have followed the
> information demands of their client media, originally for business

information, later extending to material suitable for the popular press. The average Western reporter, trained in London or Paris or New York, would probably argue or at least feel that an item of news had to be collected with care and had to be part of a comprehensive treatment of a subject, but that it would probably be of an unusual or exceptional nature in order to be "newsworthy." During the 1960's, the whole culture of journalism and the content of journalism education has been transformed with the arrival of the "new journalism" of the "investigative" journalism of the post-Watergate era. The Western journalist has come to see his role more as a kind of institutionalized permanent opposition, always looking critically askance at the doings of all those who hold official positions of power [1980: 91-93].

Finally a most important NWIO initiative has been the establishment in 1975 of the international Non-Aligned News Pool to encourage information exchanges among LDC's. Tanjug, the national news agency of Yugoslavia, acts as the principal coordinating body for the pool's activities.

The pool has offered some hope to LDC's of at least getting a foot in the door of a Western-controlled system of international newsgathering and dissemination which has been closed to them for all intents and purposes. Yet, as Rosenblum notes, there is uncertainty about the value and future of this recent international news agency:

In practice, technical difficulties have prevented the pool from expanding to any significant size. Many of the items offered are purely propaganda; and some of them are of no interest even to the most collective-minded editors in other developing nations [1979: 207].

Direct Broadcast Satellites

Closely intertwined with the NWIO and related issues addressed by WARC 79 is the controversy over broadcasting directly from satellites to home receivers. Questions of how and to what extent such broadcasting should be controlled at an international level are complex and unresolved. In addition, commencing in the 1960s, many LDC's, and some Western nations, began worrying about future uses of DBS. Psychologically, DBS came to represent to many the epitome of a foreign cultural invasion tool which could invade countries and broadcast propaganda without domestic or native content or control.

DBS, like a prior planning or reservation of orbital slots which were discussed at WARC 79, is not only an involved technical issue but also one whose resolution could have, as Ithiel de Sola Pool (1979: 196) has noted, far-reaching political and ideological implications. These turn on the question of whether the use of the airwaves and of outer space should be conditioned by considerations of national sovereignty.

While the matter of DBS was not a major item on the agenda at WARC 79 itself, previously the ITU has attempted to confront the issue head on, particularly at the Space WARC in 1971 and the Broadcast Satellite WARC in 1977.

But the ITU is not the only, nor even the most prominent, forum to which the debate over DBS has been referred. The controversy has also found its way into UNESCO, the UN General Assembly, and the UN Committee on the Peaceful Uses of Outer Space (COPUOS) plus other agencies. A genuine direct-to-home-from-satellite broadcasting service will be realized soon (*Broadcasting,* 1980). In fact, several nations will have DBS by the end of this decade.

The chief obstacle to the implementation of a true DBS service in the past has been the need for large, powerful, and elaborate earth receiving stations to pick up signals from early communication satellites which were relatively weak in power. Now technical advances have made it possible to develop increasingly powerful satellites which can transmit strong signals to be received by increasingly smaller and inexpensive dishes. Soon technology will be in place to operate satellites so powerful that they will feed small earth receivers cheap enough to be used on individual television sets. Receiving dishes under $500 are being projected and they will be suitable for the average home or community center.

Almost from the day communication satellites dawned on the scene, the possibility of using them for broadcasting was heralded as holding great promise for facilitating the flow of health and educational information and exchanges of cultural programs between the nations of the world (Queeney, 197: 45). However, DBS was also recognized as a potential threat to the cultural integrity, national sovereignty, and security of recipient nations. This has been the focal point of the heated international arguments that surround DBS's. Besides, it is the United States, Japan, Canada, and the EEC, all industrialized nations, that will introduce the service first.

If direct broadcasts from satellites could only be directed at audiences within the transmitting country's boundaries and geared toward serving domestic purposes as is more or less the case with terrestrial television broadcasting, then the issue would not have aroused such strong reaction. But because DBS's are to be stationed in a geosynchronous orbit 23,000 miles above the equator, their footprints (the area which their broadcast signal covers) will overlap various portions of other nations. In many cases, entire nations would be covered.

Many nations, particularly LDC's, fear that DBS signals, because they do not respect national borders, could be employed by foreign countries to transmit unwanted, inconvenient, or harmful messages to their own citizens. Paul Laskin and Abram Chayes (1975: 32-33) have pointed out that such fears focus on three types of messages. One of these types of messages is political propaganda which could subvert the recipient country's political and social order. Another type of message is closely related to propaganda though more subtle, and probably more profound, in its ultimate effect. We are talking here of messages which often promote the values and cultural standards of the transmitting society which persistently and appealingly diminish the receiving nation's attachment to and identification with its own native culture. The adoption of primarily American cultural tastes, habits, advertising, and other marketing characteristics, in nations in which mostly cheap American programming dominates broadcasting services, reflects the presence of this type of cultural penetration. Laskin and Chayes say:

> To some extent, the desire of some nations to have a degree of control over the content of direct-satellite broadcasts reflects a judgment . . . that the staple fare of the American networks, while visually attractive, is in large part trivial, banal and violent. These nations fear a kind of Gresham's law in which bad American programs drive out or keep out the good [1975: 33].

The third type of message which some countries fear is foreign commercials which might adversely affect local producers and depiction of high-consumption societies which might distort demand for consumer goods. These misgivings that DBS might be used for propaganda purposes, cultural intrusion, and commercialism have added to the suspicion of the free flow of information principle in general.

The emerging LDC's maintain that the preservation of a unique and healthy cultural and national identity and the right as autonomous, independent nations to pursue self-determined social, economic, political, and communication goals override the international principle of free flow of information. The free flow has in practical terms resulted in a stream of foreign mass media material consisting of "junk," sex, trivia, and violence. Much of this may violate local values and morals plus further debase local initiatives and cultural sensibilities. The LDC's claim that the free flow has been a disguise for a one-way flow and some are petrified that DBS will further exacerbate the situation.

These concerns about the possible dysfunctional effects on national sovereignty and cultural integrity by free flow supporters underline to a large extent the uneasiness among LDC's about the impact of DBS. When this is coupled with the fact that the only areas of the world in which DBS is a realistic prospect in the foreseeable future is among industrialized nations, the LDC's view DBS as a potential major component in the drift toward electronic colonialization. Schiller says this concern in the LDC's is "an outgrowth of the existing state of affairs, in which a handful of media conglomerates in the rich, industrialized, capitalist economies already dominate the international flow of news, films, magazines, TV programs, and other items" (1976: 64-65). This places the DBS issue even more squarely in the context of the demand for a NWIO.

The most common response to the anticipated dangers of DBS has been to suggest that some system of prior consent be established. This would mean that the consent of the recipient country would be required before another country transmitted into its territory by means of a DBS. Historically, the United States has been virtually alone in opposing any form of prior consent, arguing that prior consent is too restrictive a form of control which verges on censorship and violates international commitments expressed in the UN Declaration of Human Rights to freedom of information.

Since Article 19 of the Universal Declaration of Human Rights states that "Everyone has the right to freedom of opinion and expression: this right includes freedom to hold opinions without interference and to seek, receive and impart information and ideas through any media and regardless of frontiers," the United States does have some grounds in international law for its position. But as Edward Ploman (1979: 162) notes, the concepts, phrases, and terms used in this and other articles of the declaration lack precision, are open to various interpretations, and only convey a statement of general principles. He continues, "In the absence of even an only formal definition of the terms and concepts of the article, it should be no surprise that interpretations can often be no more than 'subjective,' that is, terms of national, cultural, or ideological assumptions" (1979: 162). Thus the freedom of information article is of questionable weight in international law. Indeed, the definition and enforcement of several aspects of the NWIO remain equally vague and will take years to sort out in international courts.

To support their position, prior consent advocates invoke the concept of "state sovereignty" which is enunciated in the UN Charter and has a strong tradition in international law. Prior consent advocates argue that state sovereignty guarantees the right of national governments to control their domestic broadcasting systems and that this right has priority over the right under the freedom of information principle to transmit programs to a foreign country without its approval. DBS analyst Queeney notes that an example of a practical application of the state sovereignty doctrine is the fact that "Not even the ITU assigns frequencies to licensees within a country because that is regarded as the prerogative of the country in question" (1978: 36).

The determination of whether freedom of information or state sovereignty is more consistent with the spirit of international law is yet to be resolved. Ploman notes, "Neither of these concepts state sovereignty and freedom of information represents an absolute, static, indivisible reality" (1979: 162). He suggests that both concepts should be toned down and modified to reflect real conditions such as the possibly harmful effects of a hardline free flow stance and the obsolescence of the concept of an international system of absolutely sovereign, equal, and independent states in the face of a system in which actors other than states strongly influence international behavior and in which interdependence among states is often a more significant factor than their sovereignty. DBS signals obviously know no national or geographic boundaries.

Further difficulties arise in trying to determine an appropriate legal regime to apply in the case of DBS disputes. Ploman (1979: 160) observes that some countries such as the United States take a common law approach according to which principles for regulating DBS would evolve, if at all, only after DBS services had been initiated and would be adaptable to the shape those services assumed and the conditions they imposed. On the other hand, most countries, including the Soviet Union, have a civil law orientation according to which more rigid, binding legal principles would be established early to control the development of DBS services and prevent them from generating their own imperatives. The two approaches are hard to reconcile.

The problem of evolving a consistent and coherent legal structure for dealing with DBS is again compounded by the division of the task among several international organizations each working out of different legal approaches and contexts. If the Law of the Sea conferences are indications, then any Law of Communication conferences in the future will be equally difficult. Yet future international conferences dealing with broadcasting and communications issues, despite problems, should be a serious option.

The principal forum for thrashing out the issues involved in DBS has been the UN, mainly acting through its outer space committee COPOUS. As early as 1958 the UN addressed itself to international space issues when the General Assembly adopted a resolution recognizing "the common interest of mankind in outer space." Around the same time, the General Assembly set up COPOUS which has a Legal and Technical Subcommittee and which, as of 1961, has operated according to a principle of consensus rather than through voting. According to Ploman:

> The first substantial achievement of the Committee was the elaboration of a "Declaration of Legal Principles Governing the Activities of the States in the Exploration and Use of Outer Space," which was adopted by the General Assembly in 1963. These principles were then used almost intact for the Outer Space Treaty of 1967 which is the basic international instrument in the field [1979: 157-158].

Queeney says of the treaty:

> Articles I and II have special relevance to direct broadcast satellites since these Articles affirm the sovereign equality of States to

the free use of space and its exploration on an equal basis (Article I) and state that outer space is not the domain of any one nation but the province of all nations (Article II) [1978: 26].

In 1968, the General Assembly, adopting a recommendation by Sweden and Canada, instructed COPOUS to establish a special Working Group on Direct Broadcast Satellites to study the feasibility of DBS and its possible social, cultural, and legal implications. The Working Group met five times between 1969 and 1974.

In 1972 the General Assembly voted resoundingly for a Soviet Resolution which had the effect of increasing the Working Group's mandate to include the elaboration of a set of principles requiring international agreement. On the surface the adoption of the Resolution appeared to be a victory for those countries favoring some restrictions, especially prior consent, on DBS at an international level and a defeat for the United States, which did not favor the adoption of principles. The vote was 100 to 1, with the United States standing alone.

This elaboration of principles to govern direct broadcasting was reached at the fifth session of the Working Group and represented the culmination of its deliberations over five years. Integrated in the 14 principles which were recommended were the three major positions that had gradually emerged out of the Working Group's meetings. The Soviet position, which was contained in the Soviet Convention of August 1972 and modified slightly in its Declaration of Principles in 1974, would establish "a regime of strict control: a code of broadcasting conduct and a requirement of prior consent by a recipient country" (Laskin and Chayes, 1975: 34) as well as a list of prohibited categories of broadcasts. The U.S. position "would place no restraint upon the free flow of ideas and information, either by prescribing categories of broadcast consent or by 'prior consent'" (Queeney, 1978: 199). Canada and Sweden jointly developed a compromise position with a heavy stress on regional systems of DBS in which prior consent is a requirement and participation in coverage of its territory is the right of consenting nations.

The 14 draft principles into which positions were consolidated include the question of prior consent and participation, applicability of international law, program content, copyright, and illegality of programs specifically targeted for a foreign state without that state's consent. After the Working Group's fifth and final session, the Legal Sub-Committee of COPOUS was charged with getting states to agree unanimously on the draft principles. After arduous discussions the subcommittee managed to get consensus at least in principle on the major draft principles except the key one of prior consent which is still outstanding.

UNESCO has also contributed to the DBS debate with its Declaration of Guiding Principles on the Use of Satellite Broadcasting for the Free Flow of Information, the Spread of Education and Greater Cultural Exchange in 1972. According to de Sola Pool:

> The philosophy of the Declaration is strongly restrictive, stressing sovereignty, the requirement that news broadcasts be accurate, the right of each country to decide the contents of educational programs broadcast to it, the need for broadcasters to respect cultural distinctiveness and varied laws, and the requirement for prior consent especially regarding advertising [1974: 37].

Probably the key statement of the Declaration is Article IX, which declares that "it is necessary that States, taking into account the principle of freedom of information, *reach or promote agreements* [emphasis added] concerning direct satellite broadcasting to the population of countries other than the country of origin of the transmission."

At the WARC for Space Telecommunications in 1971 an item was adopted stating that spillover should be avoided unless another nation agrees to accept the footprint reaching its territory. This provision refers to the problem of spillover, that is, parts of a satellite broadcast beam which either inadvertently or by design are transmitted beyond the borders of the country for which the broadcast is intended (due to the irregular shape of the boundaries of most countries, particularly in Europe and in LDC's, a certain amount of spillover is virtually unavoidable). Most countries interpreted the provision's mention of a previously reached agreement as an affirmation of the principle of prior consent, giving the principle status in international law, at least in international telecommunications law. But the United States and a few other countries regarded the provision as an exclusively technical regulation dealing with the carrier and not the content of the information broadcast (Ploman, 1980).

The WARC on Broadcast Satellites in 1977 adopted a plan allotting satellite television channels on a country-by-country basis. Since states represented at WARC 77 approved a plan allotting channels that can be used for the most part only for domestic broadcasting, they have implicitly recognized that at least for the time being they will not engage in direct satellite broadcasts to other countries. The only accommodation for international broadcasting made at WARC 77 was for a projected Nordic DBS system among Scandinavian countries and a possible Islamic network among Arab states and for Vatican coverage of Italy. The problem with WARC 77 is that it only applies to ITU Regions 1 and 3. The problem with ITU regulations in general concerning DBS is that they reflect the technical orientation of the union and are difficult to apply in other contexts.

The major international organizations, which are capable of adding meaningfully to the body of international law relating to DBS's and of determining legal principles whereby the implementation and use of this new technology could be properly directed, have been largely unsuccessful not only in coordinating their decisions and activities with each other but also in their individual efforts to clarify the issues. Their failure becomes more disturbing as advanced satellites become operational.

In 1979 France and West Germany announced a joint project to establish a Franco-German satellite system for direct broadcasting with each country contributing at least one satellite with a minimum of three video channels. The system may be introduced as early as 1983. In the United States, the Communications Satellite Corporation (COMSAT) also announced plans to "provide pay television by satellite to homes across the country" (*Broadcasting*, 1979: 27). It, too, may be operational by 1983. In the mid-1970s Canada and the United States jointly sponsored an experimental DBS satellite and currently Canada has further high-power DBS channels on its newer satellites.

DBS epitomizes yet another example of the rapid development of a communication technology which defies the pace of either the international bureaucracy or the legal profession. Dealing with contemporary international broadcasting issues will continue to be a growing problem. The advocates of the NWIO generally fail to take account of the complexity and slowness of the international decision-making machinery available for rulemaking or enforcing any changes in broadcasting or communications services.

Latin America Issues

It is worthwhile at this point to consider the nature, the role, and the effects of mass communication systems in a major developing region—Latin America. The Latin American experience with mass communication illustrates in an almost textbook fashion the classic pattern of problems associated with communication and development under the present international information, economic, and power order.

Perhaps one principle reason the Latin American experience is so illustrative is that Latin America, according to Alan Wells, is "the unofficial sphere of cultural, economic, and political influence for the world's richest nation, the United States" (1972: 7). Latin America provides a case study of the phenomenon of cultural imperialism, a key issue in the debate over communication, development, and an NWIO.

Another possible reason is that variables such as urbanization and, more important, mass media exposure—which have been associated with the impetus toward modernization under Western models of development and communication—are more visibly present in Latin America than in most other underdeveloped regions. In any case the level of exposure in Latin America to all three mass media—radio, television, and print—in contrast to the lower levels in most other LDC's seems to be sufficient to enable one to draw at least tentative conclusions concerning the role of communication in development and to put to the test Western assumptions about it.

A most significant feature of mass media systems, especially broadcasting, in Latin America is their commercial nature. Latin Americans generally follow the U.S. model of privately owned, print-broadcast systems. There is little alternative, educational, or public broadcasting. Antonio Pasquali describes the commercialism of Latin American broadcasting as:

> In radio, if we take the license (collecting the State in payment for the service offered) as a criticism for distinguishing broadly between two main systems—the public and the private—we find the following: in 1970, ninety-one countries (64 per cent) were using a license system, and fifty-one countries (36 per cent) were not. The first group questionably includes all the countries possessing the best broadcasting services. The second group (no license) includes: Monaco, Spain and Andorra in Europe; a group of countries (almost all small) in Africa, Asia and Oceania, in particular Egypt; North America and all three Latin American countries. The American continent therefore constitutes the only solid homogeneous and large-scale group of countries in which the radio medium is mainly controlled by private enterprise. . . .
> In Venezuela . . . the antiquated Radio Regulations of 1941 are, perhaps, less respected than any other laws; they contain a pompous declaration to the effect that broadcasting is the exclusive function of the State, which will not only exceptionally grant

authoring action to private operators... (Article 2). The exception, however, has become the rule: 128 licenses for private broadcasting up to 1973 as opposed to a single state station of 10 kw covering only a small part of the country [1975: 65].

Another problem Pasquali discusses is the proliferation in Latin America of small, commercial radio stations all competing for the same urban audiences and all lacking the financial and technical resources to serve the less profitable markets in the peripheral areas of the countries in which they operate. Pasquali says:

> The fact that Latin America has eight inhabitants per square kilometre, a jungle of diminutive stations, over 80 per cent of which have a capacity of less than 5 kw, and a radio receiving set figure that is only 6 per cent of the world total, means that 60 per cent of Latin Americans (basically the urban population) receive a super-abundance of broadcast messages, while the other 40 per cent (scattered throughout the pampas, the plains, the Andes and the jungle) cannot even receive radio programmes during the day [1975: 66].

The commercialism of the Latin American broadcasting industry applies to television as well. Wells writes:

> Unlike European in the early days of the medium, public television has not gained any substantial foothold in Latin America. Thus all of the countries have predominantly private and commercial forms of operation, even where the government has either been active in the part, or is still active in broadcasting [1972: 119].

Fred Fejes (1980) argues that, largely due to the influence of transnational advertising agencies on Latin American television, many of the images Latin Americans receive about themselves, their environment, and the outside world through that medium are inappropriate and even damaging in terms of their effects on cultural integrity and social, economic, and political development in the region. Programs and commercials are aired on the basis of their ability to continually attract large audiences and influence product sales. Commercial stations show little concern over whether the images conveyed by either programs or ads are socially useful or, on the other hand, encourage suitable values, lifestyles, and consumer habits appropriate for Latin Americans.

Research seems to indicate that television programming in Latin America follows a formula which U.S. television experience would suggest draws the most viewers, that is, a steady diet of soap operas, adventures, romances, situation comedies, programs depicting violence, and commercials, all usually reflecting the values of an affluent consumer society. Luis Ramiro Beltran notes that a study of four Venezuela television channels finds:

> Jointly, violent fare constitutes 56 per cent of their programming. Another survey in Venezuela showed that 68 per cent of television content in a typical week encouraged physical, emotional, and moral violence; this figure climbed to 73 per cent on Sundays and to 83 per cent on Saturdays. . . . Pasquali also pays attention to the "soap operas," finding that they occupy the top place in the live programming, with 30.4 per cent of the time devoted to this category. This he finds combined with abundant commercials whose interjections in the telenovelas (soap operas) amounts, at times, to a period equal to that occupied by the episode itself [1978: 65].

Beltran contends that there is a definite character to the images conveyed by such popular, commercial programming. The images conveyed, Beltran suggests, support the capitalist system and the status quo as the natural order as well as all the attendant mental attitudes, values, and modes of organizing social relationships necessary to prop up that order and prevent it from collapsing in rebellion and discontent. It is only natural that a television industry which is privately owned, highly commercialized, and thus fixed into the capitalist structure would favor, whether consciously or not, such imagery.

Beltran (1978: 75) also identifies materialism as a dominant strain of imagery in Latin American television programs; he maintains that many shows induce an adherence to the belief that the "main goals of human beings are the acquisition of wealth, the accumulation of goods, the enjoyment of services and the achievement of general well being." This promotion of materialism is also associated with the idea that material satisfaction is to be enjoyed first and foremost by the individual.

Even such apparently innocuous shows as "The Flintstones" (Los Picapiedra) and "Sesame Street" (Plaza Sesamo) betray conservative, conformist, and materialistic imagery. Citing the findings of Peruvian analyst Gorki Tapia, Beltran notes that *The Flintstones* portrays a "consumer society, plentiful in material well-being and assumedly free of contradictions and conflicts. This setting is not accidental as the consistent mention of the series is to suggest through such imagery that the only natural course of humanity is capitalism. One central value proposed is selfish individualism coupled with rugged competitiveness" (1978: 71). Beltran also refers to Mattelart's study of "Plaza Sesamo" and his conclusion that the show depicts rigid, immutable distributions of roles generally into dominant (adult-teacher) and submissive (child-learner) categories and that its setting corresponds to be U.S. middle class, implicitly accepting that model as the proper and natural one.

Considering the vast influence U.S. interests have on it, it is not surprising that Latin American television reflects the ideology of the United States and its materialistic values on an affluent, consumer-oriented middle class rather than Latin American culture and values.

Wells (1972: 102-106) outlines U.S. investment in Latin American television. The three big American networks, ABC, NBC, and CBS, account for the bulk of it. Of the three, ABC is the largest investor in Latin America, having in the 1960s invested in five Central American television stations which became known as the Central American TV Network (CATVN) and created a similar network, The Latin American

Television Network Organization (LATINO), which operates in six South American countries.

Exact figures are difficult to determine, but most estimates of the percentage of Latin American programming originating in the United States and annual sales of television programs by the United States to Latin America are in the vicinity of 30% and $25 million, respectively.

Beltran also describes how the United States exerts influence over Latin America television through advertising:

> U.S. advertising firms (mostly multinational corporations) and U.S. advertising firms (especially McCann Erickson, Walter Thompson, and Young and Rubican) dominate the Latin American advertising business through all media. Specifically in television, for instance, the top five U.S. advertising agencies controlled in Argentina 35 per cent of TV commercials, serving Standard Oil, Shell, Coca Cola, Ford, etc., and absorbing between 30 and 45 per cent of all television advertising in the country. . . . And the first five advertising clients in Columbia are Colgate-Palmolive, Lever Bros., American Home Products, Lotteries and Raffles, and Miles Laboratories; over 50 per cent of television advertising in this country is devoted to cosmetics, non-essential food stuffs and detergents, most of which are produced by U.S. multinational companies [1978: 65].

The hold of the United States on the Latin American television industry is further strengthened by the fact of Latin American dependence on U.S. technology and expertise. Luis P. Estrada and Daniel Hopen made this point:

> In Latin America the United States has a monopoly of the supply of the new technology, the basic film material, the technical experts and, of course, the large-scale capital needed to increase the size of local investments [1968: 6].

So, in effect, the content and the commercial, entertainment, and advertising-oriented structure of U.S. television has been superimposed on Latin American broadcasting systems. This position has been used, perhaps engineered, by the United States to advance its general economic, political, cultural, and ideological interests in its most important sphere of influence.

Much the same situation applies with respect to Latin American print news media. As Fernando Reyes Matta (1979: 164-171) argues, a North American system of news selection, gathering, and presentation, and of professionalism in journalism has been modeled in the Latin American press. This North American model includes values such as objectivity, currency, and accuracy and a preference for self-contained, easily reported, usually sensational, stereotyped, and thus commercially interesting stories about LDC's violence and catastrophe over eventual, probing, interpretive analysis. Latin American adoption of this news model is mainly due to the dependence of Latin American print media on Western, particularly U.S., transnational news agencies for a supply of international, and to some extent even Latin American, news. Matta says:

> The current status of the Latin American press manifests the continuing dominance of North American news values, as institutionalized in the transnational news agencies. The transnational news agencies produce and process nearly 60 per cent of the information published in Latin America. UPI and AP alone provide 30 per cent and 21 per cent of the information received by the principal Latin American dailies [1979: 165].

An illustration of how completely the North American concept of news has permeated the Latin American press is the frequent rejection by Latin American editors of fair, unsensational, and penetrating stories about Latin America in favor of more commercially reliable stories dealing with personalities or events from Central American countries or more eyecatching, sensational Latin American stories about disaster or revolution, in other words, stories more consistent with reader expectation and possibly reader demand (Matta, 1979: 166-168).

What is needed is not just a news agency to serve the region which is owned and run by Latin Americans rather than North Americans. What is needed is a regional news agency that functions in accordance with a concept of news that is better attuned to the real educational, cultural, developmental, and information needs of the region—a concept that would accommodate reports of long-term, often subtle, processes, trends, and conditions rather than obvious "snapshots" of coups and catastrophes. This concept could also accommodate accounts of actual progress toward development and modernization, no matter how small or slow or seemingly inconsistent with North American standards of newsworthiness.[3]

Perhaps as a response to this need, a proposal for a Latin American and Caribbean news agency, presumably one which would serve these areas more within the context of their development needs and an emerging NWIO than in the commercially and sensationalistically oriented fashion of Western news agencies, was put forward as a principal recommendation at the Costa Rica Inter-Governmental Conference in July 1976. Latin American researcher Raquel Salinas Bascur conducted research consisting of interviews with 61 persons including directors and owners of media institutions as well as editors and journalists to determine what their impressions of the possibilities of such a news agency were, what they felt was wrong with the service provided under the present system, and the extent of their familiarity with UNESCO and the concept of an NWIO. Among her findings were:

The main problems according to 40 per cent of the interviewees (24 persons), arise from the analysis of regional situations from a perspective of industrial countries. While 40 per cent attributed the problem to the predominance of a journalistic model associated with the sale of news or a mercantile type of news making. Many answers classified as "others" relate to these two alternatives, although they emphasize different aspects of these same questions. Thus, for instance, some sated that one of the most serious problems consist in the lack of an authentic Latin American service, and in the interference of interests corresponding to countries where transnational agencies are based [1980: 7].

While these findings are fairly encouraging in that they seem to reflect the awareness that the very concept of news is the essence of the problem, Salinas Bascur (1980: 10) also discovered that there is remarkably little knowledge among those at the forefront of Latin American print news media of a growing role of the NWIO and of UNESCO's initiatives in trying to address serious communication and development problems which stem from imbalances in the present order.

What the Latin American experience with modern mass communication seems to reveal is that foreign, particularly American, influence and control over domestic communication systems in developing nations not only fosters economic, cultural, and technical dependencies in almost all sectors of the dominated nations but also induces an acceptance of foreign communication models which for all practical purposes prevents developing societies from adopting, or even knowing about, alternatives, such as an NWIO, which might be more appropriate to their needs. Indeed, this is what electronic colonialism is about.

The Western, particularly American, conception of a free, privately owned, and market-oriented communication system linked with modernization may be a valid descriptive model of the role of communication in advanced industrial nations yet. When this model is applied to LDC's, it seems to be inappropriate. The LDC's, many in Latin America, look to the NWIO for more applicable models for them to pursue.

United States Information Policy

In discussing the U.S.'s position on both media and information policies, two major points should be kept in mind.[4]

First, the U.S.'s international media and information policies are to a great extent a reflection or enlargement of their domestic media policies and practices. The premises underlying freedom of speech, free press, market forces, and responsibility to shareholders are carried over to decision making in the international arena. (A clear exception is where some groups have formed cartels for controlling foreign markets and prices where such cartels and price-fixing arrangements are illegal within its borders.)

Second, in sharp contrast with almost all other nations, the U.S. media and communication activities take place in an open market place within a private enterprise environment. Radio and television networks and computer and telecommunications companies, including satellites, are held by private corporations, many of which are also giant transnational conglomerates soon to be further involved in the NWIO debate. Benjamin Compaine emphasizes the distinctiveness of the U.S. media empire this way:

> The mass communication industry in the United States is deeply rooted in the economic system. In this context, media technology and institutions have developed a mass communications system that is unique in the world for its independence from government control, direct or indirect. Businesses and individuals in private industry have been motivated to improve printing presses, invent typesetters and computer-driven laser composition devices, radio and television broadcasting, then color reception, two-way cable transmission communications satellites, video cassettes—the list goes on. Thousands of businesses and institutions are involved. In many ways, we are faced not with a problem of concentration but with a problem in being able to cope with the vast diversity of forms and content of the mass media [1979: 9].

This had produced a private sector orientation in both the applied and theoretical regulatory philosophy areas that favors the free enterprise system and allows the market forces and the laws of supply and demand to permeate media and information practices. There are exceptions to this, such as the "Fairness Doctrine" and telephone and cable monopolies, but the thrust of the private sector argument contrasts substantially with the public PTT's (government-owned posts, telephone, and telegraph), various media, and information systems elsewhere. The BBC is a classic example of a government-funded broadcasting corporation; the Nora and Minc (1980) report for France's President d'Estaing is indicative of future trends in Europe. These two basic points not only underlie U.S. media practices but also extend to newer, computer-based information systems.

At a 1980 meeting—the Organization for Economic Cooperation and Development (OECD), located in Paris and consisting of 24 chiefly industrial nations—the U.S. government's submission to the High Level Conference on Information, Computer, and Communications Policy reports:

> In the United States, as in other countries, there is not one grand information policy, no single national information policy, but rather a composite of policies, explicit and implicit, about information. In particular, aspects of United States domestic information policy can be divided into two broad categories: (1) the legal foundations of information dissemination and access; and (2) the economics and management of information [Bushkin and Yarow, 1980: 4].

The first category deals with the constitutional and statutory policies which impact upon the behavior of both industry and the government. The First and Fourth Amendments, The Freedom of Information Act, the Sunshine Act, and libel laws are examples.

The second category deals with, primarily in the private sector, the economic and management philosophy by which decisions are made. The ultimate goal of much decision making is to optimize profits. Much information in this category is held and coveted privately by corporations since it applies to their current market share and operations as well as their long-range planning.

For the U.S. government some deliberate restrictions are imposed, usually with legal sanctions. Three categories are:

— The government's effectiveness in protecting or promoting national security or the general welfare (e.g., military, strategic, foreign policy, law enforcement information).

— The protection of society from the influence of information that offends traditional social mores (e.g., pornography) or that is false or deceptive (e.g., false advertising or libel).

— Protection of personal privacy and of an individual's ability to control his own life to the maximum extent possible (e.g., information about individuals, particularly where held in record systems or large organizations or institutions) [Bushkin and Yarow, 1980: 8].

All this reflects the fact that, as compared with other nations, the average U.S. citizen has substantial protection from both private and public (government) interference with his or her media and information habits, preference, and tastes.

This brief review highlighting U.S. domestic policies points to certain insights as to how they also approach international issues. First, the First Amendment is central to their philosophy and practices; second, the government plays a significant role, mainly through lawmaking, in access and ownership issues. For example, the U.S. Freedom of Information Act is a model that most LDC's and Socialist governments would not tolerate. (Indeed, the U.S. Freedom of Information Act reflects an openness to government information that is almost unparalleled in the world.) Finally, as both technology, such as microprocessors and optic-fibers, makes available more choices and deregulation becomes the regulatory mode, the role and control of media and communication in the United States both at home and abroad is an evolving issue which somehow must be meshed into the movement toward an NWIO. It will be a difficult task, some maintain an irrelevant one.

A Major U.S. Foreign Policy Problem

In the overall debate about the NWIO, one of the more frequent complaints concerning U.S.'s international activities is its continual failure to produce on its promises.[5] Many rhetorical attempts have been made by the U.S. delegations at UNESCO and at other international meetings to divert the NWIO by making promises of equipment, personnel, or financial assistance. Yet, much of this never comes to pass. But it should be noted that some critics are saying that this, in retrospect, is fortuitous. Had the United States supplied all the various types of media and communication aid they had promised, particularly in providing telecommunications infrastructures and supplying software, their presence in the lives of LDC's would have been much greater than it presently is. Because of the U.S. failure to provide assistance, many LDC's are now having a second chance at establishing their own priorities or they at least are having greater say in the construction and implementation of broadcasting systems. It is not only the LDC's critics that lament U.S.'s broken promises; consider the following article with the lead, "Heading Into Trouble With The Third World."

> In his farewell address at Harvard the other day former Secretary of State Cyrus Vance used uncharacteristically sharp words ("dangerous . . . naive . . . foolish") to deplore the "new nostalgia" for military solutions as a substitute for diplomacy [*Guardian*, 1980: 17].

In the same address Vance continued:

> American aid programs . . . make the most difference in supporting our Third World diplomacy and in addressing now the causes of the later crises. Yet they are under constant assault in the Congress and elsewhere. The result is—I can think of no other word—disgraceful [*Guardian*, 1980: 17].

Basically the former Secretary of State was stating that both the executive and the legislative branches were providing little economic development assistance to LDC's; in addition, where such assistance was given, it was frequently tied to conditions favoring U.S.'s firms and policies.

In the same address Vance directly stated that the United States was in arrears in meeting pledges that it had made in the past. Vance documented that U.S. foreign aid has fallen by 26% over the last 20 years and that Vietnam represented American military solutions which were not successful. This, coupled with the fact that the United States is now 13th out of 17 for larger industrial nations in the world in terms of percentage of gross national product devoted to development assistance, provided him with little optimism. Vance maintained that greater economic assistance to LDC's would at least provide some type of diplomatic leverage when future problems arise.

Phillip Geyelyn, in commenting about Vance's speech, concludes:

> And yet there is a certain nuttiness in spending greatly increased sums of money so that sophisticated new weapons now on drawing boards will be ready 10 years from now to deal with crises and conflicts directly related to social and political unrest that relatively inexpensive economic development programs, launched today, might do much to alleviate. Foreign aid is a way of hedging bets, I suppose, and one really worth doing if you think it matters what sort of world awaits your children—and theirs [*Guardian*, 1980: 17].

The key point is that the United States frequently has made last-minute commitments of assistance—for example, at the 20th UNESCO General Assembly—in order to achieve a compromise with either little desire or ability to directly implement all promises. Eventually this alters the U.S.'s credibility in international negotiations about the NWIO or other matters.

NOTES

1. The question of cultural bias is one deserving additional research attention. Kurt Lewin's classic "gatekeeper" concept requires reanalysis (Peterson, 1979). See also McQuail's (1976) *Review of Sociological Writings on the Press,* especially pp. 39-49.

2. During the 1978 UNESCO General Assembly, the Shah of Iran was coming under daily attack and the U.S. delegation to UNESCO and their press corps were both stunned and upset. Eventually President Carter publicly chastised the head of the CIA for failing to provide an accurate assessment of the tidal wave, not a mere ripple, of opposition and hatred toward the Shah and his Westernized ways. The hostage situation extended the dislike of the American role.

Was the U.S. government or public prepared for the fall? No. The wire services projected a favorable climate surrounding a strong pro-Western ally in the troubled Middle East. Even the Shah's frequent violations of human rights failed to deter or distract the U.S. press from painting a favorable picture. The wire services, the weekly newsmagazines, television networks, and individual correspondents sent dispatches that misread both the weakness of the Shah and the resolve of the Moslems. According to Dorman and Omeed:

> By and large the American news media routinely have characterized the Iranian conflicts as the work of turbaned religious zealots in league with opportunistic Marxists, rather than—as they might have—the reaction of peoples outraged by a repressive regime. By doing so the press has helped to misinform American public opinion and narrow the range of debate on this bell-weather foreign policy crisis.
>
> This is a harsh assessment of press performance, but is one arrived at after a careful study of U.S. wire service, newsmagazine, and major daily newspaper coverage appearing since the current crisis began in January 1978 [1979: 27].

3. Latin America has many national news agencies and even a regional agency, LATIN. But none of them really operates under a concept of news appreciably different from that of North American agencies. And, as Smith points out:

> They [Latin American news agencies] have never been able to muster the resources to commence a continental, still less an international service of their own. LATIN has recently come into existence and operates in a number of South American countries, but it has been created by Reuter's and obtains its material through Reuter's. . . . So deeply has the U.S. news culture established itself in the continent's press: it would only duplicate the services already provided from the North and South American papers have come to share the same news values [1980: 71].

4. The items discussed here complement other areas where U.S. policy was discussed. In considering U.S. media policy, one must understand its central plank: the first amendment to the U.S. Constitution. It states: "Congress shall make no law respecting an establishment of religion or prohibiting the free exercise thereof; or abridging the freedom of speech, or of the press; or the right

of the people peaceably to assemble and to petition the government for a redress of grievances."

5. The change to a "free and balanced flow" has not been accepted or recognized by many senior U.S. officials. Consider the following testimony of Honorable Matthew Nimetz, U.S. Under Secretary for Security Assistance, Science and Technology before the Congressional Subcommittee on Government Information and Individual Rights on March 27, 1980: when in closing he stated "we are deeply committed to the free flow of information and will actively support and promote this principle bilaterally and in the United Nations, in the OECD, and in other forums" (Bushkin and Yarow, 1980: 20-21).

REFERENCES

BELTRAN, L. (1978) "TV exchanges in the minds of Latin Americans." Gazette 24(2): 65-81.

Broadcasting (1980) "No consensus in DBS's line of sight." October 13, pp. 25-26.

Broadcasting (1979) "From out of the blue: COMSAT designs direct-to-home subscription TV." August 6, p. 27.

BUSHKIN, A. and J. YAROW (1980) The foundations of United States information policy. U.S. Department of Commerce, NTIA-SP-80-8.

COMPAINE, B. (1979) Who Owns the Media. New York: Harmony Books.

de SOLA POOL, I. (1974a) "Direct broadcast satellites and the integrity of national cultures," in Control of the Direct Broadcast Satellite: Values in Conflict. Palo Alto, CA: Aspen Institute Occasional Paper.

de SOLA POOL, I. (1979b) "The problems of WARC." Journal of Communication 29(1): 187-196.

DORMAN, W. and E. OMEED (1979) "Reporting Iran the Shah's way." Columbia Journalism Review, January-February: 27-33.

ESTRADA, L. and D. HOPEN (1968) The Cultural Value of Film and Television in Latin America. Paris: UNESCO.

FEJES, F. (1980) "The growth of multinational advertising agencies in Latin America." Journal of Communications 30(4): 36-49.

Guardian (1980) "Heading into trouble with the Third World." July 6, p. 17.

LASKIN, P. and A. CHAYES (1975) "International satellite controversy." Society 12(6): 30-40.

MATTA, F. (1979) "The Latin American concept of news." Journal of Communications 29(2): 164-171.

McQUAIL, C. (1976) Review of Sociological Writings on the Press. London: Her Majesty's Stationery Office.

NORA, S. and A. MINC (1980) The computerization of Society. Cambridge: MIT Press.

PASQUALI, A. (1975) "Latin America: Our image or theirs?" in Getting the Message Across. Paris: UNESCO.

PETERSON, S. (1979) "Foreign news gatekeepers and criteria of newsworthiness." Journalism Quarterly 56(1): 116-125.

PLOMAN, E. (1980) "Broadcasting: The law is confused." Inter Media 8(1): 10-12.

PLOMAN, E. (1979) "Satellite broadcasting, national sovereignty, and free flow of information," in K. Nordenstreng and H. Schiller (eds.), National Sovereignty and International Communication. Norwood, NJ: Ablex.

QUEENEY, K. (1978) Direct Broadcast Satellites and the United Nations. The Hague, The Netherlands: Sijthoff and Noordhoff.

Report of the Twentieth Century Fund Task Force on the International Flow of News (1978) A Free and Balanced Flow. Lexington, MA: Lexington Books.

RIGHTER, R. (1978) Whose News? London: Burnett.

ROSENBLUM, M. (1979) Coups and Earthquakes. New York: Harper & Row.

SALINAS-BASCUR, R. (1980) "Latin America in the march towards alternative news." Democratic Journalist, May: 7-10.

SCHILLER, H. (1976) Communication and Cultural Domination. White Plains, NY: M. E. Sharpe, Inc.

SMITH, A. (1980) The Geopolitics of Information. London: Faber and Faber.

WELLS, A. (1972) Picture-Tube Imperialism? Maryknoll, NY: Orbis.

World of News Agencies (1978) Background paper for the International Commission for the Study of Communication Problems. Paris: UNESCO.

Chapter 8

THE MacBRIDE INTERNATIONAL COMMISSION

The origins and report of the International Commission for the Study of Communication Problems (1979), which is also called the MacBride Commission, are outlined here. In addition a potential successor organization to MacBride is detailed. The International Commission was in direct response to Resolution 100 of the 19th General Assembly of UNESCO, which met in Nairobi in the fall of 1976. This resolution called for the Director-General of UNESCO, Mr. Armadou-Mater M'Bow, to establish a commission to investigate international communication problems. It lasted for two years and ended in the fall of 1979. One hundred background papers were produced, plus an Interim and Final Report. Two dates were stated as being critical for its work. The first was the fall of 1978 when an Interim Report was to be completed for the 20th General Assembly of UNESCO meeting in Paris and the second was to be the Final Report.

The MacBride Commission had 16 members. The President of the commission is Sean MacBride (Ireland), barrister, politician, and journalist, President of the International Peace Bureau, former Minister for Foreign Affairs, founder and Chairman of Amnesty International, United Nations Commissioner for Namibia, holder of the Nobel and Lenin Peace Prizes. Around him are gathered the remaining 15 members:

(1) Elie Abel (United States), journalist and broadcasting expert, Dean of the Graduate School of Journalism, Colombia University

(2) Hubert Beuve-Mery (France), journalist, founder of the newspaper *Le Monde*, president of the Centre de formation et de perfectionnement des journalistes, Paris

(3) Elebe Ma Ekonzo (Zaire), journalist, Director-General of Agence Zaire-Presse

(4) Gabriel Garcia Marquez (Colombia), writer, novelist, and journalist

(5) Mochtar Lubis (Indonesia), journalist, President of the Press Foundation of Asia

(6) Mustapha Masmoudi (Tunisia), Secretary of State for Information, President of the Intergovernmental Coordinating Council for Information of the Non-Aligned Countries

(7) Marshall McLuhan (Canada), sociologist and communications expert (Initially nominated to serve on the commission, he was obliged to withdraw and has been replaced by Betty Zimmerman, Canada, broadcaster, Director of Radio Canada International, Canadian Broadcasting Corporation.)

(8) Michio Nagai (Japan), journalist and sociologist, editorialist of the newspaper *Assahi Shimbun*

(9) Fred Isaac Akporuaro Omu (Nigeria), former head of the Department of Mass Communications, University of Lagos, commissioner for Information, Social Development and Sport, Bendel State

(10) Bogdan Osolnik (Yugoslavia), journalist, politician, member of the National Assembly

(11) Gamal el Oteifi (Egypt), former Minister for Information and Culture, honorary professor, Cairo University, journalist, lawyer, and legal adviser, Deputy Speaker, Parliament

(12) Johannes Pietar Pronk (Netherlands), economist and politician, member of the National Assembly

(13) Juan Somavia (Chile), Executive Director, Institute Latino-americano de Estudios Transnacionales
(14) Boobli George Verghese (India), journalist
(15) Leonid Mitrofanovich Zamatin (USSR), member of the Supreme Soviet, ambassador, journalist (Mr. Zamatin was replaced by Sergei Losev during the study.)

Some critics have expressed surprise at the lack of a representative from Great Britain. Professor James Halloran of the University of Leicester has provided background papers and is a person of some influence at UNESCO, particularly in the area of communication research. Yet given Britain's role in developing press traditions for the Western world, the lack of representation of Britain signifies the shift of power to the LDC's.

The UNESCO Secretariat also played a major role. The Secretariat was dominated by Asher Deleon from Yugoslavia, and he formerly was with the Faure Commission of Education. He supported the NIEO and saw a need for a counter-balance to the Western press. Overall, the Secretariat accumulated power during the two years. Deleon was a powerful, skillful bureaucrat, had access to M'Bow, and continually outmaneuvered MacBride as the commission progressed. Also Deleon still occupies a major post within UNESCO and pushes NWIO resolutions.

The MacBride Commission was established to investigate: (1) the analysis of the current state of communications; (2) the problems surrounding a free and balanced flow of information and how the needs of the developing countries link with the flow; (3) how, in light of the new international economic order, a new world information order may be created; and (4) how media may become vehicles for enhancing public opinion about world problems.

Prior to the Interim Report, the commission had met three times. The meetings are reflected in the Interim Report, which also comprises aspects of several background documents; these meetings quickly turned to detailing the inadequacies of the major Western wire services.

The Interim Report is highlighted here since it caused considerable controversy at the time of its release and it was the major document on the NWIO at the time of UNESCO's General Assembly in 1978. The Interim Report was divided into six sections: (1) progress report; (2) the major issue; (3) communication structures and actors; (4) socioeconomic, sociopolitical, and sociocultural effects on communication; (5) problems today; and (6) tomorrow's trends, prospects, and ambitions. Although the report is written in UNESCOese, a message is still there.

In terms of the uneven flow of news, the Interim Report states "the present imbalance is keenly felt and denounced by some developing countries and by the movement of the nonaligned countries, there are also in all parts of the world those that feel and recognize the need to change and improve the situation speedily and substantially" (1978: 5). The LDC's believe that what is reported about them is the sensational, the negative aspects, or the catastrophes, without coverage of the gains in the educational, social, or humanitarian aspects of their societies. The report also comes down heavily upon the neocolonialism being perpetuated by LDC's when they import foreign news or video (both television and feature films) which upset domestic efforts at reflecting native values and culture. This was detailed by global statistics on various media consumption habits. For example, the Interim Report points out that the LDC's (with two-thirds of the planet's population) have less than half the newspapers, with daily circulation being one-sixth of that of the industrialized states. Similar comparisons were made for books, films, broadcasting outlets, and so on. Included in the overview was the role of advertising agencies as an integral part of the "media imperialism" of the West. Transnational corporations (TNC), exporting hardware or software, also came in for a negative critical appraisal. Representative of the comments is "one major influence of TNC imported media is that exerted on tastes and values, styles and patterns which, being adopted or copies, are largely alien in most countries of the world" (1978: 75).

The Interim Report concludes with a 10-page section of suggestions rather than conclusions. The suggestions were made with an invitation to continue the dialogue before the final report was to be completed. Four areas are covered in the final section: (1) strengthening and expansion of national capacities; (2) redressing the qualitative balance; (3) demo-cratizing communication; and (4) moving toward a New World Information Order.

In conclusion, this is what was addressed: first, to alter the one-way, top down and vertical flow of the media to a more responsive and broadly based access and participation model; second, an upgrading of journalistic codes of ethics, standards of the profession, and treatment by governments; and third, the question of "balance." The Interim Report does not equivocate here:

> It reflects the demand for more radical and complex changes. Its significance is first and foremost political. The ideas and suggestions expressed correspond to a diffuse but deep-rooted and probably irreversible aspiration to transform the models and structures inherited from past situations of hegemony or situations founded on dependence, injustice, inequality and alienation [1978: 140].

In sum, the Interim Report was a major document in legitimizing the movement toward an NWIO. Rhetorically, it levelled charges of considerable shortcomings at the Western press, particularly the major wire services. It flirts with government involvement both to correct the imbalance in the news flow and to reflect the cultural aspirations of the LDC's. It is at this point that the concept of the traditional role of the Western press (i.e., objective, free of government control, market-oriented, independent, and so on) comes into direct conflict with the missionary zeal of the new information order (i.e., promote social change, reflect indigenous cultures, balanced coverage, governmental responsibility for content, and so on).

Not much within the Interim Report caused surprise given its origins and UNESCO's previous involvement. But two paragraphs under a category labelled "Governmental Authorities" highlight Western concerns about the role of government in media activities. The Interim Report states:

> There is a trend for a continuously increasing involvement of public authorities in all fields of communication. Three major reasons are generally evoked: (i) ideological and political, since increased governmental responsibilities in all fields of public life cannot circumvent communication or at least some aspects of it; (ii) economic and financial, since the increased costs of communication often require public investments (in many cases the dilemma is not between privately-owned or publicly-owned media but between publicly-owned or no media at all); (iii) moral, since the impact of information, culture, education, and entertainment on the nation as a whole calls for attention by responsible authorities.

> Government responsibilities are mostly dispensed through: (a) inclusion of communication into overall planning; (b) regulation of conditions for media ownership and communication activities; (c) control of communication channels; (d) direct public ownership of media and other means; (e) straight involvement in various communication activities by national, regional and local public bodies; (f) limitation of imported contents and messages (e.g., in Canada for some media; it is interesting to note that in many developing countries there are fewer controls on outside cultural influence than in some developed ones) [1978: 71].

Given the thrust of the NWIO toward a significantly greater role for governments in affecting press activities, particularly print and the wire services, the West's dislike of the entire idea of the MacBride Commission grew substantially and quickly. This was in August 1978. In September 1978, the original draft of the UNESCO Draft Declaration on the Mass Media Article XI stated that "it is the duty of States to facilitate the application of the present Declaration, and to ensure that the mass media coming directly under their jurisdiction act in conformity there with" (UNESCO, 1978: 3). States, particularly Western ones, looked with shock at the thought of government (states) enforcing rules designed by UNESCO or on any other group media activities. MacBride's Interim Report generated hostile reaction because of the threat of some more active role for government in the news process. But such a view at least guaranteed close attention to the balance of the commission's work.

The final Report of the MacBride International Commission was almost a year late and runs five volumes.[1] The major volume is the final one, number five. Number five contains the major conclusions and recommendations. It is almost impossible to read due to its UNESCOese style.

Background Papers

The MacBride Commission, needless to say, generated a great deal of international activity. In fact, no fewer than 100 background papers were prepared for its use. Even had these papers not been connected in any way with the commission, the information, suggestions, and insights they provided would still have powerfully enriched the debate over a new information order. Their influence on the work and findings of a commission, which has been perhaps the most prominent focal point of that debate, enhances the significance of these documents to the study of international communication problems even further.

Obviously the limited space and purpose of our study do not allow a properly representative treatment of the documents to appear on these pages. However, probably the three most widely known of the papers are *The New World Information Order* (1979) by Mustapha Masmoudi,[2] *Communication for an Independent, Pluralistic World* (1979) by Elie Abel, and an unattributed paper entitled *The World of News Agencies* (1979).

Aside from the attention they have attracted, the first two papers have been selected because in them all the major themes and issues associated with the call for an NWIO are pulled together and compressed into a general overview. Most of the other papers, on the other hand, deal with narrow and specific issues. Also, the two papers represent two very different, in some respects opposite, perspectives, Masmoudi's paper expressing the position of the developing world and Abel's expressing a moderate U.S. or Western position.

The third paper was chosen because of the serious issues that have come to characterize the NWIO debate, that is, concentration of ownership of the international communication industry in the West, imbalances of news flow between the developed and developing countries, and cultural penetration and imperialism, and these converge most conspicuously around the question of the large transnational news agencies. The third paper may also serve to clarify Masmoudi's and Abel's papers since the news agency question arises quite prominently in them and their authors adopt sharply opposing views on the matter.

Masmoudi begins his paper by remarking that while a great many developing nations achieved political emancipation after World War II, colonialism still thrives in the form of disparities, built into the international power system, between developed and developing countries in the economic, information, and virtually all other sectors. Masmoudi divides the imbalances in the present information system into three spheres: the political, the legal, and technical-financial.

In the political sphere, Masmoudi observes that there is a "great disparity between the volume of news and information emanating from the developed world and intended for the developing countries and the volume of the flow in the opposite direction" (1979: 3). This disparity, according to Masmoudi, reflects the West's "de facto hegemony and will to dominate" with respect to international information which reflects and complements its domination in international economic, technological, and other sectors. The main agents of this Western control of news flow are the transnational news agencies, says Masmoudi.

These agencies conceive of information as a commodity, he claims. He says they are indifferent to the problems, concerns, and aspirations of the developing world and are only interested in that world insofar as it is a consumer in a market they do corner and wish to continue to corner and also a source of saluble news. Unfortunately, Masmoudi notes, the only news from the developing world that the agencies seem to feel will sell concerns disasters, coups, crime, violence, and so on, not a state of affairs that does much good for the image of LDC's abroad.

Moreover, because these transnational agencies are inextricably involved in, and in fact nourished by, the established political, economic, and ideological order in the West (see section on wire services), according to Masmoudi and other critics, the choice of what information they will carry or neglect generally reflects and supports the interests of that order. And because of their monopoly over news flows, these agencies can and do intentionally impose upon the developing world such information and the pre-Western establishment values, priorities, and biases it conveys. Often, says Masmoudi, this information is not only of no interest to those in developing countries but also, because of the Western perspectives it presents, inappropriate and damaging.

Turning to the legal sphere, Masmoudi complains that in international law as regards communication, prominence has been given to the rights of the individual over the rights of the group or community. Moreover, he notes the doctrine of freedom of information has come to mean "freedom of the informing agent" (1979: 6). The doctrine, he further claims, has become "an instrument of domination in the hands of those who control the media" (1979: 6). He goes on to note that the right of access to information has come to mean the right to those who have the resources to obtain information. He is also disappointed by the ineffectiveness of the right of states to have inaccurate, false, or misleading information about them corrected and the lack of regulations and a code of ethics to govern the profession of journalism. The legal structures that have been evolved to deal with copyright, distribution and coordination of the radio frequency spectrum, and the uses of telecommunications and satellites have failed to promote equality between developed and developing countries in these areas, adds Masmoudi.

In the technical-financial sphere, Masmoudi says, "The developed countries' technological lead and the tariff system which they have instituted have enabled them to benefit from monopoly situations and prerogatives both in fixing the rates for transport of publications and telecommunications and in the use of communication and information technology" (1979: 8). He notes existing international telecommunications links and infrastructures, largely inherited from the trade and communication patterns of the colonial past, favor a greater volume of traffic among developed countries and from developed to developing countries than among developing countries and from developing countries to developed countries. The tariff structure, too, disadvantages the type of small information outputs common to the developing world. Also in the technical-financial sphere Masmoudi notes that 90% of the radio frequency spectrum is controlled by the 10% of the world's population in the developed countries.

Masmoudi argues that a new order entailing "a thoroughgoing readjustment" of existing international information structures is necessary. This new world order would be characterized, he says, by a relationship of equality among all partners in the information system and a free and balanced flow of information as called for by UNESCO.

Among the steps the developing world should take to initiate this new order are the formulation of national communication policies as necessary to development and the motivation of citizens on behalf of such policies, the development of information centers and networks by LDC's and exchanges of news programs among them, training of professionals in the values of the new order, greater research efforts, exchanges of journalists among developing countries and between developing and developed countries, and the encouragement of viable and strong national news agencies in developing states.

He suggests developed countries for their part attempt to heighten public awareness within their borders of the problems with the present information system and the action taken by the developing world with respect to reforms of that system, pay more attention both to a larger variety of news concerning LDC's and information supplied by developing world news agencies, and treat, in their coverage of LDC's, the aspirations, concerns, and problems of those countries objectively and with respect of their values and cultures.

His main recommendations to international organizations such as UNESCO are to increase and diversify aid to developing countries, promote development of the media in LDC's, contribute to training, research, and technical assistance efforts and help coordinate such efforts, and to devise a clear-cut policy on the use of satellite transmission systems, respecting in all cases the sovereign rights of the individual states.

On the legal front, Masmoudi calls for greater emphasis on the right to objective, balanced, and accurate news, particularly about themselves and on the right of those about whom inaccurate, misleading, or incomplete information has been reported to have it rectified. He stresses the need to recognize the responsibilities as well as the rights of those transmitting information. He calls for "regulation of the right to information by preventing abusive uses of the right of access to information; definition of appropriate criteria to govern truly objective news selection; regulation of the collection, processing, and transmission of news and data across national frontiers" (1979: 16). Furthermore, he perceives a need to establish regulations and a code of ethics concerning the conduct of journalists, though he does not expressly state what principles such a deontology would include, and he also notes the need to "set up effective machinery to protect journalists against undue pressure or improper demands on the part of their employers" (1979: 17). Masmoudi also wants the laws and regulations, specifically the ITU's Radio Regulations, governing the distribution of frequencies and uses of satellites to be adjusted to guarantee a better deal and more equitable access to the developing world.

This point recurs in Masmoudi's discussion of steps to be taken toward a new information order at a technical-financial level. In the technical-financial sphere, he also notes that the present international telecommunications and tariff structure must be rethought in order to help enable the developing countries to function on a more equal footing within it and to foster the establishment of nodes or centers of communication in developing countries, setting up direct links among them where possible. He advocates more favorable terms with respect to tariffs and air freight surtaxes which hamper the transport of publications to and from developing countries. Masmoudi is now considered the chief spokesperson for the NWIO and has M'Bow's support.

In his paper, which is in large part an answer to Masmoudi's, Elie Abel agrees that there are gross imbalances in the present information system. But he denies Masmoudi's contention that these imbalances are somehow purposefully perpetuated by the Western media in order to monopolize world information flows. Rather, he says, these imbalances stem from historical processes which left the world with an uneven spread of development. He states, "Talk of conspiracies to 'dominate' information and culture flows can yield no practical outcome, save increased polarization" (1979: 6).

Abel also denies Masmoudi's allegation that the major Western transnational news agencies, by virtue of their control over international news flow, have, for all intents and purposes, "direct access to the eyes and ears of readers and listeners in developing countries" and, furthermore, use such access to intentionally impose unsuitable western values and perspectives upon LDC's. Abel writes:

> In fact, most developing countries do not allow their newspapers and broadcasting stations to subscribe directly to foreign agency services. The subscriber in most cases is the government, or government-controlled agency. In short, the picture of passive millions awash in a tidal wave of alien information is somewhat fanciful [1979: 3].

But most strenuously of all, Abel denies Masmoudi's suggestion that the rights of free circulation of information and ideas and of access to information have been exploited by the Western media for purposes of dominating international information flows and that, therefore, the solution to imbalances in the present communication order lies in placing restraints on such rights.

Abel says, "The remedy does not lie ... in measures to restrict and control the voices now being heard ... nor can the answer be found in the adoption of a single standard for the control of communication systems throughout the world" (1979: 6). There is, he says, a rich variety of communication systems among nations, systems which reflect the widely diverse and distinctive experiences and cultural, political, economic, and social structures of those nations.

Applying the same standard of controls to communication systems as far apart as those of the United States and the Soviet Union would be futile and dangerous. Understanding and respect within the information environment and the international arena in general cannot be achieved, Abel suggests, by pressuring all systems to comply with a uniform, UNESCO-approved pattern of regulations. Rather, he says, understanding and respect will only come with greater and freer flows and exchanges of a richer variety of information and ideas among nations.

Abel does concede that Masmoudi and some other advocates of a more rigidly regulated information order have offered some valid proposals for concrete action aimed at redressing some of the imbalances in the present system, actions which Abel feels could meet with near unanimous approval. For instance, Masmoudi's suggestions concerning the reduction of shipping costs and rates affecting publications are appealing, says Abel. He adds that present telecommunications tariff structures should be reformed with INTELSAT, an international satellite telecommunications services consortium, acting as the main forum for such reforms. Moves toward greater access to satellite services for LDC's should also be spearheaded by INTELSAT, he proposes. Upgraded financial, technical, and training assistance are yet other Masmoudi suggestions Abel learned.

But while Abel foresees the possibility of common ground being reached by all countries with respect to the abovementioned reforms and proposals, he also recognizes that there are information issues of such a highly sensitive political nature that no unanimity concerning them is ever likely to emerge. For instance, on the right of circulation and access issue, Abel says that many countries, such as his own United States, would never accept the demands (mentioned above) of Masmoudi and others in LDC's for internationally applied standards of objectivity which could lead to restrictions on press coverage. Abel also decries the practice of government licensing of journalists, noting that governments are not competent to properly choose who should gather and report news and that this practice negates the independence of the press by "subjecting it to influence or control by persons whose motives may have nothing to do with the pursuit of disinterested reporting, or truth" (1979: 12).

As to Masmoudi's insistence on the rights of states to correct misleading or inaccurate information concerning themselves and his insinuation that the media should be compelled to make retractions or corrections when they are in error, Abel says they would be "unthinkable" in many countries, including the United States. Abel proposes that states pursue other avenues of redress to rectify distortions

about them in the media, avenues such as libel actions, letters
to the editor, submissions to the op-ed pages, and press
councils and ombudsmen whose function it is to consider
complaints about press performance and, if a complaint is
upheld, use moral suasion or possibly legal pressure to get the
offending instituion to make amends.

Finally, Abel agrees with Masmoudi that codes of ethics be
drawn up for journalists, but considers it pointless and undesirable to attempt to apply one code of ethics for journalists
on an international basis. Each culture has its own distinct
model of journalism to which its code of journalistic ethics
must be attuned. It is useless and wrong, says Abel, to hold
an American and a Soviet journalist to the same code and
expect them to conceive of their professional functions,
duties, and moral obligations in a uniform way when their
models of journalism are so diametrically opposed. Besides a
code of ethics to which journalists would have to adhere,
Abel notes that Masmoudi also calls for rules to protect
journalists, particularly from improper demands from their
employers. "It strikes me as remarkable and somehow revealing," says Abel, "that nowhere . . . is there mention of a code
to protect journalists . . . from the dead hand of government
control" (1979: 14).

While the first two papers clearly reflect the positions of
their authors, the third paper is a fairly neutral consideration
of the spectrum of opinion regarding one of the most dominant issues connected with the call for a new information
order, that is, the performance of the major transnational
news agencies. The first part of the paper is an account of the
news agency picture in the various regions of the world. The
second part details problems encountered, especially in
LDC's, in the establishment and operation of news agencies.

The third part of the paper deals with the role of the large
transnational news agencies in the imbalances in information
flow between developed and developing countries. The paper
notes that spokesmen for the LDC's usually charge that the
news agencies give the developing world little coverage and

the coverage they do give tends to be sensationalistic with its alleged concentration on violence, dramatic social and political upheavals, and disasters. They also claim, according to the paper, that the information flowing into LDC's from the Western news agencies lacks relevance to such countries and conveys Western stereotypes, values, and perspectives in a way which induces a colonial relationship between the West and the LDC's at least at a cultural level. The news agencies, the paper says, counter that they have to provide all their customers, including those in LDC's, impartial, comprehensive, and reliable news in order to please subscribers of widely different political, ideological, cultural, and economic orientations.

Much of the debate over the role of the news agencies and how well or badly they fill it, the paper observes, can be traced to conflicting perceptions of news value and content. In the West, the model of journalism which stresses the importance of timely, "comprehensive, accurate, and objective reporting on phenomena and events of interest mainly and preferably of an unusual and exceptional nature" (World of News Agencies, 1979: 18) is still widely held. But in the developing world there is a growing feeling that journalists should focus their attention on process, long-term trends, social structure, and the complex problems of development, which are often difficult to accommodate within Western news reporting formulae. According to this model, journalists should be social analysts and educators concerned with advancing rather than obstructing the causes of development and progress.

The problem with this model,[3] the paper points out, is that there is a perilously thin line between (1) education and social analysis and (2) propaganda. On the other hand, according to the paper, the problem with the Western model has to do with journalistic responsibility, there being a fine line between (1) freedom of information and expression and (2) disregard for the responsibilities of reporting fairly and accurately and respecting the values and traditions of foreign peoples.

MacBride International Commission

The International Commission for the Study of Communication Problems produced a final report of 484 pages in length.[4] It contains five major sections which cover a very wide range of issues and statistics. The major section is Part Five: Communication Tomorrow.

Part Five of the final report is divided into two major sections: Section A, Conclusions and Recommendations, and Section B, Issues Requiring Further Study. The first section is further subdivided into five sections. Within (A) Conclusions and Recommendations, the five sections are:

    I.   *Strengthening Independence and Self-Reliance*
    II.   *Social Consequences and New Tasks*
    III. *Professional Integrity and Standards*
    IV. *Democratization of Communication*
    V.   *Fostering International Co-operation.*

The conclusions and recommendations sections commence with a summary of previous main conclusions drawn from earlier research:

1. Our review of communication the world over reveals a variety of solutions adopted in different countries—in accordance with diverse traditions, patterns of social, economic and cultural life, needs and possibilities.
2. The review has also shown that the utmost importance should be given to eliminating imbalances and disparities in communication and its structures, and particularly in information flows.
3. Our conclusions are founded on the firm conviction that communication is a basic individual right, as well as a collective one required by all communities and nations.
4. For these purposes, it is essential to develop comprehensive national communication policies linked to overall social, cultural and economic development objectives.
5. The basic considerations which are developed at length in the body of our Report are intended to provide a framework for the development of a new information and communication order [International Commission for the Study of Communication Problems, 1979: 440441].

The section ends with this paragraph:

> Thus our call for reflection and action is addressed broadly to
> governments and international organizations, to policy-makers
> and planners, to the media and professional organizations, to
> researchers, communication practitioners, to organized social
> groups and the public at large [1979: 441].

The following will be a report on the five main sections
within the conclusion of the final report.

I.   *Strengthening Independence and Self-Reliance:*
      Communication Policies

   a) All individuals and people collectively have an inalien-
      able right to a better life which, however conceived,
      must ensure a social minimum, nationally and globally.
      This calls for the strengthening of capabilities and the
      elimination of gross inequalities; such defects may
      threaten social harmony and even international peace.
      There must be a measured movement from disadvantages
      and dependence to self-reliance and the creation of more
      equal opportunities. Since communication is interwoven
      with every aspect of life, it is clearly of the utmost
      importance that the existing "communication gap" be
      rapidly narrowed and eventually eliminated [1979:
      442].

   b) *Strengthening Capabilities*
      Communication policies should offer a guide to the
      determination of information and media priorities and
      to the selection of appropriate technologies. This is
      required to plan the installation and development and
      adequate infrastructures to provide self-reliant commu-
      nications capacity [1979: 443].

   c) *Basic Needs*
      All nations have to make choices in investment priority.
      In choosing between possible alternatives and often con-

flicting interest, developing countries, in particular, must give priority to satisfying their people's essential needs. Communication is not only a system of public information but also an important part of education and development [1979: 445].

d) *Particular Challenges*
We have focused on national efforts which must be made to lead to greater independence and self-reliance. But there are three major challenges to this goal that require concerted international action. Simply, these are paper, tariff structures and the electro-magnetic spectrum [1979: 446].

II. *Social Consequences and New Tasks: Integrating Communication into Development*

a) Development strategies should incorporate communication policies as an integral part in the diagnosis of needs and in the design and implementation of selected priorities. In this respect communication should be considered a major development resource, a vehicle to ensure real political participation in decision-making, a central information base for defining policy options, and an instrument for creating awareness of national priorities [1979: 448].

b) *Facing the Technological Challenge*
The technological explosion in communication has both great potential and great danger. The outcome depends on crucial decisions and on where and by whom they are taken. Thus, it is a priority to organize the decision-making process in a participatory manner the basis of a full awareness of the social impact of different alternatives [1979: 449].

c) *Strengthening Cultural Identity*
Promoting conditions for the preservation of the cultural identity of every society is necessary to enable it to enjoy a harmonious and creative inter-relationship with other cultures. It is equally necessary to modify situations in many developed and developing countries which suffer from cultural dominance [1979: 450].

d) *Reducing the Commercialization of Communication*
The social effects of the commercialization of the mass media are a major concern in policy formulation and decision-making by private and public bodies [1979: 451].

e) *Access to Technical Information*
The flow of technical information within nations and across national boundaries is a major resource for development. Access to such information, which countries need for technical decision-making at all levels, is as crucial as access to news sources. This type of information is generally not easily available and is most often concentrated in large techno-structures. Developed countries are not providing adequate information of this type to developing countries [1979: 452].

III. *Professional Integrity and Standards: Responsibility of Journalists*

a) For the journalist, freedom and responsibility are indivisible. Freedom without responsibility invites distortion and other abuses. But in the absence of freedom there can be no exercise of responsibility. The concept of freedom with responsibility necessarily includes a concern for professional ethics, demanding an equitable approach to events, situations or processes with the attention to their diverse aspects. This is not always the case today [1979: 454].

b) *Towards Improved International Reporting*
The full and factual presentation of news about one country to others is a continuing problem. The reasons for this are manifold: principal among them are correspondents' working conditions, their skills and attitudes, varying conceptions of news and information values and government viewpoints. Remedies for the situation will require long-term, evolutionary actions towards improving the exchange of news around the world [1979: 456].

c) *Protection of Journalists*
Daily reports from around the world attest to dangers that journalists are subject to in the exercise of their

profession: harassment, threats, imprisonment, physical violence, assassination. Continual vigilance is required to focus the world's attention on such assaults to human rights [1979: 459].

IV. *Democratization of Communication: Human Rights*

a) Freedom of speech, of the press, of information and of assembly are vital for the realization of human rights. Extension of these communication freedoms to a broader individual and collective right to communicate is an evolving principle in the democratization process. Among the human rights to be emphasized are those of equality for women and between races. Defense of all human rights is one of the media's most vital tasks [1979: 460].

b) *Removal of Obstacles*
Communication, with its immense possibilities for influencing the minds and behaviour of people, can be a powerful means of promoting democratization of society and of widening public participation in the decision-making process. This depends on the structures and practices of the media and their management and to what extent they facilitate broader access and open the communication process to a free interchange of ideas, information and experience among equals, without dominance or discrimination [1979: 461].

c) *Diversity and Choice*
Diversity and choice in the content of communication are a precondition for democratic participation. Every individual and particular groups should be able to form judgments on the basis of a full range of information and a variety of messages and opinions and have the opportunity to share these ideas with others. The development of decentralized and diversified media should provide larger opportunities for a real direct involvement of the people in communication processes [1979: 463].

d) *Integration and Participation*
To be able to communicate in contemporary society, man must dispose of appropriate communication tools. New technologies offer him many devices for individual-

ized information and entertainment, but often fail to
provide appropriate tools for communication within his
community or social or cultural group. Hence, alternative means of communication are often required [1979:
463].

V.   *Fostering International Co-operation: Partners for
      Development*

a) Inequalities in communication facilities, which exist
   everywhere, are due to economic discrepancies or to
   political and economic design, still others to cultural
   imposition or neglect. But whatever the source or reasons for them, gross inequalities should no longer be
   countenanced. The very notion of a new world information order and communication order presupposes fostering international co-operation, which includes two main
   areas: international assistance and contribution towards
   international understanding. The international dimensions of communication are today of such importance
   that it has become crucial to develop co-operation on a
   world-wide scale. It is for the international community
   to take the appropriate steps to replace dependence,
   dominance, and inequality by more fruitful and more
   open relations of interdependence and complementarity,
   based on mutual interest and the equal dignity of
   nations and peoples. Such co-operation requires a major
   international commitment to redress the present situation. This clear commitment is a need not only for
   developing countries but also for the international
   community as a whole. The tensions and disruptions
   that will come from lack of action are far greater than
   the problems posed by necessary changes [1979:
   464-465].

b) *Strengthening Collective Self-Reliance*
   Developing countries have a primary responsibility for
   undertaking necessary changes to overcome their dependence in the field of communications. The actions
   needed begin at the national level, but must be com-
   plemented by forceful and decisive agreements at the
   bilateral, sub-regional, regional, and inter-regional levels.

Collective self-reliance is the cornerstone of a new world information and communication order [1979: 466].

c) *International Mechanisms*

Co-operation for the development of communication is a global concern and therefore of importance to international organizations, where all Member States can fully debate the issues involved and decide upon multinational action. Governments should therefore attentively review the structures and programmes of international agencies in the communications field and point to changes required to meet evolving needs [1979: 467].

d) *Towards International Understanding*

The strengthening of peace, international security and co-operation and the lessening of international tensions are the common concern of all nations. The mass media can make a substantial contribution towards achieving these goals. The special session of the United Nations General Assembly on disarmament called for increased efforts by the mass media to mobilize public opinion in favour of disarmament and of ending the arms race. This declaration together with the Unesco Declaration on fundamental principles concerning the contribution of the mass media to strengthening peace and international understanding, to the promotion of human rights and to countering racialism, apartheid and incitement to war should be the foundation of a new communication policy to foster international understanding. A new world information and communication order requires and must become the instrument for peaceful co-operation between nations [1979: 470].

B.   *Issues Requiring Further Study*

We have suggested some actions which may help lead towards a new world information and communication order. Some of them are for immediate undertaking; others will take more time to prepare and implement. The important thing is to start moving towards a change in the present situation.

However, there are other issues that require examination, but the International Commission lacked time or sufficient

data or expertise to deal with them. The proposals listed
below have not been approved by the Commission; several
were not, in fact, even discussed. Members felt free, nevertheless, to submit individual or group proposals which, in
their judgment, called for study in the future. While these
suggestions have not been endorsed by the Commission,
they may still indicate some preliminary ideas about issues
to be pursued, if and when they arouse interest [1979:
472].

Within this final section, several research studies are encouraged. The following areas are discussed in relation to the need
for additional studies: increased interdependence, improved
coordination, international standards and instruments, collection and dissemination of news, protection of journalists,
greater attention to neglected areas (e.g., rural studies), and
more extensive financial resources.

Part Five also contained 13 footnotes which were essentially disagreements with the thrust of the major points.
(Further comments about the Final Report are contained in
Chapter 9.) A significant interest group produced a clear and
detailed response to the Final Report of the MacBride Commission and it will be dealt with here.

World Press Freedom Committee

A major interest group in the West is the World Press
Freedom Committee (WPFC).[5] It was formed in May 1976
"to unify the free world media for major threats that
develop" (*Media Crisis*, 1980: 107). It consists of 32 journalistic organizations, ranging from the American Newspaper
Publishers Association (ANPA), AP, UPI, and the International Federation of Journalists. Both print and broadcast
associations are represented.

George Beebe, executive director of the WPFC, highlights
their response to the Final Report of MacBride Commission.
The positive aspects of the study include:

- Censorship in all forms is condemned.
- The right of access applies to private as well as public sources of
  information.

- Journalists should have no special protection; they will be protected when the rights of all citizens are guaranteed.
- Licensing of journalists is rejected because it would require stipulation by some authority as to who is eligible and on what basis.
- Employment of journalists by intelligence agencies of any country is condemned.

The negative aspects of the study include:

- A proposed International Center for Study and Planning of Information and Communications to be established within UNESCO. This appears the most troublesome of proposals to the Western world, for the center not only would monitor and establish standards for the global media, but would serve as a training centre as well.
- A consistent advocacy of pressuring if not requiring news media (including "transnationals," or the international news agencies) to promote government-set "social, cultural, economic and political goals."
- A bias against private ownership of news media and communication facilities.
- A bias against "problems created in a society by advertising."
- A suggestion that transnationals might be taxed "for the benefit of developing countries."
- Unqualified criticism of concentration of media ownership without acknowledging this sometimes is inevitable and/or desirable in a free, private enterprise society [*Media Crisis*, 1980: viii-ix].

Another group seeking less government control is the International Federation of Journalists (IFJ), which has one basic principle; it is "the promotion of a new world order of information is first and foremost the business of journalists and their trade unions and not of states, governments or any pressure group of whatever kind" (*Media Crisis*, 1980: 61).

At its 15th World Congress of the IFJ held in Athens, May 1980, they endorsed a series of wide ranging proposals. They were:

- Find the means for the organization of a seminar for anglophone African journalists, francophone African journalists and a third for journalists of the Mediterranean countries in Africa.

- Rouse initiatives in favor of training professional journalists from developing countries, both on the local and the international levels.
- Contribute to the creation of journalists' trade unions where they do not exist and to the functioning of existing ones.
- Undertake steps through affiliated organizations to promote the importance of news from developing countries.

- Endeavor to promote a more substantial participation of journalists from developing countries in world information networks.
- Examine with the International Telecommunications Agency the introduction of reduced or preferential charges for the press, both from transmissions to and from developing countries, and among developing countries themselves.
- Develop cooperation with the Federation of Arab Journalists, the Federation of African Journalists, and with other journalistic organizations in Latin America, and encourage all initiatives likely to bring about a more efficient solidarity and mutual understanding on problems in developing countries.
- Give publicity to journalists suffering from persecution, exile and banishing.
- Ensure the IFJ's representation at international and regional conferences to debate professional problems facing journalists and relating more particularly to the new world order of information.
- In the same spirit, demand that national delegations to conferences of UNESCO and of any other body debating press problems include professional journalists, representing journalists' unions, whether they be members of the IFJ or not, and not only composed of civil servants, media owners and directors.
- Undertake steps with mass media in all countries to ensure that they should adhere to basic principles of equal opportunity and pay for their local correspondents in developing countries and end financial discrimination [*Media Crisis,* 1980: 63-64].

Both the WPFC and the IFJ, as major professional organizations for journalists and publishers, are monitoring the activities of the MacBride Commission and its successor, the International Program for Development of Communication (IPDC).

MacBride's Successor—The IPDC

During the contentious 20th General Assembly of UNESCO, U.S. Ambassador Reinhardt made a suggestion to convene a conference to look at communication aid. M'Bow gladly endorsed the idea and a preparatory meeting was held in Washington, D.C., November 6-9, 1979. The purpose of this meeting was to prepare the agenda and background material for the major intergovernmental conference to be held at UNESCO in Paris during April 1980. The April meeting is a significant event in the movement toward an NWIO. Before discussing the April meeting, a few words about the November Washington meeting are illustrative.

The November meeting was labelled "Preparatory Meeting of Experts for the Intergovernmental Planning Conference to Develop Institutional Arrangements for Systematic, Collaborative Consultation on Communication Development Activities, Needs and Plans." At this meeting the ground work for the IPDC was established.

Also, at this meeting sides were quickly drawn. The chairman was Roland Homet (United States), chief of International Communications Policy Staff of the U.S.'s International Communication Agency, and the Vice-Chairman was Mustapha Masmoudi (Tunisia), permanent delegate to UNESCO and a leading spokesman for the aims of the NWIO.

A draft working paper was presented consisting of three main sections. The first section dealt with the area of communication and development, technology transfer, and self-reliance; the second section reviewed problems related to technical and international cooperation; and the third section dealt with potential mechanisms for implementing cooperation. The document contained critical references to "tied" aid and how research and projects in the Third World were dominated by the economic interests of the West.

Debate about the draft paper shifted quickly to a debate about two differing proposals for action. The one, by Homet, dealt with a proposal for an International Communications

Development Consultative Group and the other, by Masmoudi, dealing with multilateral projects for mass communication development. In addition there was considerable
debate about the overall role of UNESCO in any new program dealing with future international communication
research and development.

Most delegates sided with Masmoudi and granted UNESCO
a central role in any new initiatives. The meeting also
endorsed the view of looking at communication in a broader
perspective, involving both mass media and telecommunications. The UNESCO Secretariat was assigned the task of
developing a document for the April meeting in Paris, called
the UNESCO Intergovernmental Conference For Co-operation on Activities, Needs and Programs For Communication
Development. This intergovernmental conference was the
result of the preliminary meeting held during November in
Washington, D.C., under the auspices of the United States
Delegation for UNESCO; both were convened in accordance
with Resolution 4/9.4/9 of the 20th UNESCO General
Assembly.

Before discussing the recommendations of the intergovernmental group, it is important to realize that the mechanisms
for operationalizing the actions of the group followed differing lines:

(1) The United States initially wanted an independent body outside
    of UNESCO but shifted during the week to accept a UNESCO
    group.
(2) The LDC's were concerned with the amount and the ties and
    conditions of pledging from the Western donor nations.
(3) Issues of professionalism in terms of who would work on the
    council were raised.
(4) Interaction with other agencies, for example, the ITU, and
    associations with various intergovernmental councils that deal
    with communications were also discussed.

Much of the discussion surrounding the April meetings
dealt with funding problems, as well as whether the council

would be in or out of a United Nations Secretariat. The common denominator or unifying force was basically beating the original U.S. stand, that is, keeping it outside the UN-UNESCO structure. Once again, this represents both a mis-analysis by the United States in terms of not realizing the extent to which its particular stand was out of touch with the thrust and desires of the LDC's and, second, it represents a demonstration once again of the determination and antago-nism toward the Western donor nations. Concern about tied-funding and foreign aid designed to meet objectives of the West rather than foreign aid designed to meet the objectives and priorities of LDC's was a consistent theme.

Indicative of the LDC's stand is the preamble to the recommendations of the intergovernmental conference meet-ing. The preamble states:

> *Recalling* that the existing disparity in communication among different countries will not be eliminated by the mere material development of infrastructures and professional resources and by the transfer of know-how and technologies, but the solution depends also on the elimination of all political, ideological, psychological, economic and technical obstacles, which run coun-ter to the development of independent national communication systems and to a freer, wider and more balanced circulation of information [UNESCO, 1980: 4].

The recommendations to member states of UNESCO then proceeded to touch on traditional topics such as promotion of national and regional communication, development policies, research to identify priorities, including telecom-munications and informatics, plus the main objective of establishing an international program for development of communication. It is with the main objective that 14 subob-jectives were included in dealing with aiding LDC's in their attempts to gain control over their communication and information environment.

The structure of the international program for the develop-ment of communication, now known as the IPDC, was designed to be coordinated by a main intergovernmental council composed of representatives from 35 member states that is to be elected by the General Conference of UNESCO on the basis of seeking a fair geographical distribution. This would ensure LDC's a substantial share of the council seats. Such a council would elevate both their influence within the United Nations system and perhaps remove a very contentious problem from UNESCO's day-to-day activities. The hostility toward the NWIO and particularly government control of the press would be set aside in the council for the 1980s. The recommendation concluded with the following:

> *Expresses* the conviction that the gradual implementation of these recommendations constitutes an essential stage on the way to the establishment of a new, more just and more effective world information and communication order [UNESCO, 1980: 8].

Establishing an intergovernmental conference was a major topic at the 21st UNESCO General Assembly; the evolution of the IPDC at the Belgrade meetings is dealt with in Chapter 5.

Masmoudi, addressing the International Institute of Communications conference in September 1980, stated:

> The objectives of this UNESCO agency would be to mobilize resources in order to assist developing countries; to advise developing countries on how to gain access to modern technology in the field of information and communication; and to provide the links with regional bodies whose gradual creation should be planned in order to complement and facilitate the performance of the central agency.

> This agency, whose creation was unanimously recommended by the Conference participants, could be a providential instrument that would contribute greatly to shaping a new world information order by enabling countries to obtain the technical assistance and funds they need to meet their unlimited needs [1980: 8].

But even more controversial was the potential revenues for the new agency. Speaking for the NWIO, Masmoudi continued:

> Some members felt it was necessary to find new resources to benefit developing countries—for example, excess profits from the exploitation of raw materials; an international levy on the use of the electro-magnetic spectrum and of the geo-stationary satellite; or an international deduction on the profits of the multinationals [1980: 8].

It is interesting to note that these new revenue sources were also examined from time to time by the MacBride Commission.

NOTES

1. An indication of the enlarging split between MacBride and Deleon was the prior circulation for comment of two drafts of the Final Report, one was drafted by the UNESCO Secretariat and the other by MacBride. The bulk of the official final Report bears Deleon's stamp.

2. There is no one universally accepted definition of the NWIO; but one of the leading spokespersons for the order is M. Masmoudi. At the International Institute for Communication's 1980 Conference he stated a very broad definition:

> On the basis of the many studies that have tried to define this new order, particularly the Commission's report, what appears to be involved is the establishment of a new, open-ended conceptual framework leading to a freer more efficient, more equitable, better balanced international communication system, one founded on democratic principles and favouring equality in the relations between sovereign states.

> Moreover, it is important to put an end to disparities and inequalities between developed and developing countries in the area of communication.

> The new order would also be the ideal framework for promoting freedom of information and communication as an individual and collective right that must be guaranteed at all levels. There are no grounds for thinking that this would limit freedom of information or hamper the dissemination of information.

> It would, above all, allow individuals, communities and nations to make known their aspirations, their concerns and their problems in struggling to shape a better future. This new order would help the cause of liberty and justice, just as it would help to prevent rabble-rousing; end racism, do away

with intellectual and ideological hegemony and maintain peace in the world.

The new order must preserve cultural identity and the values of each culture, while promoting knowledge of other cultures and balanced exchanges in the sphere of culture.

To this end, two objectives must be aimed at—the cultural development of peoples and the mutual respect and appreciation of culture in the broadest sense (language, history, cultural heritage, oral traditions, etc.)—since we know that intellectual and cultural dependence has as negative an effect as economic dependence [Masmoudi, 1980: 2-3].

3. Other aspects of examining and reforming the Big Four (Western) news agencies are discussed by Oliver Boyd-Barrett (1980); John Merrill (1979) elaborates upon the divergent ethical views underlying the "free flow" mystique.

4. It is important to realize that the perception of the MacBride Commission held by Westerners—and, even at that, there are probably very few that are aware of it—is negative. It has been reported by the daily press, that is, by the very wire services—AP, UPI, and others—that are harshly attacked by LDC critics of having a distinct bias.

Also there has been very little, if any, coverage of the MacBride Commission by the electronic media. As a result it is a fair statement to say that the MacBride Commission has received bad press in the West. This is a result of earlier initiatives and speculation that some type of government control of the media, which is abhorred particularly by the printed press, would be forthcoming. The final report shows that this is not the case. In general both the quantity and quality of coverage about both UNESCO and MacBride, particularly in the United States, has been poor. For example, Elie Abel, commenting on the coverage of the Belgrade General Assembly, states, "The press has not covered itself with glory on this one. The coverage was poor" (*Broadcasting*, 1980: 28).

5. Another significant investigation of the NWIO and related issues, completed before the Final Report of MacBride, was a task force of international experts. The following are basic principles and practical proposals of the Twentieth Century Fund Task Force on the International Flow of News (1978):

1. The Task Force believes that there is a serious imbalance in the flow of information between the developing and the developed nations.
2. The Task Force is not under the illusion that the situation is amenable to quick or easy remedial action. It is convinced that some of the proposals put forward by representatives of Third World governments would be detrimental to the objective of a more equitable balance in the flow of news.
3. It is our unanimous and deeply held belief that freedom of information and economic and political development are inextricably intertwined and mutually reinforcing.
4. While the Task Force believes in a free flow of information, it also favors a more balanced flow of information, but these are two very different concepts.
5. The Task Force recommends the establishment of a private body composed of independent journalists and specialists in communications from both the developed and the developing countries, to monitor, evaluate, and report suggestions and proposals for dealing with a free and more balanced flow of information.

6. In order to emphasize that the assignment of this independent body is both temporary and discrete, devoted solely to helping resolve the current dispute, we propose that it be called the Ad Hoc Committee for the International Flow of News. We further propose that it be in operation for no more than two years, which we believe is ample time to assess the work of UNESCO's International Communications Commission as well as the reports of similar bodies.
7. The Task Force also endorses a proposal that was presented to the 1978 Cairo Conference on the International Media and the Developing World for the establishment of a Multinational News Agency (MNA) that would be supported by news agencies of both developed and developing countries.
8. The Task Force believes that the new independent and ad hoc committee that it suggests establishing—a body that would be supported by foundations and other private sources and whose members would be experts in the field of communications from both the West and the developing countries—is ideally suited to perform this function. Such a body can fill a critical gap by providing informed and disinterested analysis that no organization is at present equipped to fill.

REFERENCES

A Free and Balanced Flow (1978) Report of the Twentieth Century Fund Task Force on the International Flow of News. Lexington, MA: Lexington Books.

ABEL, E. (1979) Communication for an Interdependent, Pluralistic World. International Commission for the Study of Communication Problems. No. 33.

BOYD-BARRETT, O. (1980) The International News Agencies. Beverly Hills, CA: Sage.

Broadcasting (1980) "Split decision over UNESCO." November 3, p. 28.

Interim Report (1978) The International Commission for the Study of Communication Problems (August). Paris: UNESCO.

International Commission for the Study of Communication Problems (1979) Final Report. Paris: UNESCO.

MASMOUDI, M. (1980) "A new world information order for better human understanding." Presented at the meeting of the International Institute for Communications, Ottawa, Canada, September 10.

MASMOUDI, M. (1979) The New World Information Order. International Commission for the Study of Communication Problems. No. 31.

Media Crisis (1980) Miami: World Press Federation Committee.

MERRILL, J. (1979) " 'The free flow of news' and 'Western communication imperialism': Divergent views on ethical issues." Studies in Third World Societies 9: 27-44.

UNESCO, (1980) Document CC-80/CONF. 212/DR.8. Paris: Author.

UNESCO (1978) Document 20C2, September 6, Annex.

World of News Agencies (1979) International Commission for the Study of Communication Problems. No. 11.

Chapter 9

CONCLUSIONS AND SUMMARY

The debate about the NWIO has just begun. Resolutions or solutions are still premature; it will still take time to evolve a new international order. This is the case for economic, political, as well as information issues. The debate will also take place in several international forums. The foregoing has set the stage for the major actors in the evolving discussion over priorities in communication and information fields. What has emerged are several points, some of which will probably exacerbate the tension in the debate over electronic colonialism.

The NWIO is growing in influence. Telecommunications and transnational data flows are now part of the issues being investigated. The new recent title, "the new world information and communication order" reflects this broader concern. What started as a vague concept in the late 1960s will be a broadly based, well-researched concept by the end of this decade. Very few media systems or communication firms will escape being affected by its outcome. What the general public learns or, more important, does not learn about the LDC's will be influenced by the NWIO.

Before outlining some of the major points and implications of the NWIO, it is important to recall that the issue of foreign news gathering is critical to both national awareness and international concerns. The world is a "global village"; more extensive and accurate coverage is mandatory for the vital issues societies face in the 1980s. But the broadcasting and communication environment of the future is being decided now. It is these meetings in Belgrade, Paris, Geneva, New York, and other places that are setting the ground rules and goals for the NWIO. Some type of new order will evolve and the following deals with the major issues to date.

1. There is a major paradox. Technology is providing more choice. Optic fibers, lasers, minicomputers, cable, DBS, video discs, view data systems, and a host of other innovations could make the world of information available at one's fingertips. Yet people in both the West and in LDC's may have less international information in the future rather than more.

For the LDC's, illiteracy is growing, thus making even the newspaper a distant dream for many. Costs are keeping other media options at a meager level as well.

In the West, high costs are reducing the numbers of foreign correspondents; in addition the costs of energy, labor, and newsprint will force substantial price rises in the 1980s. A further introspective mood has editors allocating less space and priority for international items in the daily press. Whether the United States is still reacting from the Vietnam debacle or from current economic woes there is a definite movement away from foreign affairs, coverage, or concerns. Light, breezy, humorous items are the diet of the day. Dennis Schroeder makes the point well:

Nowhere is the prevailing introspective mood reflected more clearly than in the news media which, rather than using the new communication technologies to cover the Global Village more comprehensively, appear to be concentrating increasingly on their own familiar "neighbourhoods" within the village.

Such an attitude can only lead to future misunderstandings and tension. It is absolutely impossible to comprehend major domestic social, political or economic developments adequately unless they are out into the global context. Nor is it possible, in an increasingly interconnected world, to respond intelligently to developments elsewhere in the world unless we are well informed. The Third World, in particular, is assuming increasing importance to global affairs. Decisions made there strongly influence world prices of oil and other essential commodities; political unrest in Africa, the Middle East, Southeast Asia, and elsewhere affect people elsewhere. The flow of news from other parts of the world can be turned off with the flick of a dial, but the flow—and the impact—of events cannot [1980: 3-4].

The potential for more is there but the content is lacking.

2. There are two fundamentally different philosophies and outlooks in the West and LDC's. They are irreconcilable on many points and this may as well be accepted from the outset. Any future solution will involve a domestic communication policy being separate and distinct from an international communication policy. In terms of the international communication policy, the problem will then become agreement and enforcement. Moral force carries little weight given the economic and political realities of the substantial actors in both the public and private sectors. A Law of Communications Conference similar to the Law of Sea activities should be considered. The ITU-WARC meeting once every 20 years is unrealistic in the Information Age so a new forum should be contemplated.

3. Many U.S. and some EEC firms are in the transition period of making more profits outside their domestic markets than at home. In the future this reliance on foreign markets will continually emphasize the need to develop markets in LDC's. In order to develop these markets there is some need to develop a consumption mentality which is fostered by advertising.

Many LDC's lack domestic training, production facilities, and, in some cases, markets for their own products. As a result, this provides the United States and other Western nations with a significant advantage because they have a sufficiently large domestic market to cover the costs of research and production and, therefore, exports are becoming the only real challenge. Within their television, movie, and computer industries most Western societies have covered costs and their takeoff point puts them in a position to dominate markets in other areas of the world. The LDC's, on the other hand, frequently lack either the infrastructure or markets to build domestic cultural industries. The question of LDC's exporting their limited software to the West is another frustrating issue. For example, U.S. commercial television imports very little from outside its own borders.

4. LDC's want the right to control their own destinies, particularly their communication and information systems; yet at the same time, they want to be part of the international scene and play a larger role with considerable decision-making influence. This forces them to take part in international affairs. On the one hand they want a complete avoidance of foreign cultural influences, but at the same time they want to be part of the larger world which involves a substantial amount of interaction with other nations, particularly with the West which conveys certain financial, political, and cultural values.

5. A major problem in the 1980s is that with the global economic downturn there will be fewer dollars available for foreign aid. At the same time, LDC's are calling for less tied foreign aid. It is safe to predict that for the West fewer foreign aid dollars will garner closer scrutiny and as a result there will be greater ties attached to aid rather than less.

6. Information is the basis of culture. The greater the foreign information, the greater the threat to a native or domestic culture. More national concern about foreign, mainly American, cultural intrusions will occur in both industrialized and LDC's alike in the 1980s. The television

show "Dallas" does represent the pervasiveness internationally of U.S. television.

7. The question of electronic colonialism ranges from a single printed page to sophisticated computerized data transferred via satellite and stored on video discs. To develop an information policy at the international level dealing with this enormous range of technologies is an almost impossible task, yet at the same time there needs to be some recognition and resolution of the disparities in information traffic. Western nations are concerned with Information Age issues such as new technologies like video discs which are blurring traditional distinctions like the separation of carrier and content or the vital issue of privacy, while LDC's are worried about literacy or imported comic books. All these concerns are legitimate but voting solutions to them via UNESCO resolutions will not resolve them in a substantial way.

8. Resolution of the debate about the NWIO has significant implications for foreign policy. The West's concept of the LDC's is mediated by information they receive via newspapers, radio, television, and other media. If coverage of the LDC's shifts substantially, then the role of the public may shift also. Since there currently is a strong reaction in Western nations about issues such as bureaucracy, big government, high taxes, and accountability, any reduction in coverage of LDC's could quickly reduce foreign aid budgets and assistance initiatives.

9. The LDC's newspapers are becoming more difficult to maintain. High illiteracy, escalating costs of newsprint, plus the growing costs of energy and transportation make increases in print-oriented products difficult. Radio appears to be the best medium for LDC's. Yet the ITU will have to allocate more and better frequencies for radio transmission in many areas; this may require cutting back on existing, overly powerful high transmitters in both North America and Europe. Radio, and not color television, has much to offer as a preferred medium to aid development.

10. Basically we are talking about the elites on both sides of the issue. In terms of the Western press we are talking about either academic elites or publisher elites represented in many cases by giant transnational corporations. Critics from LDC's are also either academic elites, many educated in the West, or bureaucratic and government elites whether in home nations or as representatives within international organizations. The average person on the street, whether in the West or in an LDC, is totally unaware of the NWIO debate; indeed, even if he or she was aware, he or she probably would not care a great deal about it unless he were to lose his popular game shows, soap-operas, or Hollywood feature films. Very few are aware of either the NIEO or the NWIO. Many more should become aware of them.

11. The MacBride Commission performed no original research. In essence it pulled together existing information from studies and statistics on both international as well as national information systems. It is unfortunate that no original research was undertaken given both the need for it as well as implications of what the overall investigation sought to establish. It turned out that there was little cooperation between the Secretariat of UNESCO, headed by Asher Deleon, and MacBride. In addition there was considerable tension among the members of the commission. Yet the commission did produce a report and already there is serious talk of it appearing on the UNESCO 1983 General Assembly agenda. In parallel a three-year study (1980-1983) of the NWIO and its meaning is underway under UNESCO's direction.

12. There should be more field and applied training in LDC's. Much training (both academic and technical) takes place in the West. This involves sophisticated hardware and the latest in multimedia equipment. But these learning systems often leave foreign students with little realistic and applicable skills in terms of what they will confront upon returning home.

In addition, there is a related issue. When Western nations send a team of experts to LDC's in connection with various development projects, one of their goals should include training a local successor rather than being replaced by other Western experts or evaluators. Each Western development project should include a timeframe for its own conclusion. This would avoid some of the self-serving aid projects that assist Western donors to a greater extent than the recipient nations. Aid projects that perpetuate themselves at the expense of excluding local assistance or leadership should be phased out. Paternalistic aid is not a solution.

13. Some type of tax on the spectrum, or a tax on international data or advertising traffic, will likely emerge as a potential source of revenue for NWIO projects. This is a sensitive area, but it again illustrates the lack of political finesse by many Western nations in dealing with the entire NIEO and NWIO movements. Indeed, the West, with the notable exception of Great Britain, thinks it is winning the debate. This is not the case. The LDC's are committed to activities that will alter free press media systems and ultimately will have significant effects on the four Western wire services. This is in spite of gains, as Mort Rosenblum states:

> Many editors, sensitized by the confrontation, have decided to take a more positive approach toward developing countries. Reporters are cautioned to avoid gratuitous sidelights which might be taken as slurs and to seek balancing "good points" when reporting on development setbacks. And they are asked to see things from the point of view of the society they are covering. But a deep-seated conflict remains, not only over how stories should be written but also over what subjects should be broached at all. Western newsmen contend that slight improvement over status quo is not news; violent change is. Coups, upheavals and economic failures, therefore, must be reported fully. Stories on peaceful development must take their place with other world stories in the selection process. Third World leaders argue that for them violent changes has been status quo; their slight improve-

ment is news. By harping on discord, they say, reporters are failing to note their hard won progress.

Whether justified or not, frustrated governments have imposed a dazzling array of restrictive measures to hinder reporting. Border after border was closed to Western newsmen in 1970's, and there have been expulsions of some type in almost every part of the Third World. Censorship has been developed to a high art. As a result, correspondents have no access at all to many countries, and in others they can gather news only with difficulty [1979: 13].

Summary

The consolidation and expansion of international media and communication activities is now being altered by highly political and vocal forces seeking to further the NWIO. Based upon a series of grievances against Western transnational information industries, particularly the wire services, a coalition of LDC's and socialist nations through organizations like UNESCO is providing alternative conceptions of and rules for international communication.

The theory of development journalism is an alternative to the traditional free press theoretical orientation of the West. Concerns about the effects of becoming an electronic colony of the West have heightened the awareness of many about the consequences of continued and expanding acceptance of foreign media products.

The issue is not going to be solved or disappear. Media questions will continue to dominate UNESCO, WARC meetings, North-South meetings, and the newly created International Program for Development of Communication. They will both further define the concept of the NWIO as well as operationalize both technical and theoretical research projects aimed at altering the historical ways of dealing with transnational information flows of all types. The February 1981 UNESCO meeting to work out details for foreign press cards is but one of many forthcoming moves to implement the NWIO.

The Western press has the most to lose, yet many appear unaware of the potential negative consequences of the NWIO.[1] While national daily newspapers transmitted via satellite directly to home videotext systems are being planned by progressive information providers, at the same time, less and less news from around the world may be the reality of the future if government control and restrictive measures are sanctioned as part of the NWIO.

But others will argue that the NWIO will create a better international information picture, with greater sensitivity, more of a two-way flow, and meaningful pieces on development projects and issues, to the benefit of all concerned.

There is little doubt that the NWIO is in place. The issue now is how will it evolve, either to aid international communication or to restrict it. The outcome will alter the Western press in some way, perhaps in a profound way. That is why additional study and empirical research about the NWIO is a concern to students and professionals of international broadcasting and communication alike.

NOTE

1. The debate about MacBride, the NIEO and NWIO, the IPDC, and various international meetings has received scant attention in the daily Western press. This is in spite of the considerable consequences that various aspects of a new order will have on their profession and business. Even when considerable copy is dispatched from UNESCO General Assemblies to various newsrooms via the wire services, little priority is assigned to such items. The following item, "UN quietly enters UNESCO communication fray," from Presstime illustrates the above all too well:

The international debate on how to build a "new world information order" surfaced in the United Nations in December when the General Assembly passed a resolution expressing satisfaction with UNESCO's actions on communications issues in Belgrade, Yugoslavia, last fall (Presstime, December 1980, p. 26).

The resolution specifically mentioned the MacBride Report, a document whose recommendations trouble many Western journalists (Presstime, June 1980, p. 14). Yet the American press was anything but alert to this latest development, and no press reports on it appeared for about a month [1981: 18].

REFERENCES

Presstime (1981) "UN quietly enters UNESCO communication fray." February, p. 18.

ROSENBLUM, M. (1979) Coups and Earthquakes: Reporting the World for America. New York: Harper & Row.

SCHROEDER, D. (1980) A survey of international news coverage by the Canadian media. IDRC Manuscript Reports 20.

APPENDIX A

ALIGNMENTS OF THE NONALIGNED

The nonaligned movement encompasses nearly every shade of political opinion. But on most issues, the members fall into three broad groups. The radicals generally lean toward Russia or China. The conservatives usually tilt toward the West. And the independents stick to the original purpose of their movement: nonalignment with any superpower Newsweek (1979). September 17, p. 50.

Radical

Afghanistan	Congo	Iraq	Mozambique	Patriotic Front of Zimbabwe	S.W. Africa People's Organization
Algeria	Cuba	Laos	North Korea	P.D.R. Yemen	Syria
Angola	Ethiopia	Libya	Palestine Liberation Organization	Sao Tomé and Principe	Vietnam
Cambodia	Guinea-Bissau	Mauritania			

Conservative

Argentina	Cyprus	Ivory Coast	Malta	Senegal	Yemen Arab Republic
Bahrain	Djibouti	Kenya	Morocco	Seychelles	Zaire
Bolivia	Egypt	Liberia	Oman	Singapore	
Central African Republic	Gabon	Malawi	Qatar	Togo	
	Indonesia	Malaysia	Saudi Arabia	United Arab Emirates	

Independent

Bangladesh	Chad	India	Mali	Peru	Tanzania
Benin	Comoros	Iran	Mauritius	Rwanda	Trinidad and Tobago
Bhutan	Equatorial Guinea	Jamaica	Nepal	Sierra Leone	Tunisia
Botswana	Gambia	Jordan	Nicaragua	Somalia	Uganda
Burma	Ghana	Lebanon	Niger	Sri Lanka	Upper Volta
Burundi	Grenada	Lesotho	Nigeria	Sudan	Yugoslavia
Cameroon	Guinea	Madagascar	Pakistan	Surinam	Zambia
Cape Verde Islands	Guyana	Maldives	Panama	Swaziland	

APPENDIX B

DRAFT DECLARATION ON FUNDAMENTAL PRINCIPLES CONCERNING THE CONTRIBUTION OF THE MASS MEDIA TO STRENGTHINING PEACE AND INTERNATIONAL UNDERSTANDING THE PROMOTION OF HUMAN RIGHTS AND TO COUNTERING RACIALISM, APARTHEID AND INCITEMENT TO WAR

Article I

The strengthening of peace and international understanding, and promotion of human rights and the countering of racialism, apartheid and incitement to war demand a free flow and a wider and better balanced dissemination of information. To this end, the mass media have a leading contribution to make. This contribution will be the more effective to the extent that the information reflects the different aspects of the subject dealt with.

Article II

1. The exercise of freedom of opinion, expression and information, recognized as an integral part of human rights and fundamental freedoms, is a vital factor in the strengthening of peace and international understanding.

2. Access by the public to information should be guaranteed by the diversity of the sources and means of information available to it, thus enabling each individual to check the accuracy of facts and to appraise events objectively. To this end, journalists must have freedom to report

and the fullest possible facilities of access to information. Similarly, it is important that the mass media be responsive to concerns of peoples and individuals, thus promoting the participation of the public in the elaboration of information.

3. With a view to the strengthening of peace and international understanding, to promoting human rights and to countering racialism, apartheid and incitement to war, the mass media throughout the world, by reason of their role, contribute effectively to promoting human rights, in particular by giving expression to oppressed peoples who struggle against colonialism, neocolonialism, foreign occupation and all forms of racial discrimination and oppression and who are unable to make their voices heard within their own territories.

4. If the mass media are to be in a position to promote the principles of this Declaration in their activities, it is essential that journalists and other agents of the mass media, in their own country or abroad, be assured of protection guaranteeing them the best conditions for the exercise of their profession.

Article III

1. The mass media have an important contribution to make to the strengthening of peace and international understanding and in countering racialism, apartheid and incitement to war.

2. In countering aggressive war, racialism, apartheid and other violations of human rights which are *inter alia* spawned by prejudice and ignorance, the mass media, by disseminating information on the aims, aspirations, cultures and needs of all people, contribute to eliminate ignorance and misunderstanding between peoples, to make nationals of a country sensitive to the needs and desires of others, to ensure the respect of the rights and dignity of all nations, all peoples and all individuals without distinction of race, sex, language, religion or nationality and to draw attention to the great evils which afflict humanity, such as poverty, malnutrition and diseases, thereby promoting the formulation by States of policies best able to promote the reduction of international tension and the peaceful and the equitable settlement of international disputes.

Article IV

The mass media have an essential part to play in the education of young people in a spirit of peace, justice, freedom, mutual respect and understanding, in order to promote human rights, equality or rights as between all human beings and all nations, and economic and social progress. Equally they have an important role to play in making known the views and aspirations of the younger generation.

Article V

In order to respect freedom of opinion, expression and information and in order that information may reflect all points of view, it is important that the points of view presented by those who consider that the information published or disseminated about them has seriously prejudiced their effort to strengthen peace and international understanding, to promote human rights or to counter racialism, apartheid and incitement to war be disseminated.

Article VI

For the establishment of a new equilibrium and greater reciprocity in the flow of information, which will be conducive of the institution of a just and lasting peace and to the economic and political independence of the developing countries, it is necessary to correct the inequalities in the flow of information to and from developing countries, and between those countries. To this end, it is essential that their mass media should have conditions and resources enabling them to gain strength and expand, and to cooperate both among themselves and with the mass media in developed countries.

Article VII

By disseminating more widely all of the information concerning the objectives and principles universally accepted which are the bases of the resolutions adopted by the different organs of the United Nations, the mass media contribute effectively to the strengthening of peace and international understanding, to the promotion of human rights, as well as to the establishment of a more just and equitable international economic order.

Article VIII

Professional organizations, and people who participate in the professional training of journalists and other agents of the mass media and who assist them in performing their functions in a responsible manner, should attach special importance to the principles of this Declaration when drawing up and ensuring application of their codes of ethics.

Article IX

In the spirit of this Declaration, it is for the international community to contribute to the creation of the conditions for a free flow and wider and more balanced dissemination of information, and the conditions for the protection, in the exercise of their functions, of journalists and other agents of the mass media. UNESCO is well placed to make a valuable contribution in this respect.

Article X

1. With due respect for constitutional provisions designed to guarantee freedom of information and for the applicable international instruments and agreements, it is indispensable to create and maintain throughout the world the conditions which make it possible for the organizations and persons professionally involved in the dissemination of information to achieve the objectives of this Declaration.

2. It is important that a free flow and wider and better balanced dissemination of information be encouraged.

3. To this end, it is necessary that States should facilitate the procurement, by the mass media in the developing countries, of adequate conditions and resources enabling them to gain strength and expand, and that they should support cooperation by the latter both among themselves and with the mass media in developed countries.

4. Similarly, on a basis of equality of rights, mutual advantage, and respect for the diversity of cultures which go to make up the common heritage of mankind, it is essential that bilateral and multilateral exchanges of information among all States, and in particular between those which have different economic and social systems be encouraged and developed.

Article XI

For this Declaration to be fully effective it is necessary, with due respect for the legislative and administrative provisions and other obligations of Member States, to guarantee the existence of favourable conditions for the operation of the mass media, in conformity with the provisions of the Universal Declaration of Human Rights and with the corresponding principles proclaimed in the International Covenant on Civil and Political Rights adopted by the General Assembly of the United Nations in 1966.

AUTHOR INDEX

Abel, E., 143, 208, 213, 214, 218, 219, 220, 221
Ahumada, R., 36
Alexander, J., 51

Ball-Rokeach, S., 76
Barghouti, S., 81
Beaulne, Y., 119, 125
Becker, C., 43
Beebe, G., 98, 119, 230
Behr, E., 115
Beltran, L., 70, 73, 80, 81, 192, 193, 194
Briggs, A., 26, 27
Bullen, D., 39
Bury, J., 40, 41
Bushkin, A., 199, 20

Cato: (John Trenchard & Thomas Gordon), 51
Chayes, A., 181, 182, 186
Chutkow, P., 134
Clement, W., 25, 26
Clippinger, J., 76, 79
Clyde, W., 44, 45
Clyne, J., 30, 31
Compaine, B., 33, 198
Crane, B., 102, 104, 105
Crouse, T., 17
Cruse-O'Brien, R., 79
Curran, J., 78

Davey, K., 26

de Sola Pool, I., 180, 187
DeFleur, M., 76
Deleon, A., 209, 246
Denning, Lord, 59
Duke, R., 143
Dunkley, C., 122, 123

Eisenstadt, S., 63, 65, 66, 67, 71
Ellul, J., 18
Emery, E., 43, 46, 53
Emery, M., 43, 46, 53
Epstein, J., 17
Estrada, P., 194

Faure, E., 93, 96, 209
Fejes, F., 191
Finkle, J., 102, 104, 105
Fitchett, J., 135
Francuski, B., 135
Frey, F., 67, 73
Fuller, J., 142

Geyelyn, P., 202
Giroud, F., 134
Golding, P., 80
Gordon-Lennox, Lord, 140
Grierson, J., 29
Guback, T., 78
Guebenlian, S., 173

Haley, W., 138, 139
Halloran, J., 83, 209
Hart, J., 115, 121, 124, 125

Heacock, R., 92, 97
Hirst, D., 132
Hoggart, R., 91, 109, 111
Homet, R., 233
Hoppen, D., 194
Howkins, J., 150, 151, 153, 156, 159, 164, 167
Huxley, J., 110

Inayatullah, I., 66
Innis, H., 18

Jasperse, S., 74, 75, 80

Klapper, J., 24

Laskin, P., 181, 182, 186
Lasswell, H., 70
Lazarsfeld, P., 70, 74
LeBlanc, N., 119
Lerner, D., 62, 64, 71
Levy, L., 47, 48, 51, 52, 53, 54
Lewis, P., 142, 144
Lilburne, J., 48
Losev, S., 209

M'Bow, A., 68, 89, 98, 99, 100, 109, 110, 111, 112, 113, 114, 121, 122, 129, 131, 132, 135, 137, 144, 207, 209
MacBride, S., 32, 35, 37, 100, 106, 110, 111, 112, 117, 125, 126, 137, 138, 141, 142, 175, 207, 209, 212, 213, 219, 223, 233, 246
Manley, M., 119
Marsden, E., 132
Masmoudi, M., 125, 208, 213, 214, 215, 216, 217, 218, 219, 220, 221, 233, 234, 235, 236
Matta, F., 195, 196
McLuhan, M., 18, 208
Merton, R., 70
Mill, J., 58
Milton, J., 47, 48
Mott, F., 52
Murdock, G., 80

Munnion, C., 132
Murray, I., 131, 136
Muscat, P., 121

Nathan, B., 173
Nolan, K., 173
Nora, S., 199
Nordenstreng, K., 83

Ornes, G. 98
Overton, R., 48

Paley, W., 33, 34
Pasquali, A., 190, 191
Ploman, E., 183, 184, 185, 188
Porter, J., 24, 25
Powers, S., 142

Queeney, K., 181, 184, 185, 186

Rana, T., 120
Read, W., 20
Reinhardt, J., 116, 117, 118, 121, 123, 124, 130, 132, 134, 233
Righter, R., 23, 140, 141, 142, 175 177
Roberts, J., 118, 125, 133, 134
Robinson, G., 158
Robinson, H., 48
Romantsov, U., 174
Rogers, E., 68, 70, 72, 73, 81, 84
Rosenblum, M., 15, 17, 21, 23, 176, 179, 247
Rostow, W., 65
Rutherford, P., 27

Salinas Bascur, R., 196, 197
Schiller, H., 63, 76, 77, 78, 183
Schramm, W., 62, 66, 72
Schroeder, D., 242
Schumacher, E., 85
Severini, R., 158
Sharp, R., 69
Shihepo, S., 120
Siebert, F., 40, 41, 42, 44, 45, 46, 47, 49, 50, 54, 55, 56, 57
Smith, A., 23, 33, 174, 178

Sussman, L., 97, 98

Tunstall, J., 20

Vance, C., 201, 200
Varis, T., 63

Walwyn, W., 48
Waugh, E., 13

Wells, A., 63, 189, 191, 193
Wicker, T., 132
Williams, R., 80

Yarrow, J., 199, 200
Yu, F., 84

Zenger, J., 51, 52, 53
Zimmerman, B., 208

ABOUT THE AUTHOR

THOMAS L. McPHAIL teaches Mass Communication and Journalism at Carleton University in Ottawa, Canada. He holds degrees in Economics and Communication (Ph.D., Purdue), which aid him in discussing both the New International Economic Order and the rapidly evolving New World Information Order. Dr. McPhail has worked as a consultant to the United Nations Educational, Scientific and Cultural Organization in both North America and Europe and is a widely recognized international consultant in broadcasting and communication fields. His current research focuses on international telecommunications and broadcasting with an emphasis on policy and cultural implications. He is also writing about the future of the newspaper.